Awakening the Spirit
Moving Forward in Child Welfare
Voices from the Prairies

Awakening the Spirit
Moving Forward in Child Welfare
Voices from the Prairies

Editors

Don Fuchs
Faculty of Social Work, University of Manitoba
& Prairie Child Welfare Consortium

Sharon McKay
Faculty of Social Work, University of Regina
& Prairie Child Welfare Consortium

Ivan Brown
Centre of Excellence for Child Welfare, Factor-Inwentash Faculty
of Social Work, University of Toronto

2012

Copyright © 2012 Canadian Plains Research Center. All rights reserved.

Awakening the Spirit: Moving Forward in Child Welfare: Voices from the Prairies may be downloaded free of charge from www.uregina.ca/spr/prairiechild/index.html or www.cecw-cepb.ca/ or may be reprinted or copied, in whole or in part, **for educational, service, or research purposes** without permission.

For all other purposes, written permission to reprint or use is required. Requests for written permission should be sent to the publisher. Any request for photocopying, recording, taping or placement in information storage and retrieval systems of any sort shall be directed in writing to Access Copyright.

Production of *Awakening the Spirit: Moving Forward in Child Welfare: Voices from the Prairies* has been made possible through funding from the Public Health Agency of Canada. The views expressed herein do not necessarily represent the views of the Public Health Agency of Canada or those of the editors. Every reasonable effort has been made to secure necessary permissions, but errors or omissions should be brought to the attention of Don Fuchs at fuchs@cc.umanitoba.ca.

Suggested Citation: Fuchs, D., McKay, S., & Brown, I. (Eds.). (2012). *Awakening the Spirit: Moving Forward in Child Welfare: Voices from the Prairies.* Regina, SK: Canadian Plains Research Center.

Printed and bound in Canada by Friesens. This book is printed on 100% post-consumer recycled paper.

Library and Archives Canada Cataloguing in Publication

Awakening the spirit : moving forward in child welfare : voices from the Prairies / editors, Don Fuchs, Sharon McKay, Ivan Brown.

(University of Regina publications series, ISSN 1480-0004 ; 29)
Based on papers presented at the Prairie Child Welfare Consortium's fifth biennial symposium, Awakening the Spirit, held in Winnipeg, Man., on Oct. 23-25, 2009.
Book is the third joint publication of the Prairie Child Welfare Consortium and the Centre of Excellence for Child Welfare.
Includes bibliographical references and index.
Also issued in electronic format.
ISBN 978-0-88977-278-6

1. Native children--Services for--Prairie Provinces. 2. Child welfare--Prairie Provinces. I. Fuchs, Don, 1948- II. McKay, Sharon, 1940- III. Brown, Ivan, 1947- IV. University of Regina. Canadian Plains Research Center V. Centre of Excellence for Child Welfare VI. Prairie Child Welfare Consortium. Symposium (5th : 2009 : Winnipeg, Man.) VII. Series: University of Regina publications ; 29

HV745.A6A93 2012   362.77'8970712   C2012-901411-7

Canadian Plains Research Center, University of Regina
Regina, Saskatchewan S4S 0A2 Canada
Tel: (306) 585-4758 • Fax: (306) 585-4699
E-mail: canadian.plains@uregina.ca • http://www.cprcpress.ca

CPRC Press acknowledges the financial support of the Government of Canada through the Canada Book Fund for our publishing activities.

CPRC Press acknowledges the financial support of the Creative Industry Growth and Sustainability program, which is made possible through funding provided to the Saskatchewan Arts Board by the Government of Saskatchewan through the Ministry of Tourism, Parks, Culture, and Sport.

Dedication

To all those who work to *awaken the spirit*
and generate hope through their actions
to address the needs of children and families

Contents

ix	Foreword • *Cindy Blackstock*
xii	From the Editors
xv	Acknowledgements
xvii	INTRODUCTION: Moving Forward in Hope • *Don Fuchs*
1	CHAPTER 1: Legacy of the Centre of Excellence for Child Welfare on Child Welfare in Canada: The Manager's Perspective • *Ivan Brown and Nicole Petrowski*
23	CHAPTER 2: A Day's Discourse among Indigenous Scholars and Practitioners about Indigenous Child Welfare Work in Canada • *Gwen Gosek and Marlyn Bennett*
37	CHAPTER 3: The Bent Arrow Study: A Way Forward in Leadership for Child Welfare • *Jean Lafrance and Linda Kreitzer*
71	CHAPTER 4: Awakening to the Spirit of Family: The Family Group Conference as a Strengths-Based Assessment Process • *Donald Keith Robinson*
93	CHAPTER 5: Cultural Safety and Child Welfare Systems • *Eveline Milliken*
117	CHAPTER 6: A Conceptual Framework for Child Welfare Service Coordination, Collaboration, and Integration • *Alexandra Wright*
135	CHAPTER 7: Fathers in the Frame: Protecting Children by Engaging Fathers when Violence against Mothers Is Present • *Carla Navid*
157	CHAPTER 8: Hitting the Target: Transitioning Youth with High-Risk Behaviours • *Kathryn A. Levine and Rick Rennpferd*

179   CHAPTER 9: Fetal Alcohol Spectrum Disorder Communities of Practice in Alberta: Innovations in Child Welfare Practice • *Dorothy Badry, William Pelech, and Sandra Stoddard*

213   CHAPTER 10: Awakening the Caring Spirit for Children and Youth with FASD: Social and Economic Costs to the Child Welfare System in Manitoba • *Don Fuchs, Linda Burnside, Shelagh Marchenski, and Andria Mudry*

233   CHAPTER 11: Awakening the Spirit of Caring by Creating a Community Response for Children with Special Needs: A Presentation of the Innovative Efforts of the Kinosao Sipi Minisowin Agency • *Madeline Gamblin and Rachel Barber*

249   CHAPTER 12: Substance Use during Pregnancy and a Woman-Centred Harm-Reduction Approach: Challenging the Mother and Baby Divide to Support Family Well-Being • *Noela Crowe-Salazar*

273   Epilogue

277   Abstracts

283   Contributors

289   Subject Index

295   Author Index

FOREWORD

Child Welfare: Lessons from
The Emperor's New Clothes

It is a story for the ages. An emperor walks down the street believing that he is wearing a beautiful robe visible only to the intelligentsia and those of suitable social station. The emperor's subjects can all plainly see that he is naked and, despite a child telling him so, the emperor continues to believe he has a beautiful robe on.

Hans Christian Anderson's 1837 story of the emperor with no clothes reminds me of the child welfare system in Canada. Neglect is the most prevalent type of maltreatment reported to child welfare authorities across Canada,[1] and yet it typically gets bottom-drawer attention compared to other forms of maltreatment such as physical or sexual abuse. The failure to pay adequate attention to neglect and its underlying factors of poverty, poor housing, substance misuse and, in the case of First Nations children on reserves, dramatic child welfare funding inequalities, has contributed to growing numbers of First Nations children being placed in child welfare care. Although child welfare authorities across the nation say that they are failing First Nations children, the system itself is not fundamentally changing. Worse than the naked emperor, Canadian

---

1   See Nico Trocmé, Barbara Fallon, Bruce MacLaurin, Joanne Daciuk, Caroline Felstiner, Tara Black, Lil Tonmyr, Cindy Blackstock, Ken Barter, Daniel Turcotte, Richard Cloutier (2005), *Canadian Incidence Study of Reported Child Abuse and Neglect – 2003: Major Findings*, Minister of Public Works and Government Services Canada.

child welfare *knows* it is naked, yet keeps on walking in increasing irrelevance at the expense of many children and families.

Authors in this collection call for increased alignment between those in need and the response of the child welfare system to them. These include women misusing substances during pregnancy and children with FASD, intellectual disabilities, and other disabilities. Others discuss promising interventions and highlight the need to centre interventions within a cultural context. Still others contend that, in order to free space for innovation and broad-based change, child welfare policy must be based on good evidence and must resist fear-based policy development driven primarily by child death reviews.

As much as I believe that good research coupled with respect for other types of knowledge needs to be the basis of child welfare, I also worry that we can produce endless amounts of research without ever acting on it. The Canadian Incidence Study (CIS),[2] which looked at reporting of child abuse and neglect, is a good example. Today, nearly 15 years after the factors driving the over-representation of First Nations children were identified in this leading study, very few child welfare workers across the country get any significant training on how to assess and respond to poverty and substance misuse. This is very troubling and makes me wonder why a system that is premised on ensuring the safety and well-being of children would not *do* better when it *knows* better.

As noted earlier, I think misapplication of child death review recommendations is part of the problem. I also wonder about the lack of moral courage among child welfare policy-makers and social workers to simply do the right thing for children. It seems that most of us know that the child welfare emperor has no clothes but we do not muster the courage to simply call it as we see it and demand that the system act on the best evidence and be willing to accept and endure all the risks that come from challenging the status quo.

To truly honour the works in this volume, we must take this knowledge and make it real in the lives of children. It is not going to be easy

---

2   See Nico Trocmé, Bruce MacLaurin, Barbara Fallon, Joanne Daciuk, Diane Billingsley, Marc Tourigny, Micheline Mayer, John Wright, Ken Barter, Gale Burford, Joe Hornick, Richard Sullivan, Brad McKenzie (2001), *Canadian Incidence Study of Reported Child Abuse and Neglect: Final Report*, Ottawa, Ontario: Minister of Public Works and Government Services Canada.

and it will require creativity and a combination of strategies to compel the system to change even when it does not want to. Jordan's Principle[3] provides a good example of such an approach. This is a child-first principle aimed at resolving government-based jurisdictional disputes that prevent First Nations children from accessing government services available to all other children. The Canadian Government and several provincial governments claim to fully support Jordan's Principle, but have failed to properly implement it. Supporters of Jordan's Principle, therefore, are deploying a mix of voluntary strategies (e.g., discussions with governments) and non-voluntary strategies (e.g., legal action and citizen engagement) to ensure that governments and child welfare systems do the right thing for children even if they don't want to.[4] For the sake of the children and families in Canada, we must demand full and proper implementation of good ideas like Jordan's Principle, along with culturally based interventions to address poverty, poor housing, and the special needs of children in Canadian child welfare while being courageously prepared to be insubordinate to bad ideas. "Awakening the Spirit" means that, like Hans Christian Anderson's emperor, we need to listen to the children's truth and act on it.

Cindy Blackstock
Executive Director, First Nations Child
and Family Caring Society of Canada and
Associate Professor, University of Alberta

---

[3] See www.jordansprinciple.ca.
[4] See C. Blackstock (2011), The Canadian Human Rights Tribunal on First Nations Child Welfare: Why if Canada wins, Canadians lose, *Children and Youth Services Review, 33,* 187-194.

From the Editors

We are very pleased to bring you this book, *Awakening the Spirit: Moving Forward in Child Welfare: Voices from the Prairies*. The book is the third joint publication of the Prairie Child Welfare Consortium (PCWC) and the Centre of Excellence for Child Welfare (CECW). It is strongly supported by the Social Policy Research Unit of the Faculty of Social Work, University of Regina; The Faculty of Social Work, University of Manitoba; and the Centre of Excellence for Child Welfare, administered through the Factor-Inwentash Faculty of Social Work, University of Toronto, and was partially supported by the Public Health Agency of Canada.

The chapters in the book represent a selection of some of the excellent presentations made at the Prairie Child Welfare Consortium's fifth biennial symposium, Awakening the Spirit: Moving Forward in Child Welfare, held in Winnipeg, October 21–23, 2009. Individuals attending previous PCWC Symposia (Saskatoon, 2001; Winnipeg, 2003; Edmonton, 2005; and Regina, 2007) emphasized the great importance of sharing information about programs, policies, and initiatives found to be supportive and effective when working with at-risk children and families. Building on this recommendation, the Call for Papers for the 2009 Symposium encouraged potential presenters to speak to their own innovative efforts to awaken the spirit in moving child welfare forward respecting work that is being done, and to present new and emerging policies, programs, and initiatives that hold promise for more effectively meeting the needs of at-risk children, youth, and their families. Holding to this idea, conference planners incorporated a day of training workshops for participants, an event widely appreciated in the 2007 symposium in Regina. Significantly, the planners also provided an opportunity on the day preceding the conference for a unique Indigenous scholars meeting to be held. This meeting brought together Indigenous scholars involved in child welfare research and practice together to share their ideas for moving child welfare forward. In their report on this meeting, the participants indicated that the Indigenous scholars present reaffirmed the perspective that "children are seen as gifts from the Creator, gifts to be cherished and cared for" by families and communities. The implications of this theme for child welfare with Indigenous peoples framed the discourse at the fifth biennial PCWC symposium. Together the three conference days stimulated numerous informative, enthusiastic, and passionate exchanges between and among participants and presenters. This book has attempted to capture the spirit of innovation and reform that was part of all the conference presentations and activities.

Consistent with the mandates of both the PCWC and the CECW, this book is intended to convey the work of presenters who were able to dedicate time and energy to the hard task of presenting their experiences, ideas, and research in print form for publication purposes. The outstanding contributions that have resulted reflect the dedication, commitment, and passionate zeal of the authors. Our contention in this book is that respectful inquiry, action-based research, and innovative, community-based, culturally anchored approaches are the necessary and integral driving force that will bring about transformative change in child and family serving systems. Such change is essential if Canada's children, youth, and families are to truly thrive and enjoy well-being.

The PCWC is a tri-provincial and northern multi-sector, cross-cultural, child and family services network representing university educators, government, First Nations, and Métis in-service training and service delivery administrators. Members of the network are dedicated to working together collaboratively for the purpose of strengthening and advancing education and training, policy, service delivery, and research in aid of children and families in need across the prairie provinces. The development of the PCWC has been powerfully and fundamentally influenced by the urgent voices of Aboriginal people deeply concerned with the escalating numbers of their children and youth in the care of the state. This influence permeates the PCWC's vision, mission, and goals, which are directed towards ensuring that child and family services in the Prairie Provinces and the North meet the needs of the children, families, and communities they support. Working together across many levels and sectors, PCWC partners seek to influence, advocate and change education, training, research, policy, and practice/service delivery through collaboration, innovation, and partnering. Ensuring respect for the needs of Aboriginal communities in the delivery of child welfare services is fundamental. In this quest, the PCWC seeks affiliation with other national child welfare bodies for joint initiatives that would further the PCWC mission and present a Prairie/Northern perspective at the national level. Readers interested in the history and development of the Consortium may wish to look up the introductory chapter of the first joint PCWC/CECW publication, *Putting a Human Face on Child Welfare: Voices from the Prairies* (McKay, 2007).

The CECW has been a major supporter and an important national resource for the PCWC. The CECW was established in early 2001 with a mandate to help develop child welfare research across Canada; to disseminate child welfare knowledge broadly among researchers, service providers, policy-makers, and other stakeholders; to provide policy advice to governments and service; and to build networks of child welfare professional and other stakeholders across Canada. In addressing this mandate, the CECW has attempted to bridge gaps that existed among provinces and territories; among researchers, policymakers, and practitioners; between those who speak French and English; and between Aboriginal and non-Aboriginal peoples. The CECW worked collaboratively with the PCWC over several years as one way of making child welfare a truly national community in Canada. Unfortunately, funding for the CECW ended in 2010 and it was not able to continue to function as a national organization. One of the main chapters of this book outlines the significant impact that the CECW had in moving child welfare forward in Canada.

It is the intention of the editors and the authors of this book to help strengthen the child welfare community in Canada by adding to its distinctive body of child welfare knowledge. Further, it is our hope that the perspectives contained within this book will help "awaken a spirit" to move forward child welfare research, policy, services, and practices to more effectively meet the emergent needs of children and families.

Don Fuchs, Sharon McKay, and Ivan Brown

REFERENCES

McKay, S. (2007). Introduction: Development of the Prairie Child Welfare Consortium and this book. In I. Brown, F. Chaze, D. Fuchs, J. Lafrance, S. McKay, & S. Thomas Prokop (Eds.). *Putting a human face on child welfare: Voices from the Prairies* (pp. xv–xxxvi). Prairie Child Welfare Consortium www.uregina.ca/spr/prairiechild/index.html/ Centre of Excellence for Child Welfare, www.cecw-cepb.ca.

McKay, S., Fuchs, D., & Brown, I. (Eds.). (2009). *Passion for action in child and family services: Voices from the prairies.* Regina, SK: Canadian Plains Research Center.

Acknowledgements

This book would not have been possible without the contribution of many people and, as editors, we would like to thank each of them for their hard work and support. We must begin by acknowledging the outstanding contributions of the chapter authors, whose expertise, wisdom, and patience with the editing process have created a manuscript that will benefit the field of child welfare research and practice. The chapters reflect the breadth of the authors' considerable experiences as practitioners, program planners, and academics. Readers can learn more about the chapter authors in the "Contributors" section of the book.

The following persons served as peer reviewers and provided feedback and suggestions on the chapters. Their comments help sharpen the focus and the messages in each chapter and we are sincerely grateful for their input: Gary Cameron, Jeannine Carriere, Peter Dudding, Rachel Greenbaum, Valerie Temple, Michael Hart, Jean Lafrance, Duane Lesperance, Bruce Leslie, Lynn Martin, Brad McKenzie, Monty Montgomery, Maire Percy, Gayla Rogers, Nico Trocmé, Chris Wekerle, Jonathan Weiss, and Fred Wien.

We are grateful to Brian Mlazgar, publications manager at the Canadian Plains Research Center (CPRC), who agreed to publish and distribute the hard copies of the book. For the considerable work in copy editing and designing the book's interior, we are grateful to Donna Grant and we acknowledge the fine work of Duncan Campbell on cover design. Staff members from CPRC Press meticulously corrected all the inconsistencies across chapter formats and contributed substantially to the overall quality of the book.

We wish to acknowledge the time and commitment of the planning committee members of the PCWC's 5th Biennial Symposium held in Winnipeg, Manitoba, October 21–23, 2009: Alex Wright, Alana Courtney, Marlyn Bennett, Leilani Buschau, Elsie Flett, Gwen Gosek, Robin Jackson, Kathy Kristjanson, Billie Schibbler, Eveline Milliken, Don Robinson, Mallory Newman, Bruce Unfried, and Jan Christianson-Wood.

The presentations of that Symposium were the basis of the chapters contained in this book.

We wish to thank the Faculties of Social Work at the University of Manitoba and the University of Toronto, and the School of Social Work at the University of Regina for providing us with the encouragement and administrative infrastructure support to carry out much of the work of this book. The editors had valuable assistance from a number of people within their universities.

Finally, we would like to thank the Public Health Agency of Canada, which provided funding support for PCWC's Symposium through the Centre for Excellence for Child Welfare. As well we would like to thank the core partners of the Prairie Child Welfare Consortium and the Centre of Excellence for Child Welfare, listed below, for their cooperation and support.

PRAIRIE CHILD WELFARE CONSORTIUM

University of Manitoba, Faculty of Social Work
University of Calgary, Faculty of Social Work
University of Regina, Faculty of Social Work
Manitoba Family Services and Consumer Affairs
Alberta Children's Services
Saskatchewan Social Services
Federation of Saskatchewan Indian Nations
Metis Association Alberta

CENTRE OF EXCELLENCE FOR CHILD WELFARE

Factor-Inwentash Faculty of Social Work, University of Toronto
École de service social, Université de Montreal
Child Welfare League of Canada
First Nations Child & Family Caring Society of Canada
School of Social Work, McGill University

INTRODUCTION

Moving Forward in Hope

Don Fuchs

"From the beginning of time Indigenous children, families and communities have been at the spiritual centre of the universe," proclaimed Bennett and Gosek in their report on the meeting of Indigenous scholars that took place at the Awakening the Spirit: Moving Forward in Child Welfare Conference. The Indigenous scholars meeting reaffirmed that "children are seen as gifts from the Creator, gifts to be cherished and cared for." The implications of this theme for child welfare with Indigenous peoples framed the discourse amongst the scholars who were part of the Indigenous scholars meeting. This theme of social and community responsibility to support and care for vulnerable children and families regardless of their diverse backgrounds or minority status was reflected in all the conference presentations. The themes of research, promising programs built on Indigenous perspectives of child welfare, notions of caring community, and holistic approaches framed the discussion throughout the conference.

SUGGESTED CITATION: Fuchs, D. (2012). Introduction: Moving Forward in Hope. In D. Fuchs, S. McKay, & I. Brown (Eds.), *Awakening the Spirit: Moving Forward in Child Welfare: Voices from the Prairies* (pp. xvii–xxiv). Regina, SK: Canadian Plains Research Center.

This book is the third joint publication of the Prairie Child Welfare Consortium (PCWC) and the Centre of Excellence for Child Welfare (CECW). All of the chapters in the book are based on presentations made at the Prairie Child Welfare Consortium's fifth biennial symposium, Awakening the Spirit: Moving Forward in Child Welfare, held in Winnipeg, Manitoba, on October 23-25, 2009. Passion for action to promote child welfare has led to an awakening of the spirit in Indigenous families, in communities, and in child and family service agencies to provide leadership to move forward in child welfare. The awakening of the spirit has led to an increased awareness of the need for more practice that is informed by respective inquiry and action research.

Increasing awareness of the alarming overrepresentation of Aboriginal children in Canada's child welfare system and the awareness that these numbers continue to grow has heavily influenced the development of the PCWC and the planning of successive symposia. Fundamental to the structure and processes of the Consortium is respect for the needs of Aboriginal communities in the delivery of child welfare services.

Aboriginal families, largely located in the Prairie provinces and in the North, have statistically significantly less-stable housing, greater dependence on social assistance, younger parents, more parents who were maltreated as children, and higher rates of alcohol and drug abuse. They are more likely to be investigated for neglect or emotional maltreatment (Trocmé, Knoke, & Blackstock, 2004). The demographics of this unprecedented growth in the numbers of children and youth needs to be understood and the implications for health, education, and social services require thorough examination to address more effectively the changing needs of marginalized children, youth, and their families.

The fifth bi-annual conference examined some of these implications and helped identify several of the major issues that need to be addressed in meeting these changing needs. Presentations at the conference examined the applications of some innovative and promising culturally anchored approaches to the growing need for child and family services. Other presentations discussed the need for more effective alternatives to existing child welfare systems to decrease the number of children being removed from their families. Resources need to be invested or reallocated to support and strengthen families. Interventions for families at-risk need to be introduced early, before problems escalate and lead to family breakdown (Shangreaux, 2004). The conference identified some of the progress that has been made in addressing these needs and presented many promising innovative approaches that build on traditional areas of community strength.

The first chapter, by Ivan Brown and Nancy Petrowski, speaks about the role of the Centre of Excellence in Child Welfare (CECW) in collaboration with the PCWC and other groups across the country in stimulating knowledge generation and dissemination to inform the practice of child welfare with current knowledge based on needs and promising practices across the country. Brown and Petrowski indicate that the funding provided to establish and operate the Centre of Excellence for Child Welfare for 10 years created a leaven for research activity and renewed interest and excitement in child welfare across Canada. Brown and Petrowski point out that the CECW was a unique organizational entity whose primary purpose was to bring together the many diverse aspects of child welfare across Canada. They maintain that there had never before been a structure that simultaneously generated new ideas for child welfare, promoted a culture of research and evaluation within child welfare practice, took an active role in providing policy advice, produced and disseminated child welfare information, and brought together several types of people and networks. The CECW demonstrated that a Canada-wide voice and set of research activities were desirable and possible to attain, and that attaining them was indeed very helpful to the ongoing enhancement of child welfare in Canada. The Centre stimulated the development of a culture of child welfare research across Canada. The CECW worked on building the capacity for this type of research in child welfare jurisdictions and agencies across Canada. It provided a major contribution to the development of research relating to Aboriginal child welfare practice and assisted in building the capacity of Aboriginal researchers in child welfare all across Canada. In addition, it provided a major resource for the dissemination of knowledge to Aboriginal child welfare in Canada.

Building on the theme "awakening of the spirit of child welfare research," the second chapter, by Gwen Gosek and Marlyn Bennett, reports on the conclusions and recommendations that came out of the discourse of an Indigenous scholars meeting in Winnipeg at the Awakening the Spirit Conference. The chapter elaborates on the discussions of the three themes that appear to be at the heart of Indigenous child welfare practice for the participating scholars and practitioners: 1) the importance of valuing and incorporating Indigenous world views and cultural ways of being into practice; 2) recognizing the structural barriers that exist for Indigenous families who become tangled up in child welfare services and that result primarily from inadequate policies and resources; and 3) the need for post-secondary education that incorporates Indigenous world views, practices, and knowledge. The chapter identifies and celebrates some of the successes and progress in areas that have led to a collective consciousness and the development of resources that promote traditional and contemporary Indigenous knowledge and ways of practice. In addition, the chapter puts forward several recommendations about where future concerted efforts must be expended or continued in order to advance collective action in decolonizing child welfare services for Indigenous families in Canada.

The third chapter, by Jean Lafrance and Linda Kreitzer, points to the need for child welfare services to use and build on the lessons learned from the promising practices of urban Aboriginal and child and family service resources. Using the Broken Arrow initiative in Edmonton, the authors demonstrate how services can be built on Aboriginal world views and the strengths of the growing numbers of innovative programs emerging in First Nations communities as they try to move child welfare forward.

While it is crucially important to work at awakening the spirit of communities, there is also a need to focus on supporting and strengthening families in their community contexts. Chapter Four speaks directly to this in its discussion of family group conferencing (FGC). Don Robinson outlines the origins of FGC and connects Aboriginal historical traditional practices with the FGC model. Robinson's discussion of the model's potential for decolonization of Aboriginal families is well-grounded in practice.

Awakening the spirit involves risks in developing and implementing culturally anchored programs and practices. In Chapter Five, Eveline Milliken discusses the importance of understanding cultural safety as part of social work practice in child welfare. She describes a key shift of perspective involving cultural safety that will assist educators and practitioners who struggle to move away from systemic inequality toward conceptualizing and operationalizing inclusion, respect, and sensitivity.

Milliken builds on her research with Aboriginal social work graduates of an inner-city Bachelor of Social Work program to identify ten suggestions through which the child welfare practitioner may begin to move toward "cultural safety."

The growing numbers of children in care, child deaths, and youth suicides, as well as the overrepresentation of Aboriginal children and youth in the child welfare system, are a signal that regular fundamental re-examination of the service delivery system is required to ensure that new developments do not perpetuate colonial cycles of oppression. Awakening the spirit and changing practices at an organizational level requires new patterns of relationships between service providers, funders, and service users. There is a great need for research into social service delivery systems. Alex Wright's chapter provides an important conceptual framework for awakening the spirit of service coordination, collaboration, and integration to promote the effective post-colonial management, development, and delivery of culturally sensitive and relevant child welfare services.

In Chapter Seven, Carla Navid addresses the invisibility of fathers, an often neglected area of child welfare. Drawing upon discourse analysis methods from a number of sources she reveals how the discourse of "mothers failing to protect" has emerged, and how this discourse informs child welfare practice and policy in ways that harm mothers and children. Navid argues that, in order to realize a feminist perspective in our work with families, men need to be included as both risks and assets in the frame of our child welfare lens.

A recurrent theme in the conference was that many youth who are in care or involved with the child welfare system have great difficulties transitioning out of care. In Chapter Eight, Kathryn Levine and Rick Rennpferd discuss a specific, and particularly vulnerable, group: adolescents with cognitive disabilities who sexually offend. Adolescents with intellectual disabilities and these types of high-risk behaviours present a complex challenge to the service system. Levine and Rennpferd indicate that one of the key factors that hinders successful transition to the adult disability system is the absence of disability-specific knowledge within child welfare systems regarding children and adolescents with intellectual disabilities. This, in conjunction with contradictory mandates of the various service systems with potential involvement, prevents professionals from responding to these youth in a thoughtful and planned manner.

This book contains a group of chapters that address the challenges of meeting the needs of a growing number of children with Fetal Alcohol Spectrum Disorder (FASD) in the care of child welfare in many jurisdictions across Canada. In Chapter Nine, Dorothy Badry, William Pelech, and Sandra Stoddard reflect on the development of an FASD Communities of Practice model. The term "promising practices" also identifies a philosophical shift in child welfare caseload management such that risks need to be taken to benefit children and youth with FASD, who face multiple struggles in their lives and in care, and who live with a lifelong disability. In this chapter, early and promising results of this research are profiled as well as the importance of considering a new model of practice for children and youth in care with FASD.

In Chapter Ten, Don Fuchs, Linda Burnside, Shelagh Marchenski and Andria Mudry look at the prevalence of FASD and its cost implications for health, education, and training. They conclude that closing the gap in knowledge around the economic costs of FASD-affected individuals can help to make better public policy, which partly focuses on prevention of FASD. An emphasis on primary prevention would effectively expand the public policy approach to FASD in Canada, as well as creating efficiencies in the allocation of scarce resources. This research clearly identifies the inordinate and growing economic and social costs of children who have been affected by prenatal alcohol use. It demonstrates the importance for prioritizing and addressing future programming in the area of services to FASD-affected children, as well as confronting challenges faced by children affected by problematic parental drinking.

Chapter Eleven, by Madeline Gamblin and Rachel Barber, provides a description of an innovative community-based model grounded in Aboriginal traditions. Norway House Cree Nation is a northern Cree community that follows an holistic approach in its services to children with FASD and other cognitive disabilities and their families. While the program itself is an excellent resource, its creation highlights the challenges faced by Aboriginal children with special needs and their families in regards to accessing services. Specifically, the creation of the program draws attention to the service vacuum that Aboriginal children with special needs must face. The chapter discusses the structural and resource issues—particularly the inequitable treatment of children living on- and off-reserve—that the community needed to address in creating a response for providing services to children and youth and their families. The authors highlight the importance of Jordan's Principle in providing direction for the sustainability and ongoing development of the Children's Special Services Program.

In the final chapter, Noela Crowe-Salazar discusses the important and difficult issue of substance use during pregnancy and the need for support programs that use a woman-centred and harm-reduction approach. She provides an extensive review of the literature and discusses four examples of effective programs in various parts of Canada. A comprehensive program plan is suggested from knowledge garnered from these programs and from the scholarly literature.

In keeping with the theme of our conference, "Awakening the spirit—moving forward in child welfare," these scholars focus on children and families as the spiritual centre of our community and society; and they write from this basic position—that children, youth, and families are gifts to be cherished, cared for, and nurtured, as they represent the future of our society. We hear in their voices a sense of urgency about the need to develop more caring policies, programs, and practices that respect and build on individual community strengths. *Awakening the Spirit* clearly identifies the importance of research in child welfare, especially research that focuses on Indigenous knowledge and Indigenous research approaches. The goal of such research is to foster efforts toward change that are accurately informed, sensitive to Indigenous cultural practices, and respectful of the people for whom and the communities in which the programs are being delivered.

According to the Aboriginal Peoples 2006 Canadian Census, between 1996 and 2006 the Aboriginal population grew by 45%, nearly six times faster than the rate of increase for the non-Aboriginal population. Almost half of the Aboriginal population consists of children and youth aged twenty-four and under, compared with 31% of the non-Aboriginal population (Statistics Canada, 2006).

In addition the conference discussed alternate policy and practice approaches based on research and demonstrated promising policy and practices grounded in Aboriginal traditions and culture, as the means of awakening the spirit and moving forward in child welfare.

The PCWC has emerged from a collective tri-provincial and Northern effort to share information, conduct research, and consult, collaborate, and partner with one another to enhance and strengthen child welfare service delivery, education and training, and research and policy development in the Prairie region (PCWC, 2011). Fundamental to the structure and processes of the Consortium is respect for the needs of Aboriginal communities in the delivery of child welfare services. Additionally, the Consortium seeks affiliation with other national child welfare bodies for joint initiatives, in order to further the PCWC mission and present a Prairie perspective at the national level (McKay, Fuchs, & Brown, 2009). This book is a part of the ongoing efforts of the PCWC to carry out its mission.

REFERENCES

McKay, S., Fuchs, D., & Brown, I. (Eds.) (2009). *Passion for action in child and family services: Voices from the prairies*. Regina, SK: Canadian Plains Research Center.

Prairie Child Welfare Consortium. (2011). History, Vision and Goals, downloaded from cat.uregina.ca/spr/pcwc-about.html.

Shangreaux, C. (2004). *Staying at home: Examining the implications of least disruptive measures in First Nations Child and Family Service Agencies*. Ottawa: First Nations Caring Society.

Statistics Canada. (2006). *Aboriginal Peoples 2006 Canadian Census*. Downloaded from www12.statcan.ca/census-recensement/2006/rt-td/ap-pa-eng.cfm.

Trocmé, N., Knoke, D., & Blackstock, C. (2004). Pathways to the overrepresentation of Aboriginal children in Canada's child welfare system. *Social Service Review* (December), 577–600.

CHAPTER 1

Legacy of the Centre of Excellence for Child Welfare on Child Welfare in Canada: The Manager's Perspective

Ivan Brown and Nicole Petrowski

First author's note: The Centre of Excellence for Child Welfare (CECW) emerged from a number of interests, involved a large network of people all across Canada, and initiated or partnered in carrying out a huge number of activities. It is not possible to detail all these in one chapter, and readers are encouraged to consult the body of work of the CECW that now forms part of the Canadian Child Welfare Research Portal (www.cecw-cepb.ca) and other sources of information such as issues of Canada's Children, published by the Child Welfare League of Canada. It is also not possible here to reflect the perspectives of all those who contributed so actively to the CECW over the years, especially its directors. As manager of the CECW for most of its ten years of operation, my role was to oversee all its day-to-day activities, and thus the content of this chapter necessarily reflects my own experience and perspective. Part of this perspective—something that forms an implicit part of this chapter—was the very positive relationship that developed over the years with the Prairie Child Welfare Consortium and the many people associated with it across Manitoba, Saskatchewan, and Alberta.

SUGGESTED CITATION: Brown, I., & Petrowski, N. (2012). Legacy of the Centre of Excellence for Child Welfare on child welfare in Canada: The manager's perspective. In D. Fuchs, S. McKay, & I. Brown (Eds.), *Awakening the Spirit: Moving Forward in Child Welfare: Voices from the Prairies* (pp. 1–22). Regina, SK: Canadian Plains Research Center.

One of the most challenging aspects of trying to stimulate the evolution of Canadian child welfare in positive ways is that we are bound by features of our history. Two such features are of particular importance, one for influencing how we think about child welfare in the first place, and the other for determining who has authority and responsibility for child welfare.

First, because the lands that came to be known as Canada were colonized by Europeans who assumed governance of the country, our way of looking at social structures and social problems has been distinctly European. When European adventurers, traders, settlers, and military personnel "discovered" our lands, and proceeded to come by the thousands to live here, they brought with them the assumption that was common in Europe at the time that the rest of the world was theirs for the taking, and that any resources they encountered were theirs because they "discovered" them. This point of view led, over several centuries, to a claim on all the land and to the right to govern it. Sometimes this was done peacefully and at other times it was not. However it was accomplished, people of European descent and customs became the dominant power throughout the various settlements of Canada, and for centuries the Indigenous peoples were forced off their lands, were left to live in poverty, and experienced extreme powerlessness. One legacy of the European viewpoint is that it has shaped the way child welfare itself has been conceptualized and how child welfare systems have developed. This legacy is helpful in many ways, but it also acts as a barrier to making improvements in the system.

Second, at the time of Confederation in 1867, the responsibilities of the federal government and those of the four provinces that composed Canada at the time were set out. Although health, education, and social services are important areas of governance in today's world, they were not so at the time of Confederation. As a result, responsibility for these areas was given to the provinces. The result of this historic decision is that today each of Canada's ten provinces and three territories has its own systems of health, education, and social services. Health is regulated to some extent federally, but social services, including child welfare, are not considered to be within the scope of federal influence. This has made the task of improving the child welfare system in Canada—essentially thirteen separate systems—a very difficult one indeed.

Within this context, there emerged in the late 1990s a minor groundswell of enthusiasm for developing some type of Canada-wide voice in child welfare. At about the same time, UNICEF's report entitled *A World Fit for Children* (United Nations General Assembly, 2002) was stimulating thought and discussion about improving children's lives more generally through its clear statement of goals and description of a way forward. The Canadian government's response to this was the drafting of *A Canada Fit for Children* (Government of Canada, 2004) and the creation of its own national action plan for children. A variety of initiatives—both continuing and new—contributed to Canada's national action plan for children. One new initiative, following strong advocacy and active involvement of child welfare experts and organizations, was the establishment of the Centres of Excellence for Children's Well-Being Program, funded by the federal Ministry of Health. One centre within this program, the Centre of Excellence for Child Welfare (CECW), would focus specifically on issues related to child welfare across Canada. This chapter describes the impact of the CECW, as perceived by its manager, on the field of child welfare in Canada by chronicling its major activities and accomplishments over the ten years that it operated (2000–2010).

THE CENTRES OF EXCELLENCE FOR CHILDREN'S WELL-BEING PROGRAM

The Centres of Excellence for Children's Well-Being Program was launched in October 2000, and was originally set up as a series of autonomous centres. Following a call for proposals and adjudication of the submissions, five centres of excellence were established for a funding period of five years. This original configuration was later reduced to four: the Centre of Excellence for Child Welfare (CECW), based at the University of Toronto; the Centre of Excellence for Early Childhood Development (CEECD), based at the Université de Montréal; the Centre of Excellence for Children and Adolescents with Special Needs (CECASN), based at Lakehead University; and the Centre of Excellence for Youth Engagement (CEYE), based at The Students Commission of Canada, Toronto.

A secretariat was established within Health Canada to support the work of the program and to ensure accountability. Later, when the Public Health Agency of Canada (PHAC) was formed, the entire program, including the secretariat, was housed within PHAC. From the beginning, the program set up a National Expert Advisory Committee (NEAC) that consisted of experts in children's issues from across Canada and that was appointed by the minister of Health. The role of the NEAC was to provide timely advice to PHAC to ensure the program met its mandate and objectives. Over time, the NEAC also provided helpful advice and support to the centres themselves.

The mandate of the Centres of Excellence Program was to ensure that advanced knowledge on key issues of children's health was generated and disseminated effectively to those who need it most. This included researchers; service providers; parents, children, and youth; community groups; non-governmental organizations; and the federal, provincial, and territorial governments. The centres also were to promote partnerships among governments and government departments, service providers, community-based and non-profit organizations, and academics and families to make a difference in the health and well-being of Canada's children and youth.

In more specific terms, the Centres of Excellence for Children's Well-Being Program set out five functions for its centres to address:
1. Analyze existing data.
2. Conduct original research.
3. Provide policy advice.
4. Disseminate knowledge.
5. Forge networks.

ESTABLISHING THE CENTRE OF EXCELLENCE FOR CHILD WELFARE

A number of people were instrumental in establishing the Centre of Excellence for Child Welfare. Dr. Paul Steinhauer (1934–2000) envisioned a Canada in which all children were physically and emotionally healthy; safe and free from neglect or abuse; cared for in a manner that would optimize their academic, emotional, and social potential; and able to form stable and nurturing attachments (Steinhauer, 1999). Dr. Steinhauer was instrumental in providing recommendations that would shape the federal government's National Children's Agenda. In early 1999, Dr. Steinhauer and the newly-appointed executive director of the Child Welfare League

CHAPTER 1: Legacy of the Centre of Excellence for Child Welfare

of Canada (CWLC), Peter Dudding, discussed the creation of a national organization to promote and disseminate information on effective, evidence-based policy and practice to those involved with the child welfare systems in Canada. These leaders felt strongly about the lack of Canadian research in child welfare and the lack of understanding and dissemination of such research.

Support for the idea of building a Centre of Excellence for Child Welfare came from many others working in the field. In 1999, Nico Trocmé, then the director of the Bell Canada Child Welfare Research Unit at the University of Toronto, and Claire Chamberland, director of the Institut de recherche pour le développement social des jeunes (IRDS) at Université de Montréal, partnered with Peter Dudding and the CWLC to submit a proposal to Health Canada to create and manage the Centre of Excellence for Child Welfare. This collaboration bridged two important historical divides in Canadian child welfare: the divide between the service and academic worlds, and the divide between English-language and French-language knowledge, activities, and systems. In October 2000, the Centre of Excellence for Child Welfare was selected as one of five Centres of Excellence for Children's Well-Being to receive five-year funding. Nico Trocmé became the principal investigator of the CECW for administrative purposes. Sadly, Dr. Steinhauer passed away just six months prior to seeing his vision of the CECW become a reality; it was his tireless commitment and advocacy on behalf of Canada's most vulnerable children and youth that resulted in the founding of the CECW.

It was recognized from the beginning that the collaboration included three organizations that were based in Ottawa, Toronto, and Montréal, and thus brought in experts from only central Canada. On the other hand, the Child Welfare League of Canada was a national organization that represented child welfare agencies from all parts of Canada. It was also considered that establishing the CECW first in Ontario and Québec would make accomplishing this rather substantial undertaking more feasible. The longer-term plan was to expand interest and activities to all parts of Canada as additional partnerships were developed.

The CECW added two more core partners in subsequent years. In 2002, the First Nations Child & Family Caring Society of Canada (FNCFCS) was formed as the umbrella organization for Canada's more than one hundred First Nations child welfare agencies. Offices were set up in Ottawa, and an executive director, Cindy Blackstock, was hired by a newly-appointed board of directors. Soon afterward, the CECW invited the Caring Society to join it, and invited Cindy Blackstock to become a CECW director. In 2004, Nico Trocmé accepted a faculty position at the School of Social Work at McGill University in Montréal and became the new director of the Centre for Research on Children and Families (CRCF). With this change, Nico became the scientific director of CECW, with McGill as a core organization. At the University of Toronto, Cheryl Regehr took over as principal investigator and executive director of CECW, and child welfare expert Aron Shlonsky later also joined as a director.

The Centre of Excellence for Child Welfare was set up on a platform model, using the facilities, expertise, infrastructure, and many resources of its core partner organizations and, in turn, contributing to them by providing funding and a program of activities that were of specific interest to the core partners. Ivan Brown filled the role of manager from 2001–2007. From July 2007 to June 2008, Michael Saini, at the time a recent graduate of the Ph.D. program in the Faculty of Social Work at the University of Toronto, stepped into the role of manager, with Ivan once again taking up this position from 2008–2010. A strength of the platform model and partnership of organizations was that every partner organization could access, utilize, and benefit from the skills and knowledge of the other organizations within the common CECW infrastructure. In addition, all the organizations had opportunities to network with numerous other organizations and create partnerships to work collaboratively and in a multidisciplinary manner.

The CECW set up its own advisory committee, a body of 20 experts in child welfare policy, practice, and research from across Canada. This body met annually for the first three years, and was consulted regularly by telephone, letter, and e-mail on a wide variety of matters pertaining to the mission and activities of the CECW. Such expert advice was highly instrumental in establishing the CECW and, although it became less essential as the activities of the CECW developed momentum and was consequently disbanded, its value to the new entity taking root cannot be overstated.

Mission of the CECW

The CECW's mission was to promote excellence in child welfare practice, policy, and research. The CECW has been committed to contributing to academic knowledge, research, and policy development at the federal, provincial/territorial, and local levels. The CECW has always been guided by the principle that all children in Canada are entitled to a life free from violence and neglect. The CECW's mandate has been to work at a national level to disseminate evidence-based knowledge on the incidence, characteristics, and effects of abuse and neglect on children and youth, as well as to transfer knowledge on the most effective ways to alleviate and prevent child maltreatment.

NEEDS PERCEIVED BY THE CECW

The CECW considered that the five functions set out by the Centres of Excellence for Children's Well-Being Program were highly appropriate for addressing child welfare needs it perceived to be priorities. The most important of these are described in the sub-sections that follow.

Need for Canada-wide child welfare data

The decision at the time of Confederation to create two levels of government—a federal and a provincial system—continues to influence policy today in many areas of governance. Perhaps the legacy of federalism is no more evident than in the decentralized structure of contemporary child welfare services in Canada. The responsibility for protecting children and youth at risk of abuse or neglect is under the jurisdiction of the thirteen Canadian provinces and territories, and a system of Aboriginal child welfare agencies. Although provinces and territories are obligated to provide a system of child protection services, as with health care and education, provincial/territorial governments differ considerably in the ways they organize and implement their child welfare systems (see the series of information sheets on provincial/territorial child welfare systems available on the Canadian Child Welfare Research Portal, CCWRP). This has created a mosaic of child welfare systems across Canada that range from centralized government-run systems to those operated by agencies delegated to provide mandated services. Further complicating the picture are differences among jurisdictions in legislation and statutes and wide variations in the way service statistics are collected and recorded.

In its earliest stages, the CECW recognized the need for a mechanism to bring together child welfare as a field within Canada, and for national information and data on the extent and types of child maltreatment. This gap in the knowledge base has changed in large part due to the Canadian Incidence Study of Reported Child Abuse and Neglect (CIS). The CIS provides reliable data on families and children receiving child welfare services in every province and territory every five years beginning in 1998. The study released its Major Findings Report from the third cycle in October 2010 (see the Canadian Child Welfare Research Portal website to view the report). The CECW was a strong support for the CIS at all stages of the study in both the 2003 and 2008 cycles.

Recently, the University of Toronto-McGill University partnership within CECW has been working on the National Outcomes Matrix (NOM) Data Support project, which has created an outcomes-monitoring system that provinces and territories can adapt to collect data on ten key child welfare indicators. The project began with a close collaboration between the research team and the provincial/territorial directors of child welfare and has been slowly progressing.

Need to establish dialogue between French and English languages

The CECW always envisioned itself as a Canada-wide organization that would be sufficiently broad and inclusive to help bring together the field of child welfare within Canada. A vital part of this vision included a desire to consolidate the networks of francophone and anglophone researchers and practitioners in child welfare. The original partnership between the Child Welfare League of Canada, the University of Toronto, and the Université de Montréal, which established the CECW, set an atmosphere of collaboration. To support the dialogue between French and English, a decision was made by the CECW in 2001 to produce all of its products and materials in both official languages.

Need to establish a dialogue between Aboriginals and non-Aboriginals

The devastating consequences of the residential school system and the "Sixties Scoop," in which mass numbers of First Nations children were removed from their homes and adopted into euro-Canadian families between 1960 and the mid-1980s, has left a legacy of distrust, by many people in Aboriginal communities, of the mainstream child welfare system. This has resulted in a strong thrust, in recent years, toward developing child welfare services that are more in keeping with Aboriginal knowledge and culture. It has also underscored the need for Aboriginal and non-Aboriginal child welfare professionals, policy-makers, and service users to understand one another much more fully than has been the case in the past.

Because child maltreatment is of particular importance to First Nations, the CECW set as one of its key priorities an emphasis on promoting knowledge and understanding of Aboriginal child welfare. In large part due to its close partnership with the First Nations Child & Family Caring Society of Canada, the CECW has been instrumental in creating a profound change in thinking that has been critically important for First Nations and other Aboriginal children, families, and communities (see *Touchstones of Hope* on the CCWRP website to view the philosophical context for this change in thinking). Numerous activities have been generated by the *Touchstones* document and have been successful, in large part, because of the enormous groundswell of Aboriginal initiatives that have sprung up across Canada. With regard to child welfare in particular, in recent years many child welfare agencies have developed culturally relevant programs and supports, in consultation with Aboriginal stakeholders, to meet the specific needs of Aboriginal children and families using child welfare services. In addition, there are a growing number of fully mandated Aboriginal agencies that provide the full range of child protection services to Aboriginal families. These developments made sharing knowledge, values, policies, and practices between Aboriginal and non-Aboriginal communities, agencies, policy-makers, and researchers all the more important. For this reason, the CECW placed a strong priority on developing and expanding a fruitful dialogue that would be beneficial to both Aboriginal and non-Aboriginal child welfare across Canada.

Need to bridge gaps among academia, policy, and service

Knowledge created through research has always been applied to some extent to policy and practice and, conversely, the needs of policy and practice have always helped to inform research agendas. This exchange of ideas has not always been as frequent or as fluid as might be desired, however. In recent years, there has been an increasing emphasis on bridging the gaps among research, policy-making, and providing best practice. Evidence-based policy and evidence-based practice are attempts to make use of research knowledge to develop policy and practice plans, and there is a growing requirement within funding agencies to base new research on the real needs of policy and practice.

The CECW recognized that there was a need to draw together academia, policy, and service in Canadian child welfare in a more comprehensive way. The research agenda that was initiated in 2001 set out to link child welfare service needs and university-based researchers in projects that would create new knowledge and also help establish a research culture that valued the collaboration of universities and community organizations. The policy advice agenda evolved over the first years of the CECW's operation, but increasingly involved ties with key policy-makers in child welfare from Canada's provinces and territories and direct evidence-based advice to policy-makers as occasions arose. In addition, over the ten years that the CECW functioned, the CECW developed numerous plain language documents and summaries that helped to bridge former gaps, as well as a comprehensive communications system to disseminate knowledge across Canada. Overall, addressing the need to bridge gaps among academia, policy, and services was seen as essential, and efforts to do so were undertaken following a comprehensive strategy.

Need to develop a national network of child welfare professionals

During its inception, the CECW regarded the notable lack of a national network of professionals working in the field of child welfare as a considerable barrier to the sharing of information and knowledge. This gap is largely attributable to the discrepancies in provincial and territorial child welfare legislation and practices. The Centre saw great value in utilizing the many new and available electronic technologies to build a community of child welfare researchers, policy-makers, and practitioners in universities and institutes in various parts of the country. Soon after its formation, the CECW began working to build a comprehensive and linked network of those working in child welfare. The electronic community grew dramatically over the years to include over 2,500 subscribers to the CECW's list-serve. The Centre also developed a searchable database (accessible on the CCWRP) of Canadian researchers working on topics related to children's well-being and child welfare-related issues.

Need to have a way to disseminate child welfare knowledge and information

In the beginning, the CECW's work featured knowledge generation through original research partnerships. In carrying out this work, it was essential first to determine both a need and a desire for such information among those working in child welfare across Canada. Various stakeholders in universities, non-governmental organizations, and community organizations were consulted in helping to frame questions on pressing topics within child welfare, and in working collaboratively over the years on generating this new knowledge.

Due to changes in the CECW's funding structure in its final four years, the focus shifted from knowledge creation through new research and data analysis to knowledge transfer, exchange, and dissemination. Dissemination is the act of putting information out into the world, and the CECW perceived identifying and disseminating research knowledge generated and carried out by others as a central reason for its existence, particularly in its last few years. This shift in the CECW's focus was not only pragmatic, but also seen as a much-needed response in the broader field of children's health to make research knowledge more readily accessible to policy-makers and practitioners who are in a position to use and apply the knowledge in practice.

Need to initiate a longer-term evaluation strategy

It is not enough simply to create and then circulate new knowledge without some thought of monitoring how the knowledge is being used and whether it is exerting any impact. This part of the process is also the most challenging, as it can be difficult to account for all the factors that might influence knowledge use, such as relevance of the knowledge, frequency of use, and accessibility of the product. Longer-term impacts and outcomes (e.g., changes in awareness, knowledge, behaviours, or attitudes) are even more difficult to measure and document. Evaluating system-wide outcomes has received very little attention in most fields, including child welfare, but is a task that should receive more collective investment and collaboration.

To begin to address this issue, the CECW realized that use of research-based knowledge was directly related to the relevance of research to practice, as well as to the direct involvement of practitioners who were in a position to effect practice changes. Thus, the research agenda developed was based on developing knowledge that would help assess the efficacy of a variety of child welfare practices. The assumption was that such information would then be of use to practitioners who could make changes to improve their services and outcomes.

During the last two years of the CECW, there arose a need to explain this process in a more formal and conceptual way. As a result, all four centres undertook a joint project to develop a Knowledge Transfer and Exchange (KTE) model that was uniquely adapted to the needs of children's well-being. This work identified and expanded upon four key aspects: knowledge generation, knowledge dissemination, knowledge use, and impact of knowledge. This KTE conceptual model (available at www.cecw-cepb.ca) appears to offer a solid framework for evaluating the longer-term effects of knowledge creation and dissemination.

MAJOR ACCOMPLISHMENTS OF THE CECW

The scope of CECW's activities and achievements over the years has been broad and far-reaching. It is important to note that the Centre's work has gone well beyond the written products and resources available on the Canadian Child Welfare Research Portal (formerly the CECW website). The range and reach of the CECW has extended much farther than its core infrastructure to include activities carried out by its partner sites and numerous affiliates. Perhaps the Centre's greatest accomplishment has been the development of strong and meaningful partnerships, collaborations, and relationships among all those who have been involved with its work over the years.

The five functions established by the Centre of Excellence for Children's Well-being Program—analyze existing data, conduct original research, provide policy advice, disseminate knowledge, and forge networks—have guided the work of CECW over the years.

Analyze existing data

The CECW has worked over the years to gather, consolidate, and analyze existing information and data on child maltreatment in Canada and abroad. This crucial work has been a foundation for more extensive research and has shaped the Centre's dissemination activities and products.

The CECW actively supported and conducted numerous secondary analyses and produced dissemination materials for the 1998 and 2003 cycles of the CIS, as well as the provincial studies in Ontario and Quebec. The Centre assisted with the 2008 cycle of the CIS (in the final stages of completion) and supported the enhanced First Nations component of the study.

Conduct original research

Carrying out and funding original research was an initial core objective of the CECW. A large part of this work in the early years of the Centre included funding and carrying out eleven evaluations of promising child welfare interventions, as well as four 5-year research projects in child welfare funded by CIHR. In April 2002, the CECW and the First Nations Child & Family Caring Society of Canada officially opened the First Nations Research Site in Winnipeg to create the infrastructure to conduct research on First Nations issues in child welfare. The NOM Data Support project team has been working to build provincial and territorial capacity to utilize the outcomes monitoring system and indicators, and to conduct trend and comparative analyses of service data to enhance evidence-based policy-making and program development. In the fall of 2009, McGill hosted the second Canadian Roundtable on Child Welfare Outcomes, attended by representatives from all provinces and territories as well as several international researchers. In addition, provinces and territories participating in the Child Welfare Outcomes Coordinating Committee have provided two years of data on one or more of the indicators and agreed to a four-stage process for measuring the indicators of child development and parenting. The CECW has also been involved with a number of systematic reviews with the Canadian partner of the Campbell Collaboration, an international research network that produces systematic reviews of the effects of social interventions (The Campbell

Collaboration, n.d.), to consolidate best available evidence for select child welfare issues.

In addition to this research agenda of activities that were directly initiated by the CECW, the platform model provided an opportunity for the CECW to become a partner in numerous other research activities. These included research by directors and other faculty at the three universities, and partnerships with numerous universities and community organizations across Canada (especially in the Prairie provinces). Throughout its ten years, the CECW was involved in some way in much of the major child welfare research that was conducted in Canada. The impact of initiating such a research agenda is not yet known, but the intention was to help set the basis for a stronger ongoing research culture within Canadian child welfare and to "kick-start" this process by supporting specific research projects in various cities across the country.

Provide policy advice

The CECW and its associated researchers have worked closely with all levels of government to provide direction for child welfare policies in Canada. For example, CECW Scientific Director Nico Trocmé was seconded in 2004 by the Child Welfare Secretariat of Ontario and has consulted with the Alberta government in its development of differential response policies within the province.

Over the years, the CECW has actively promoted links between policy development, research, and practice through its sponsorship and participation in numerous meetings, consultations, forums, and other events. Notably, the CECW hosted the National Child Welfare Policy Symposium annually from 2001–2006 to address immediate and pressing policy issues within child welfare in Canada. The CECW also published a policy book on community collaboration and emerging models of differential response by international researchers and practitioners from Canada, the United States, England, and Australia.

Disseminate knowledge

The timely and effective dissemination of child welfare information has been a particular strength and commitment of the CECW. The CECW has striven to make credible research and evidence-based knowledge in child welfare that were previously unexplored or underexplored widely accessible. The CECW's main vehicle for dissemination over the years was its website, which offered all CECW products free for download in both English and French. Success of the website was demonstrated by the fact that it received more than one million hits on average per year. The website recently transitioned into the Canadian Child Welfare Research Portal (www.cwrp.ca). The website is designed to serve as a comprehensive child welfare research database, as well as a dynamic networking platform for both international and Canadian academics, researchers, policy-makers, professionals, and students in the child welfare field. The websites of our core partner organizations provided a great deal of additional information.

Two important products featured on the website are Research Watch (RW), which produces summaries of the most pertinent and recent child welfare research publications, and Canadian Research in Brief (CRIB), summaries of selected published Canadian child welfare-related studies. RW and CRIB summaries were sent out on a monthly basis to the CECW list-serve of 2,500 subscribers, who in turn forwarded it to other list-serves, reaching a total audience of approximately 4,200 readers across Canada. The website houses online catalogues of all past editions of RW and CRIB, available for searching and viewing.

The Centre's most popular product throughout the years was the more than 75 plain-language Information Sheets on various child welfare topics, all available for download on the website. These Information Sheets were accessed by numerous child welfare researchers, practitioners, policy-makers, service providers, and students.

The First Nations Research Site, the Caring Society, and the CECW created an online journal entitled the *First Peoples Child & Family Review* to promote and publish research articles primarily focused on First Nations/Aboriginal child welfare. The *Review* has been an extremely popular online journal, perhaps because it fills a unique and badly needed niche in Canadian child welfare. An online archive of all past issues of the journal is accessible at www.fncfcs.com.

Forge networks

An important part of the CECW's work has been promoting multidisciplinary collaboration between professionals in child welfare and related areas in Canada and internationally. The CECW established an impressive number of strategic partnerships with a diverse group of stakeholders, including various Canadian universities, government policy-makers, community organizations, and graduate students in various disciplines and from various universities.

The CECW's work in the area of First Nations child welfare has led to many important and fruitful partnerships and collaborations over the years. One of the Centre's most significant accomplishments was the Reconciliation conference held in 2005 and attended by more than 200 Indigenous and non-Indigenous leaders from across North America within child welfare. This event and numerous activities before and after it were developed through a strong partnership with the Child Welfare League of America and the National Indian Child Welfare Agency in the United States. The goal of the three-day event was to create a collaborative vision of how to better serve Aboriginal families and children involved with the child welfare system. The gathering resulted in the development of the important *Touchstones of Hope for Indigenous Children, Youth, and Families* document which outlines five guiding principles and four phases of reconciliation for working with Indigenous peoples in child welfare. The movement has led to the training of over 200 facilitators in the *Touchstones* process, presentations of the *Touchstones* document to several international audiences, influences on policy development both within Canada and in other parts of the world (e.g., northern British Columbia, Australia, New Zealand), and contributions to curriculum development for university-based courses in an effort to apply *Touchstones* within academia. The bulk of this work has been undertaken by the First Nations Child & Family Caring Society of Canada and, in particular, by the executive director, Cindy Blackstock.

The CECW established a strong partnership with the Prairie Child Welfare Consortium (PCWC), a group of researchers, practitioners, and policy-makers throughout Alberta, Saskatchewan, and Manitoba. The CECW funded several research projects carried out through the PCWC, and helped fund and organize three PCWC's bi-annual symposia that brought together more than 200 participants from the Prairies as well as from other provinces. The CECW also worked with the PCWC on the publication of two collaborative books, *Putting a Human Face on Child Welfare: Voices from the Prairies,* released in 2007, and *Passion for Action in Child and Family Services: Voices from the Prairies,* published in 2009.

The CECW was instrumental in encouraging the development of the Atlantic Canada Child Welfare Forum to bring together child welfare professionals in the Atlantic provinces. The Centre sponsored and helped to organize the group's meetings in 2007, 2008, and 2010.

These and numerous other less formal associations with individuals and organizations over the CECW's 10 years had a wide variety of effects. A great many research projects were proposed and undertaken that included the CECW as a partner in some way. Academics, policy-makers, and others were attracted to the activity and funding of the CECW and voluntarily made their expertise available to one or more of the activities. The funding was very helpful to the core partner organizations, especially by putting in place a strong federally-funded infrastructure that provided research and leveraging opportunities for university faculty; part-time employment and learning for graduate students; and training for service providers, students, and other stakeholders. Thus, the networks were valuable to develop for their own sake, but they also resulted in numerous other advantages for the CECW and many other people and organizations.

Specifically, the CECW has excelled in four essential areas of Canadian child welfare:

1. Developing and disseminating new knowledge in both French and English, and bridging the French-language/English-language divide. The CECW functioned in both official languages and all of its products were made available in both French and English.
2. Developing and disseminating new knowledge and creating new relationships between those involved in Aboriginal and non-Aboriginal child welfare in Canada. The First Nations Child and Family Caring Society was an integral partner in this process and an invaluable ally in establishing a dialogue between Aboriginal and non-Aboriginal professionals.
3. Having a pan-Canadian, broad, and inclusive mandate to unify and bring together the previously discrete provincial/territorial child welfare services and legislation within Canada.
4. Working extensively to promote linkages between policy development, practice, and research to promote evidence-based practice with respect to child welfare in Canada.

TRANSITIONING FROM THE PHAC FUNDING MANDATE

The CECW was fortunate to receive one-year funding contracts beyond its original five-year mandate, beginning in April 2006 and ending in March 2010, to help it firmly establish its program of activities and to transition away from its PHAC funding. In response to the year-by-year funding structure, the CECW's focus shifted to conducting secondary data analyses of existing research, supporting the development of research capacity through support and consultation, and continuing the development of knowledge transfer and dissemination products. From 2008–2010, the focus of the Centre's activities narrowed to shift much of the responsibility for its key activities and projects to the core partner organizations to ensure that much of the work will be carried on. In its final two years, the CECW directors developed sustainability plans for the ongoing projects and a major focus became the transformation of the CECW website into the redesigned Canadian Child Welfare Research Portal. A partnership between the University of Toronto and McGill was forged to harness the collective energies of their faculty and graduate students to ensure that the website will be kept current through the inter-university Journal Watch club.

LEGACY OF THE CECW

The CECW became a unifying "voice" and presence of Canadian child welfare when no such entity existed, and has been proud to act as a mechanism that ties together child welfare as a field within Canada. The inclusive and broad mandate of the Centre has helped to bring together the previously discrete field of provincial/territorial child welfare services and legislation within Canada. This uniting of child welfare as a field in Canada will be maintained and carried on, in part, through the core partnership of the University of Toronto, McGill University (through the work of the Centre for Research on Children and Families), Institut de recherché sur le development social des jeunes (IRDS) at the Université de Montréal, the Child Welfare League of Canada, and the First Nations Child and Family Caring Society of Canada. The strong and enduring partnership among these organizations is perhaps one of the greatest legacies left by the CECW, as is the larger network of affiliated researchers, policy-makers, practitioners, and students who were brought together through the work and efforts of the Centre.

The CECW has prided itself on making resources and information on child welfare research widely available and easily accessible. The recent transformation of the CECW's former website into the Canadian Child Welfare Research Portal has strengthened and expanded this function and will serve to enhance knowledge transfer and dissemination of child welfare, particularly Canadian child welfare, information, and research.

The many and varied research initiatives and projects that have grown out of and/or been supported by the CECW will serve as continual reminders of the ways in which the Centre influenced the focus and direction of child welfare research within the Canadian context. Many of these research initiatives are leading the way in shaping the face of child welfare research and knowledge of the scope and characteristics of child maltreatment in Canada, such as the National Outcomes Matrix, the CIS studies, and the Maltreatment and Adolescent Pathways (MAP) longitudinal study being led by Christine Wekerle at the University of Western Ontario.

The CECW was proud and honoured to play an integral role in opening the doors of communication and understanding among Aboriginal and non-Aboriginal child welfare professionals. The creation of the *First Peoples Child & Family Review* has been a catalyst for increasing the capacity and visibility of First Nations child welfare researchers to publish their work. It is hoped that the CECW's attention to the important issues facing First Nations children and families involved with the child welfare system in Canada has been a stepping-stone in laying the foundation for a spirit of respect and compassion that will endure long into the future.

THE WAY FORWARD

The Centres of Excellence for Children's Well-Being Program completed its mandate on March 31, 2010, and is no longer receiving financial support from the Public Health Agency of Canada. With the end of the Program, each centre has developed strategies for continuing its goals and activities into the future.

The way forward for CECW Activities

The end of core funding for the Centre of Excellence for Child Welfare has resulted in a considerable change in the way that the activities of the former CECW are carried out. Some of the activities are continuing under the leadership of one or more of the partner organizations, while others have ended. The CECW directors and sponsoring organizations are committed to enriching their many collaborations and partnerships that have developed over the past ten years by developing new research initiatives and setting strategic directions in child welfare research, collaborating further with provincial and territorial governments in setting future child welfare policy, and disseminating scientific and plain-language child welfare information to a broad child welfare audience throughout Canada in both official languages. Dissemination of Canadian child welfare knowledge will continue to expand through the website developed by the CECW, which has transitioned into the Canadian Child Welfare Research Portal.

The way forward for child welfare in Canada

Although the CECW as an established entity has ended, and some of the national voice for child welfare has been lost, the difficult but crucial work of child welfare research carries on in the CECW's partner organizations and by the numerous professionals across the country committed to caring for the children and families involved with the child welfare system. There is a need to create and support more networks of multi-disciplinary collaborations among those working in the fields of child welfare, health, early childhood development, education, youth justice, mental health, and addictions to consolidate and share knowledge to improve children's health and well-being in all areas of their lives.

New knowledge produces new questions and there is a pressing need for more Canadian research in all areas of child welfare. Critical questions about the health status and needs of children in care, the effectiveness of emerging child welfare interventions such as family group conferencing, appropriate service delivery models for working with First Nations children and families, and the long-term profiles and outcomes of children in care are some of the many questions that remain unanswered.

The way forward for children's well-being in Canada

On March 1, 2010, the managers of the four centres in the Centres of Excellence for Children's Well-Being Program met in Toronto to finalize their collective report for the program. Those attending the meeting felt strongly that they wanted to develop a short but helpful statement that would reflect the key lessons they learned in setting up and running national children's well-being sets of activities. Their statement below (taken from the Centres of Excellence for Children's Well-Being Summary Report 2010, available at www.cecw-cepb.ca) is meant to provide an overall strategy for others to follow.

Funders and others interested in children's well-being should recognize:

- the need to develop national strategies to improve children's well-being;
- that strategies should be developed around broad issues and are inclusive of the social determinants of health;
- that strategies should be comprehensive and include: knowledge development, dissemination, and action; action needs to include capacity building;
- that multi-year funding support for infrastructure is essential for success;
- that the implementation of the strategies should build on existing networks.

IN SUMMARY

The funding provided to establish and operate the Centre of Excellence for Child Welfare for ten years created a stir of activity and excitement in child welfare. There had never before been a structure whose primary purpose was to bring together the many diverse aspects of child welfare across Canada. There had never before been a structure that simultaneously generated new ideas for child welfare, promoted a culture of research and evaluation within child welfare practice, took an active role in providing policy advice, produced and disseminated child welfare information, and brought together several types of people and networks. A lesson from the CECW that we are left with is that a Canada-wide voice and set of activities are absolutely possible to attain, and that attaining them is indeed very helpful to the ongoing enhancement of child welfare in Canada.

ACKNOWLEDGEMENTS

The CECW is grateful to its talented and dedicated staff between 2001 and 2010: Wendy James, Caroline Felstiner, Sarah Dufour, Ivan Brown,

Shannon Woodward, Sue Sullivan, Catherine Roy, Marlyn Bennett, Sophie Léveillé, Tina Crockford, Véronique Bouchard, Ferzana Chase, Pamela Gough, Carrie Reid, Jules Lajoie, Michael Saini, Amanda Bello, Nicole Petrowski, Andrew Hauser, Tobi Baker, Jonathan Schmidt, and numerous M.S.W. students and Ph.D. candidates.

REFERENCES

Government of Canada. (2004). A Canada fit for children. Retrieved October 30, 2011, from www.canadiancrc.com/PDFs/Canadas_Plan_Action_April2004-EN.pdf.

Steinhauer, P. (1999). The National Children's Agenda – what should it look like?: A submission to the Federal Government from The Sparrow Lake Alliance. Toronto, ON: The Centre for Health Promotion, University of Toronto and Canadians Against Child Poverty.

The Campbell Collaboration. (n.d.). The Campbell Collaboration: What helps? What harms? Based on what evidence? Retrieved October 29, 2011 from www.campbellcollaboration.org.

United Nations General Assembly. (2002). A world fit for children. Resolution adopted by the General Assembly at the Twenty-Seventh Special Session on Children. Retrieved May 12, 2010, from www.unicef.org/specialsession/wffc.

CHAPTER 2

A Day's Discourse among Indigenous Scholars and Practitioners about Indigenous Child Welfare Work in Canada

Gwen Gosek and Marlyn Bennett

From time immemorial, Indigenous families and communities have been the centre of the universe for their children and vice versa. Today, in Indigenous communities across Canada, children continue to be seen as valued and precious gifts from the Creator, gifts to be cherished and cared for by their communities. This has persisted in spite of all the interruptions created by colonizing forces, such as residential schools and child welfare systems. But these forces have taken their toll. Indigenous children continue to represent approximately 40% of children and youth in the care of child welfare in Canada (Blackstock, Trocmé, & Bennett,

---

SUGGESTED CITATION: Gosek, G., & Bennett, M. (2012). A Day's Discourse among Indigenous Scholars and Practitioners about Indigenous Child Welfare Work in Canada. In D. Fuchs, S. McKay, & I. Brown (Eds.), *Awakening the Spirit: Moving Forward in Child Welfare: Voices from the Prairies* (pp. 23–36). Regina, SK: Canadian Plains Research Center.

2004), and Indigenous communities and families continue to experience a loss that has become too familiar.[1]

The sense of loss and grief experienced by families and communities through the residential school era has been compounded and further complicated over subsequent decades in which thousands of Indigenous children have been continuously removed from families and communities and placed in out-of-home care by child welfare systems. Changes have been made to legislation, standards, and policies since the sixties scoop that are designed to stem the loss of Indigenous children and youth from their homes and communities, but still the number of children in out-of-home care has continued to rise (Trocmé, Knoke, & Blackstock, 2004). When one considers that 40% of the estimated 76,000 children and youth in out-of-home care are Indigenous and that less than 10 percent of those individuals are placed in Indigenous homes[2] (Trocmé, Knoke, Shangreaux, Fallon, & MacLaurin, 2005), it becomes obvious that literally thousands of Indigenous children and youth are being raised outside of their families and communities. This strongly suggests that current policies, based on practices of the past, are not working well for Indigenous people and that innovative new policy is clearly required (Blackstock, 2008). Some First Nations communities have made considerable progress in bringing about such changes to their child welfare practices in order to keep their children in community care, although many continue to struggle to overcome systemic barriers (McKay & Thomas Prokop, 2007).

If there is one lesson we should have taken from the residential school experience and the "Sixties Scoop," it is that the cost of wholesale removal of children and youth from their families, communities, and cultures has long-term consequences for those individuals, their

---

1   A note about terms: The terms "Indigenous" and "Aboriginal" are used interchangeably in this paper in reference to the Canadian context; both include Métis, Inuit, and First Nations regardless of where they live in Canada and regardless of whether they are "registered"under the Indian Act of Canada (Lavallée, 2009). The terms "First Nations" and "Indians" are also used to refer specifically to those identified and registered as "Indians" under the federal Indian Act. "First Nations" is a term that is not legally defined.

2   According to B.C.'s Ministry of Children and Family Development, "in 2007, only 15.8 percent of B.C.'s Indigenous youth and children were placed with Indigenous caregivers" (Quoted by Feduniw, 2009, p. 165).

families and communities, and for society as a whole. Like the survivors of residential schools and the "Sixties Scoop," the majority of Indigenous children who spend long periods of time growing up in care away from their own cultures will contribute to yet another generation that will not be fluent in its own cultural languages, and will continue to struggle to feel connected to their families, communities, and territories (Carriere, 2007; Locust, 2000). These young people have reduced opportunities to participate in spiritual and cultural events, and they do not have opportunities to learn firsthand about the values, norms, and practices of their biological families and communities (Bertsch & Bidgood, 2010).

THE INDIGENOUS SCHOLARS MEETING

It was not surprising, then, that when Indigenous scholars and practitioners met for a one-day workshop to discuss Indigenous child welfare issues the day prior to the Prairie Child Welfare Consortium (PCWC) conference in Winnipeg in October 2009, they brought with them a sense of urgency. The participants' knowledge and experience were based not only in their relationships to child welfare as child protection workers, managers, community support practitioners, elders, and academics—many in attendance were also Indigenous community and family members who had been directly impacted by the child welfare system either through removal of close family members or through their own childhood experiences in foster care or adoption situations (Reid, 2005; Sinclair, 2007).

Planning for the one-day preconference workshop was initiated through the PCWC. Indigenous members of the PCWC identified the need to bring together other Indigenous scholars and practitioners in a setting where participants could begin identifying and discussing the common themes reflected in Indigenous child welfare work and the reality of that work within Canada. The purpose of this chapter is to describe briefly the process of that meeting, and to highlight main points of the discussion that emanated from this day of talking and sharing amongst Indigenous scholars and practitioners.

Workshop Process

The workshop was held at Whaka Pimadiziiwii Pinaysiiwigamic (Circle of Life Thunderbird House, www.thunderbirdhouse.com), which is an Indigenous gathering place in Winnipeg. The Circle of Life Thunderbird

House provided a practical and esthetic environment for meeting, particularly because it reflected the cultures of the territories. Two Elders, a woman and a man, accepted tobacco to attend and to fully engage with participants as spiritual advisors and carriers of sacred knowledge as well as to support the process with opening and closing ceremonies.

In planning for the workshop, committee members agreed to an agenda that would be used to structure the day's events in a manner that allowed for the process to unfold in response to what would emerge from the participants. For example, the agenda included opening comments and introductions, followed by small group discussions in which participants responded to the questions, "What is happening in Indigenous child welfare now?" and "What needs to change?" The afternoon session included having each group report on their group's discussions, and the day's activities were rounded out by a focused discussion in response to the question, "What concrete action do we take and how do we do this?"

As the group participants engaged in the process, it became evident that each group represented diversity in terms of Indigenous identity and culture, work and lived experience, and current location and practice. It was also immediately evident that people were invested in the issues they brought to the discussion, and that the issues shared by individuals were familiar to others regardless of their different locales within western Canada. Participants broke into four groups for the morning session and recorded their main ideas on flipchart paper. The following discussion is based on the main themes that were identified from the four groups.

Theme 1: Valuing Indigenous world views and cultural ways of being

Valuing Indigenous world views and cultural ways of being was the first theme that flowed from the day's discussion. This theme focused on the importance of valuing Indigenous world views and cultural ways of being in all areas of child welfare. The discussion identified a number of "needs": 1) a need for home studies to be relevant to Indigenous realities; 2) a need for teams identified as "Aboriginal" to have Indigenous representation; 3) a need to incorporate Indigenous cultural practices rather than relying solely on mainstream psychological assessments; 4) a need to ensure that assessments are strengths-based and that they include culturally rooted approaches rather than being based on the deficit models currently in use; 5) a need to ensure that practice standards are inclusive of all Indigenous groups; 6) a need to provide a space to listen to the children's and youths' voices and to create empowering situations; and 7) a need to ensure kinship care is rooted in an Indigenous community's cultural traditions.

The workshop participants were clear in their message that in order for child welfare services to be effective in Indigenous communities those services must reflect the values, norms, and practices of the communities. The sentiments expressed above are not necessarily new to the discussion of Indigenous child welfare, as the people involved with child welfare are only too aware of the shortcomings and barriers within this system (Blackstock, Brown, & Bennett, 2007). What made this workshop discussion distinctive was the opportunity it provided to individuals working in the child welfare system and academic circles to sit down together to discuss their concerns and to problem solve.

The need to keep these conversations going is critical if positive changes that support Indigenous ways of being are to be reflected in social work policies, practices, research, and education (Giwa, Sethi, Smith, & Wabano, 2006). As Jeffery (2009) pointed out, "The mission and practices of the profession evolved out of a history of elites 'helping' marginalized groups of people," and the profession, like so many others, developed out of European ideology in its "understandings of social difference, hierarchy and systems of marginality" (p. 46). In view of their historical and contemporary knowledge, Indigenous people not only have an intimate understanding of the urgent need for change but they also have the knowledge of what needs to change and how those changes must come about in order for their communities to become healthy once again. Unfortunately, the road to change is complex, full of roadblocks, and not readily embraced by all of society.

In our efforts to bring about positive change for Indigenous communities, we often believe that we are on the right track only to discover in hindsight that we are repeating the same mistakes using a different approach (Blackstock, 2005). An example of this is the seemingly "progressive" recognition that residential schools were devastating families and communities and then moving to close them down—while, at the same time, the "Sixties Scoop" was being implemented, basically taking over where residential schools left off (Hudson & McKenzie, 1981).

Providing services that fit with Indigenous world views and ways of being is made difficult by a number of underlying factors: first, our inability to step outside of the Eurocentric world views and values that have been ingrained in all of us since birth; second, the related assumption that social workers are, for the most part, "culture free" (Maiter, 2009); and third, a general lack of trust in the ability of Indigenous people to govern themselves.

Social workers have recognized the need to acknowledge cultural diversity and, in recent decades, have supported the cultural competence or cross-cultural model, which is "seen to encourage openness to differences, expertise in the use of cultural resources, and respect for cultural integrity" (Jeffery, 2009, p. 49). While these are worthy aspirations, what needs to be considered is the question of whether or not the model actually reflects these goals in intent and practice. As with so many theories, models, and approaches, the cross-cultural approach has been developed within a mainstream perspective as a "method" for professional social service workers, who reflect the values of the dominant society, to work "effectively" with people who do *not* reflect the dominant society's ways of being. Rather than having real conversations with people from different cultures in which they listen and learn from their stories, social workers are encouraged to become cultural experts in such a way that cultural attributes are "catalogued, evaluated and managed" (Jeffery, 2009, p. 49).

Although it takes a lifetime for one person to learn his or her culture in order to pass on the knowledge to the next generations, social workers are expected to learn about multiple cultures in a relatively short period of time. The oversimplification of complex cultures, which also represent a wide range of diversity within cultures, results in stereotyping of people and misrepresentation of their actions. Therefore, rather than closing the gap on cultural understanding, the cross-cultural approach highlights difference and nurtures stereotypical views and practices. One way to avoid these pitfalls is to pause long enough to listen and learn from the people we are committed to support, whether it is in the role of community members or allies (Gray, Coates, & Hetherington, 2008). As we continue to work together we must always remember to stop along the way to re-evaluate our policies and practices in order to ensure we are hearing the peoples' voices and that we are working *with* diversity and not against it (Lavallée, 2009).

Theme 2: Inadequate policies and resources as barriers

The second theme identified barriers such as inadequate policies and resources experienced by First Nations and Métis child and family services in the provision of services. Among the concerns expressed were: 1) legislation that does not reflect Indigenous culture; 2) paperwork that overwhelms workers and interferes with their ability to spend time with the families on their caseload; 3) the lack of resources for fathers; 4) the lack of prevention services across the system; 5) the lack of supports for people experiencing grief and loss issues, attachment disorders, and post-traumatic stress disorder; and 6) the lack of housing.

Inadequate policies and resources as barriers were highlighted in the day's initial discussions. These focused on the status of the Human Rights complaint that was jointly filed in 2007 by the First Nations Child & Family Caring Society and the Assembly of First Nations against Indian and Northern Affairs Canada for discriminating against First Nations children on the basis of race and national ethnic origin. The complaint was launched after the Government of Canada failed to implement the recommendations arising from two joint initiatives it commissioned (the 1991 National Joint Policy Review and the 2005 *Wen:De* Report; Blackstock, Loxley, Prakash, & Wien, 2005) to address the inequality stemming from funding practices to First Nations child welfare services on reserve. While the federal government has failed to act, growing numbers of First Nations children continue to go into child welfare care because they are denied services to keep them safely at home. This historic case marked the first time that Canada has been held to account before a legal body for its current treatment of First Nations children and their families (Blackstock, 2011).

Theme 3: Post-secondary education needs

Theme three was the need for post-secondary education, and includes the need for: 1) increased Indigenous-based training and education; 2) the inclusion of Elders and ceremonies in the university environment; 3) educators to have an increased level of knowledge related to Indigenous people; 4) academia to link to frontline/grassroots; and 5) an increase in the number of Aboriginal people teaching in universities.

In speaking to the difficulties faced by newly graduated non-Indigenous social workers, who have theoretical knowledge but have not had the opportunity to be immersed in Indigenous communities, Walmsley (2009) noted, "...without the experience of living or growing up in an Indigenous community, it is not possible to be an expert in child protection intervention with Indigenous children and families" (p. 103). This insight takes us back to the question of how well-prepared social work graduates are to work with the diversity that exists within Indigenous communities.

Academics and their institutions often have trouble with the idea that they may practice racism. But discrimination "is a matter of impact and not intent," wrote Frances Henry and Carol Tator (2009), both social scientists, in the book they co-edited, *Racism in the Canadian University: Demanding Social Justice, Inclusion and Equity*. The issue really starts with representation, or who gets in and how. According to the 2006 Census, about 14 percent of visible minorities held faculty positions, whereas 24 percent of all Ph.D.-holders in Canada were visible minorities. Aboriginal professors in the humanities and social sciences essentially make up a smaller percentage of the faculty-held positions in universities across Canada—Aboriginal professors with a Ph.D. designation hold only two percent of faculty posts. Sadly, the social issues facing Indigenous children, families, and communities remain objects of study, rather than producers of knowledge.

Successes and Progress

The group also spoke of the successes and progress they have witnessed in recent years. For instance, it was observed that communities are now more aware of the issues and solutions and, collectively, they agreed that "We have an understanding of who we are in our efforts and we're moving in a good direction." To summarize, the participants proposed the belief that "We are getting wiser!"

Some specific areas of progress identified by participants included: successes in reconnecting children and adoptees with family members (Carriere & Scarth, 2007); community building efforts in community support agencies such as Ma Mawi Wi Chi Itata Centre in Winnipeg, Manitoba (Silver, 2004); the devolution of Child and Family Services in Manitoba through the Aboriginal Justice Inquiry – Child Welfare Initiative, which has allowed for more control over how and where services are provided (Hudson & McKenzie, 2003); and the increase in online Indigenous journals that encapsulate and promote Indigenous knowledge such as *The First Peoples Child and Family Review* (www.fncaringsociety.ca) and *Pimatisiwin: A Journal of Aboriginal and Indigenous Community Health* (www.pimatisiwin.com), among many other Indigenous journals that are now just beginning to emerge that support and celebrate the emancipation of Indigenous knowledge from colonial forces (Heyd, 1995; Smith, 1999).

RECOMMENDATIONS FOR MOVING AHEAD

In the final part of the afternoon, the discussion groups came together in a large circle to brainstorm concrete actions for beginning to address some of the issues raised in the morning session. The following list represents the main statements that were recorded on a flipchart at the time of the discussion.

1. We need jurisdiction over our children!
2. We must shift the mandate of agencies to a focus on prevention and keep prevention in the forefront.
3. We need to work together.
   - Our fight is politically similar to the fight for our treaty rights; and
   - We need to do the groundwork, gather the facts, and work collaboratively with the chief, counsellors and lawyers working on the collective behalf of Indigenous peoples.
4. We need to remember that we still own the process (in other words, we can decide how we deliver the programs).
5. We must ensure that we continue to incorporate the seven teachings (Honesty. Humility. Truth. Wisdom. Love. Respect. Bravery.) (Benton-Banai, 1988).
   - Ask, "Is this how you do your social work?";
   - Walk tenderly among the people; and
   - Always use compassion and kindness.
6. Remember that regardless of the type of work we do, we are facilitators (for example, we can only facilitate healing for a family —we cannot heal them).
   - What we view as "helping" may not be considered helping by the other person, so we need to be mindful in asking people whom we work with what they need.

7. The stories must continue to be told.
   - Incorporate and implement events and ceremonies (like the Creating Hope Society's "Blanket of Remembrance Round Dance") held for children who have died in the care of child welfare; and
   - Recognize that our Nations have gone from losing children in residential schools to losing children in child welfare.
8. Partner more with other provinces and organizations.
9. We still need a safe place to talk about our experiences.
   - Invite people who are working with our children in other areas of the system to attend future discussions so they can hear the stories first hand.
10. We must do our healing *before* working with our communities.
    - Be hyper-vigilant to ensure that the people who are working with others are healthy / balanced.
11. Be involved in community development.
    - Access the communities' resources;
    - Be inclusive of our Elders;
    - Ensure that we *fully engage* our Elders in our forums / dialogues and make them central to the process;
    - Advocate for more money for prevention services in child welfare; and
    - Shift away from a focus on individuals to a focus on community.
12. Disseminate what we know is working.
    - Use our voices by writing and aspire toward publishing;
    - Educate by sharing our knowledge with other professions; and
    - Be creative and use different formats (i.e., presentations, workshops, technology, photography, art).

CONCLUSION

First Nations families and communities have a long history of child welfare involvement (Hamilton & Sinclair, 1991). First Nations leaders have long argued that their people are better placed in providing child and family–related services to their own families because they have provided for their children for thousands of years (Blackstock, 2007). This paper has highlighted some of the discourse that emerged during the one-day gathering of Indigenous scholars and practitioners who expounded on the state of child welfare in First Nation communities today. The day's discussions centered on three themes that appeared to be at the heart of Indigenous child welfare practice for the participating scholars and practitioners: 1) the importance of valuing and incorporating Indigenous worldviews and cultural ways of being into practice; 2) recognizing the structural barriers that exist for Indigenous families who become tangled up in child welfare services, and that result primarily from inadequate policies and resources; and 3) the need for post-secondary education that must incorporate Indigenous world views, practices, and knowledge. The discussion concluded with recognition that there have been successes and progress in many areas that have led to a collective consciousness and the development of resources that celebrate and promote traditional and contemporary Indigenous knowledge and ways of practice. The discussion ended with recommendations about where future concerted effort must be expended or continued in order to advance collective action in decolonizing child welfare services for Indigenous families in Canada.

Unfortunately, the discrimination inherent in the colonial system of child welfare is still all too apparent. At the time of the publication of this chapter, the Canadian Human Rights Tribunal had recently ruled against First Nations children (Chotalia, 2011). The Tribunal Chair, Shirish P. Chotalia, dismissed the discrimination complaint (discussed earlier) jointly filed by the First Nations Child and Family Caring Society of Canada and the Assembly of First Nations, on a technicality. In her ruling, Chotalia stated that the federal government can continue to provide a different, and inequitable, level of service to First Nations children so long as the provinces/territories provide the service to all other children. The decision of the Canadian Human Rights Tribunal to dismiss the allegation that the Federal government practices racial discrimination against First Nations children came as an enormous shock and disappointment to all those who know the history of mistreatment of Indigenous peoples in communities across Canada. Although an appeal to this ruling was subsequently filed, the day's discussions highlighted in this chapter sadly evidences that the discrimination inherent in the colonial system of child welfare may well continue unabated. The ruling legitimizes discrimination against Aboriginal children. Until this matter is resolved, inferior services will continue to be provided to the most vulnerable members residing in First Nations communities across Canada. In the meantime, Indigenous scholars and practitioners have little choice but to work within the systems that exist, but are endeavouring to improve them by bringing their voices and perspectives to both philosophy and practice.

REFERENCES

Benton-Banai, E. (1988). *The mishomis book: The voice of the Ojibway*. Hayward, WI: Indian Country Communications, Inc.

Bertsch, M., & Bidgood, B. A. (2010). Why is adoption like a First Nations' feast?: Lax Kw'alaam Indigenizing adoptions in child welfare. *First Peoples Child & Family Review, 5*(1), 96–105.

Blackstock, C. (2005). The occasional evil of angels: Learning from the experiences of Aboriginal peoples and social work. Special edition "World Indigenous Peoples Congress on Education." *Journal of Entrepreneurship, Advancement, Strategy and Education, 1*, 1–5.

Blackstock, C. (2007). If reindeer could fly: Dreams and real solutions for Aboriginal children. *Education Canada, 47*(1), 4–8.

Blackstock, C. (2008). Reconciliation means not saying sorry twice: Lessons from child welfare in Canada. In M. Brant Castellano, L. Archibald, & M. DeGagné (Eds.), *From truth to reconciliation: Transforming the legacy of residential schools* (pp. 163–178). Ottawa, ON: The Aboriginal Healing Foundation.

Blackstock, C. (2011). The Canadian Human Rights Tribunal on First Nations Child Welfare: Why if Canada wins, equality and justice lose. *Children and Youth Services Review, 33*, 187–194.

Blackstock, C., Brown, I., & Bennett, M. (2007). Reconciliation: Rebuilding the Canadian child welfare system to better serve Aboriginal children and youth. In I. Brown, F. Chaze, D. Fuchs, J. Lafrance, S. McKay, & S. Thomas Prokop (Eds.), *Putting a human face on child welfare: Voices from the Prairies* (pp. 59–87). www.cecw-cepb.ca/sites/default/files/publications/prairiebook/Chapter3.pdf.

Blackstock, C., Loxley, J., Prakash, T., & Wien, F. (2005). *Wen:De: We are coming to the light of day*. Ottawa, ON: First Nations Child and Family Caring Society of Canada. Available from http://www.fncaringsociety.com/sites/default/files/docs/WendeReport.pdf

Blackstock, C., Trocmé, N., & Bennett M. (2004). Child maltreatment investigations among Aboriginal and Non-Aboriginal families in Canada. *Violence Against Women: An International and Interdisciplinary Journal, 10*(8), 901–916.

Carriere, J. (2007). Promising practice for maintaining identities in First Nation adoption. *First Peoples Child & Family Review*, 3(1), 46–64. Available from http://www.olc.edu/local_links/socialwork/OnlineLibrary/Carriere%20(2007)%20Promising%20practice%20for%20maintaining%20identities%20in%20first%20national%20adoption.pdf.

Carriere, J., & Scarth, S. (2007). Aboriginal children: Maintaining connections in adoption. In I. Brown, F. Chaze, D. Fuchs, J. Lafrance, S. McKay, & S. Thomas-Prokop, S. (Eds.), *Putting a human face on child welfare: Voices from the prairies* (pp. 203–221). Available from http://dev.cecw-cepb.ca/files/file/prairebook/Chapter10.pdf.

Chotalia, S. P. (March 14, 2011). Ruling. Canadian Human Rights Tribunal. Available from https://docs.google.com/viewer?a=v&pid=explorer&chrome=true&srcid=1ss03ch-9XoFnWJWqqxMrlo5oAe5kAv7oDmO6am7osvsFaNkYMrW4LMPdCIYW&hl=en

Feduniw, A. (2009). Supporting youth in care through anti-oppressive practice. In S. Strega & Sohki Aski Esquao (J. Carriere) (Eds.), *Walking this path together: Anti-racist and anti-oppressive child welfare practice* (pp. 158–172). Halifax: Fernwood Publishing.

Giwa, S., Sethi, A., Smith, B., & Wabano, M. (2006). *Reconciliation: Looking back, reaching forward, Indigenous peoples and child welfare*. A Research Project for the First Nations Child and Family Caring Society of Canada (FNCFCSC). Available from http://reconciliationmovement.org/docs/Reconciliation_Evaluation_April2006.pdf.

Gray, M., Coates, J., & Hetherington, T. (2008). Hearing Indigenous and local voices in mainstream social work. In M. Gray, J. Coates, & M. Yellow Bird (Eds.), *Indigenous social work around the world* (pp. 257–269). Hampshire, UK: Ashgate Publishing Limited.

Hamilton, A. C., & Sinclair, C. M. (Commissioners). (1991). Report of the Aboriginal justice inquiry of Manitoba. Winnipeg, MB: Queen's Printer.

Henry, F., & Tator, C. (2009). *Racism in the Canadian university: Demanding social justice, inclusion and equity*. Toronto, ON: University of Toronto Press.

Heyd, T. (1995). Indigenous knowledge, emancipation and alienation. *Knowledge and Policy: The International Journal of Knowledge Transfer and Utilization*, 8(1), 63–73.

Hudson, P., & McKenzie, B. (1981). Child welfare and native people: The extension of colonialism. *The Social Worker*, 49(2), 63–88.

Hudson, P., & McKenzie, B. (2003). Extending Aboriginal control over child welfare services: The Manitoba Child Welfare Initiative. *Canadian Review of Social Policy/Revue Canadienne de politique sociale*, 51, 49–66.

Jeffery, D. (2009). Meeting here and now: Reflections on racial and cultural difference in social work encounters. In S. Strega & Sohki Aski Esquao (J. Carriere) (Eds.), *Walking this path together: Anti-racist and anti-oppressive child welfare practice* (pp. 45–61). Halifax: Fernwood Publishing.

Lavallée, L. (2009). Practical application of an Indigenous research framework and two qualitative Indigenous research methods: Sharing circles and Anishnaabe symbol-based reflection. *International Journal of Qualitative Methods, 8*(1), 21–40.

Locust, C. (2000). Split feathers. Adult American Indians who were placed in non-Indian families as children. *Ontario Association of Children's Aid Society, 44*(3), 11–16.

McKay, S., & Thomas Prokop, S. (2007). Identity, community, resilience: The transmission of values project. In I. Brown, F. Chaze, D. Fuchs, J. Lafrance, S. McKay, & S. Thomas Prokop (Eds.), *Putting a human face on child welfare: Voices from the prairies* (pp. 25–57). Prairie Child Welfare Consortium. Available online at http://www.cecw-cepb.ca/sites/default/files/publications/prairiebook/Chapter2.pdf.

Reid, M. (2005). First Nations women workers' speak, write and research back: Child welfare and decolonizing stories. *First Peoples Child & Family Review, 2*(1), 21–40. Available from http://www.fncfcs.com/sites/default/files/online-journal/vol2num1/Reid_pp21.pdf.

Silver, J. (2004). To help one another: The story of Ma Mawi. Fast facts. Canadian Centre for Policy Alternatives, Manitoba. Available from http://www.policyalternatives.ca/sites/default/files/uploads/publications/Manitoba_Pubs/FastFactsJune25_04.pdf.

Sinclair, R. (2007). All my relations: Native transracial adoption: A critical case study of cultural identity. Unpublished doctoral thesis, University of Calgary.

Smith, L. T. (1999). *Decolonizing methodologies: Research and Indigenous peoples*. London: Zed Books Ltd.

Trocmé, N., Knoke, D., & Blackstock, C. (2004). Pathways to the overrepresentation of Aboriginal children in Canada's child welfare system. *Social Services Review, 78*, 577–60.

Trocmé, N., Knoke, D., Shangreaux, C., Fallon, B., & MacLaurin, B. (2005). The experience of First Nations children coming into contact with the child welfare system in Canada. The Canadian Incidence study on reported abuse and neglect. In *Wen:De: We are coming to the light of day* (pp. 60–86). Ottawa, ON: First Nations Child and Family Caring Society of Canada.

Walmsley, C. (2009) The practice of child welfare in Indigenous communities: A perspective for the non-Indigenous social worker. In S. Strega & Sohki Aski Esquao (J. Carriere) (Eds.), *Walking this path together: Anti-racist and anti-oppressive child welfare practice,* (pp. 96–109). Halifax: Fernwood Publishing.

CHAPTER 3

The Bent Arrow Study: A Way Forward in Leadership for Child Welfare

Jean Lafrance and Linda Kreitzer

This chapter describes a research project that took place in Alberta from 2007 to 2009 among three different child and family services organizations: 1) Bent Arrow Traditional Healing Society (non-government organization serving Aboriginal families in Edmonton); 2) Edmonton and Area Child and Family Services, Region 6, Family Enhancement Unit (government organization located in Bent Arrow Traditional Healing Society); and 3) Southeast Neighbourhood Centre Child and Family Services (located in a local neighbourhood). Two faculty members from the University of Calgary, Faculty of Social Work, facilitated the project.

The purpose of the Bent Arrow research project was to provide the opportunity for all three partner agencies to explore—in a supportive environment that allowed for creative thinking—ways to improve child and family practices within Aboriginal communities. The overall objectives of the project were threefold: 1) to explore effective collaboration

---

SUGGESTED CITATION: Lafrance, J., & Kreitzer, L. (2012). The Bent Arrow Study: A way forward in leadership for child welfare. In D. Fuchs, S. McKay, & I. Brown (Eds.), *Awakening the Spirit: Moving Forward in Child Welfare: Voices from the Prairies* (pp. 37–69). Regina, SK: Canadian Plains Research Center.

between agencies in child and family services with Aboriginal families; 2) to compare and contrast differences in organizational contexts of a traditional non-government organization (NGO) and a government agency; and 3) to discover new ways of providing child and family services that combine traditional world views and western theories of child and family practice that supports Aboriginal communities.

Key findings included the importance of relationship in child welfare practice, the desire of child welfare workers for greater creativity in their responses to children and families, and the need for more supportive organizational and political leadership in the creation of the conditions necessary for this to happen. This chapter is one of a series of writings that focuses on one aspect of the findings.[1] It will focus on leadership issues within an organizational structure that has shifted from rehabilitation and treatment to surveillance and investigation, highlighting changes that need to be made and proposed actions for improving leadership in human services organizations.

RATIONALE

Wagner, van Reyk, and Spence (2001) cite research by Voigt and Tregeagle and by Markiewicz that identified some interesting characteristics affecting staff performance in child welfare programs. Both of these studies, Wagner et al. note, list "the complexity of problems, emotional stress, tensions between bureaucratic organizational structures and professional practices as stressors for child welfare workers" (p. 162). Although there is much literature on effective collaboration in agencies, little focuses on system management among agencies, similarities and differences between organizational contexts, working relationships (subjective components of partnerships) and outcomes (quality of service) (Horwath & Morrison, 2007). Leadership issues emerging from the Bent Arrow study add to this knowledge base by linking organizational success (i.e., an organization where clients and staff are working well together for the clients they serve) with patterns of leadership. In particular, we were interested in learning how effective leadership skills and the co-location of two of the three organizations met the challenges of dealing

---

[1] See Kreitzer & Lafrance (2010) for complete findings.

with philosophical differences in organizational contexts. The meeting of these challenges called upon the participants to learn and accept each other's world views, particularly where one of these world views, that of surveillance and investigation, is becoming normal practice.

LITERATURE REVIEW

Introduction

Several researchers have noted a growing trend in the evolution of child welfare practice from a casework orientation to a primarily forensic approach (e.g., Heinonen & Spearman, 2010; Howe, 1992; Parton & Parton, 1989). This is particularly so in the United Kingdom (UK) and Canada, in response to a series of high profile cases that have affected leadership responses over the past twenty-five years. In their research examining child protection and bureaucratization of social work, Howe (1992) and Parton & Parton (1989) have each revealed practice that is concerned less with rehabilitation and treatment and more with surveillance and investigation. Alternatives to this latter approach are becoming rare; however, an Aboriginal approach to running organizations seems to have a more open approach to serving families, creating an atmosphere of acceptance and trust, as opposed to one that seems to focus on security and mistrust. Further understanding of this change is explored below.

Changes in child welfare organizational practice

Some twenty years ago, David Howe (1992) proposed an explanation for the bureaucratization of child welfare work in the UK that seems closely related to the evolution of child protection services in Canada. Howe suggested that organizational changes imposed upon social workers and child welfare agencies were to prevent children from being killed by their parents and caretakers. He feared that the focus on family work would or might become less of a priority, to be replaced by an emphasis on the protection of children from dangerous parents. These changes fundamentally affect practice and organization in child protection services. Howe suggested that this change in thinking, and therefore practice, arose in response to the numerous public inquiries and extensive media criticism that led government departments to frame the problem of child abuse and neglect in ways that were "essentially legalistic and bureaucratic"

(p. 491). This made it more important to recognize which families were dangerous and which were not, so that child welfare could more quickly identify "high risk" cases, that is, those that were creating unfavourable political and public attention. This redefinition of child abuse in turn reduced the importance of professional social work practice in child welfare. As cited in Howe (1992), Jamous and Peloille (1970) claimed that "when the amount of 'technicality' in the job is increased, the element of 'indeterminacy' must decrease. When this happens, professional occupations are likely to find themselves more susceptible to managerial control and prescription. This appears to be the fate of social work practice in the field of child welfare" (p. 492).

Parton (1985) examined child abuse as a social phenomenon and how society has responded to it over the past century. He described a gradual shift from punishment to reform and noted that by the 1950s and 1960s the switch from control and punishment to treatment and welfare was well-advanced. Heinonen & Spearman (2010) also supported this trend. Parton (1985) made a convincing argument that in the UK the inquiry into the death of Maria Colwell in 1973 was the crucial event in establishing the issue as a major social problem, for providing the catalyst for the rapid emergence of a moral panic (p. 97), and for a shift to surveillance and investigation. Her story is summarized here.

> *Maria Colwell, seven, died in Brighton after being starved and beaten by her stepfather, William Kepple. She had suffered brain damage, a fractured rib, black eyes, extensive external bruising and internal injuries. Maria had been fostered by her aunt and uncle because her mother, Pauline, could not cope with bringing up five children on her own. Five years later Pauline decided she wanted her daughter back. But an inquiry by the Department of Health found that East Sussex county council had insufficient evidence to return the girl. There were 50 official visits to the family, including from social workers, health visitors, police and housing officers. All agencies involved in the case were criticized.* (Batty, 2003, p. 1, par. 2)

Howe (1992) proposed two assumptions that are being made in cases like this one. The first is that families with children at risk possess characteristics and behaviours (indicators) that, if detected, should alert child welfare workers of those children who are in danger. The Beckford report (1985), quoted below, asserted that "research designed to refine techniques for predicting more accurately those children who will continue to be at risk is urgently required" (p. 89). It also noted the failure of child welfare organizations to handle the information about the character and behaviour of families, even when they have it, in a systematic and coordinated way, as well as their failure to highlight the need for sufficient resources to work with families. Here is a summary of the Beckford situation.

> *Jasmine Beckford was starved and battered to death by her stepfather, Maurice Beckford. He was found guilty of the four-year old's manslaughter and jailed for 10 years. Her mother, Beverley Lorrington, was jailed for 18 months for neglect. Jasmine had been in the care of Brent social services for two-and-a-half years before she died, after Beckford was convicted of assaulting her younger sister. She was seen by a social worker only once in 10 months.* (Batty, 2003, p. 1, par. 3)

Such beliefs became dominant in the minds of policy-makers and program planners. Good practice was no longer vested in the treatment and rehabilitation of the family, and was superseded by a focus on surveillance and investigation. The key question became, "How can we protect children from being killed by their parents?" Put this way, the question supported approaches that were administrative and judicial in attitude, rather than those that were professional and rehabilitative. Consequently, therapeutic approaches were no longer seen to be appropriate. The caseworker's question "How can we treat parents to be more competent and less dangerous?" fell outside the emerging discourse, which began to centre primarily on the protection of children and less on the rehabilitation of the family unit.

The emphasis on protection instead of rehabilitation redefined the roles needed if the problem was to be solved. Howe (1992) posited that "social workers would have to become investigators and not family caseworkers. Managers would have to become designers of surveillance systems and not casework consultants. Parents would have to become objects of inquiry whose behaviour could be predicted and people whose skills could be improved. The shift was from therapy to surveillance and control" (p. 497). Noting this change in focus, Parton and Parton (1989) highlighted the growing demands for social workers to become more authoritative and intrusive in their dealings with families where children were thought to be at risk. They quoted the Tyra Henry report in 1984, suggesting "that preventing danger and taking firm protective steps are the two fundamental pillars on which modern practice should be based. The inter-relationship between the law, child protection and the assessment of dangerousness is therefore at the core of the social work task in this area of work" (p. 59). Here is a summary of the Henry situation.

> *Tyra Henry died after being battered and bitten by her father, Andrew Neil, while in local authority care. Neil was subsequently sentenced to life imprisonment for the 21-month-old baby's murder. A report on the case found that the white social workers from Lambeth council tended to be too trusting of the family because they were black. John Patten, then a junior social services minister, published new guidelines on child abuse cases for social workers soon after.* (Batty, 2003, p. 1, par. 4)

Howe (1992) suggested that since most child welfare inquiries are conducted by lawyers and judges it is not surprising that they recommend practices and procedures that fit within the legal framework in which they are trained. If children were to be protected from dangerous parents, it would be logical to first identify which parents were dangerous and then, having recognized unsafe situations, plan to remove the child. Protection became the primary objective and was to be achieved by closely monitoring risky situations. In the same way that the police do not protect property by attempting to cure suspect populations of any tendencies they might have towards burglary, child welfare became less concerned about social issues such as poverty, race, and oppression that were such important factors in the identification of children at risk. In this environment a fundamental assumption evolved that it was possible to anticipate and predict human behaviour in complex situations. The pattern has grown with each public crisis of confidence in the child welfare system, with each new review adding layers of complexity to child welfare practice in an effort to ensure that such an error could never take place again.

Changes in social work practice

This logic led to the gradual bureaucratization of social work practice in child welfare. As this concept of child protection work was refined, social work was repeatedly diminished by administrative processes that seemed necessary if the systems were to function properly. However, in spite of the best efforts of researchers, predicting whether or not particular parents are going to be dangerous is extremely difficult. Unless all children thought to be at risk are removed, some children will be killed, even when the systems are working well (Hollis & Howe, 1987). The response, nevertheless, has been to create more procedures and more guidelines.

The sheer scale and complexity of these documents makes it almost inevitable that the social worker with a dead child on her caseload will have failed in some aspect of a highly regulated practice. Tragically, simply adding new procedures in the wake of yet another tragedy merely compounds the problem. This pushes the social workers into ever more defensive forms of practice, which makes them less sensitive to the people involved, and more concerned with the procedures that govern their behaviour.

This is where greater understanding is needed between all levels of staff in child welfare. Front-line workers need to understand why rules and regulations have been created, and management needs to understand the fears, constraints, and challenges that these regulations put on front-line workers. Trust between the managerial and the front line has to be established, knowing that a manager will back the front-line worker no matter the outcome of the case. When this trust is not well-established, front-line workers fear repercussions from management. Further and most importantly, when this trust is not well-established, a consistent and ongoing dialogue concerning which rules and regulations work and which ones do not, so crucial to child welfare practice, is diminished.

In the end, it comes down to relationships with colleagues and with families. Benefits of risk assessment emphasise the primary concern of the welfare of the child. But if this risk assessment is not balanced by good relationships with the families and a reflective time to understand what is happening when "things go wrong," then a "knee-jerk reaction" can take place and more restraining policies put in place that, in the end, benefit neither families nor the agencies that serve them. This is where good leadership skills can help in balancing rehabilitative/supportive services with protection services, and can help in providing the wisdom to know the difference and to know which is appropriate under different circumstances.

Can Aboriginal people help to restore the balance?

The way in which organizations are established and managed has a direct impact on the leadership in human services (Horwath & Morrison, 2007; Hyde, 2004; O'Connor & Netting, 2009; Strier & Binyamin, 2010). In planning this research, it seemed clear that something very different was taking place at Bent Arrow than existed in most child serving systems. Knowing the background of colonialism and the role of social work in the assimilation of Aboriginal peoples as well as the 1960s and 1970s child welfare scoops (Blackstock, 2009), we were encouraged by what we saw at the agency. The atmosphere of collegiality, respect for clients, and spirituality was most intriguing and refreshing. We knew that Aboriginal communities that are grounded in their culture and traditions could provide a community environment that is conducive to child, youth, and family wellness (Chandler & Lalonde, 1998). One way to ensure this can be found is in the way that services are established, administered, and delivered.

Briskman (2007) outlined widely accepted values for Indigenous peoples. They include: the earth is our Mother; preservation and conservation; sharing and caring; being each other's keeper; group-based society; decision-making by consensus; harmony between people, and between people and land; knowledge to be sought, acquired, given and used in a proper way; and importance of oral tradition. When implemented in organizations, each of these aspects, along with localized values and beliefs, can create an atmosphere that will directly challenge the mainstream way of providing services. This is a form of decolonizing organizations. bell hooks (as quoted in Graveline, 1998) said, "Even in the face of powerful structures of domination, it remains possible for each of us, especially those of us who are members of opposed and/or exploited groups... to define and determine alternative standards, to decide on the nature and extent of the compromise" (p. 11). This means that it is possible for Indigenous organizations, despite living in a colonized world and having to meet certain imposed standards for funding requirements, to change various aspects of the way in which services are provided and operated. Initiating, leading, and maintaining such changes requires wise leaders who understand oppression and power issues in organizations.

RESEARCH METHODOLOGY

Participatory Action Research (PAR) was the methodology selected for the Bent Arrow project. PAR engages people involved in the issue being researched and considers those involved as co-researchers from the beginning to the end (Fals Borda, 1988). Creating space for future thinking around service provision is a rare but valuable process in any organization (Lafrance & Bastien, 2007).

The study began in 2006, when an advisory board was created to oversee the project. This advisory board continued throughout the project. The Bent Arrow PAR group began with fifteen people, representing all three agencies, in January 2007. Over time, the group decreased to seven. Two faculty members from the University of Calgary, co-authors of this chapter, facilitated the project. The research began with a one-day workshop, which provided detail about the project. The group met once a month for three hours at the Bent Arrow Traditional Healing Society until January 2009. Near the end of these sessions, the group participated in a two-day retreat to reflect upon the learning that had taken place and to consolidate the findings.

Data collection included participatory critical thinking exercises, audiotaped three-hour group discussions, videotape of the first and last workshops, individual reflections, and guest speakers. Each group member was given a digital recorder so that journals could be orally recorded outside the meetings for further reflection. The reflection/action process aimed to raise the critical consciousness of the individuals and the group in order to explore issues. First-, second-, and third-level coding was used for data analysis. An atmosphere of mutual respect and understanding was established, wherein people could speak their minds and think critically about their own practices. As one participant explained:

> *Initially, the researchers stated that this would be a safe environment for discourse and they really have made that happen. I've never felt the need to worry about something that I've needed to say in this group, which is wonderful to hear.*

For more information concerning this process, see Kreitzer and Lafrance (2010).

The major research questions posed from the front-line perspective with specific regard to leadership issues were as follows: 1) What organizational factors support effective collaboration practice? 2) What organizational factors constrain the implementation of effective collaborative practice? 3) How has co-location made a difference with this partnership and is it possible for partnerships to flourish without co-location? and 4) What beliefs, values and philosophical orientations have affected the way in which child and family services are practiced in this setting among Aboriginal families?

FINDINGS

With the shift from treatment and rehabilitation of the family to one of surveillance and investigation, there seems to be a growing gap between senior management and front-line workers in mainstream agencies concerning philosophical understandings in practice (Howe, 1992; Hyde, 2004; Jaskyte & Dressler, 2005). For example, front-line social workers are trained through educational systems to work with families to promote treatment and rehabilitation that keeps families together; yet they are expected to become investigators whose purpose is to protect the child. This incongruence in philosophy and practice brings about dissatisfaction with the job and, as a result, there is a high turnover of staff, creating a work environment where people who understand the system are no longer there, and new people are asked to provide leadership that they may not be trained for. There is a sense that senior leadership has lost touch due to an overriding concern with optics and political considerations. At the mid-management level, onerous policy and paperwork demands interfere with clear and transparent communication. According to many of our participants, this situation is creating a sense of chaos in the system, and it is restricting their capacity to meet commitments. It has been suggested that a lack of effective leadership is largely attributable to an overemphasis on what was perceived as cost-effectiveness and a corresponding underemphasis on family needs, a focus on filling out forms rather than on casework. Although this is not a completely new issue, in this study, it seemed that, following the opportunity to reflect upon their circumstances, staff members were able to more clearly understand and express themselves about these important issues.

Question 1. What organizational factors support effective collaborative practice?

The key issues to come out of the research project concerning the organizational factors that support effective collaborative practice were: 1) the importance of a mentor; 2) good relationships between front-line workers and senior management; 3) leaders that are experienced and understand the philosophical underpinnings of the agency; 4) training of supervisors in Aboriginal world view and family life; 5) supporting creative practice; 6) promoting teamwork and joint decision-making; and 7) respecting wisdom born out of experience.

Importance of a mentor

One of the strengths of any agency is the people who have worked there for a long period of time and understand the philosophy of the organization, its structures, and its relationship to the community. These people also serve as mentors to new people coming to the agency. With a large turnover of staff members in many government organizations, the importance of mentoring has been lost, and this loss is not fully appreciated. Nor is putting time and effort into mentoring seen as a priority. One of the group members expressed how much she appreciated her mentor at Bent Arrow Traditional Healing Society.

> *Something that leads to good practice that my supervisor taught me was that the ability to have a mentor and the ability to be a mentor is really critically important in this field because... there was someone in our lives that had an impact on us.... she was a strong mentor that without sort of watching or realizing, that over the years I've sponged up the things she's taught me*

> and I portray those traits in my day-to-day practice and in so doing have become a mentor to many of the staff that are at Bent Arrow.

Good mentoring can not only encourage good practice but also will contribute to maintaining a strong foundation for the organization. Along with good mentors in one's own workplace, it was also suggested that experts in different areas of child welfare should be available to mentor staff in other regional offices when necessary. For example, there are several people who have expertise in Aboriginal communities or high-risk youth, and their expertise would be helpful on an individual basis and in workshop settings.

Good relationships between front-line workers and management

Good relationships between front-line workers and senior management was an important issue to research participants. There was a general feeling amongst mainstream participants that policy-makers and practitioners did not see eye to eye, and that senior managers were not really in touch with practice in the field. One participant suggested that senior managers should be required to "do a certain amount of hours a month in a group home or be a foster parent to know what the children are like that they are serving. I think there needs to be a mandatory element so that they understand what these kids really are like, what some of the issues really are, because I think when you get away from the clients you are serving and the population you serve, you don't know what the issues are." Another participant stated: "Staff should invite their senior and mid-level leaders to their work; to reconnect with them and to support staff and help set the tone to better assist families... their priority should be on supporting healthy relationships and freeing up staff for more creative work." Every effort should be made to promote direct communication between front-line workers, supervisors, and senior management concerning practice issues.

Leaders that are experienced and understand the philosophical underpinnings of the agency

Another area of concern raised by the group members was the constant turnover of staff at all levels. This turnover means that when people who know the agency and understand the philosophy behind the agency and its importance to the community leave, the history and purpose of the organization is lost. It was noted by one participant that, during the time period of the research project, staff at Bent Arrow seemed to stay longer than government staff. There are many reasons for this, but one was that Bent Arrow offered support to its staff that was not always seen in government offices. Further, because staff members stayed for longer periods, members understood the philosophy and purpose of the agency. It seems clear from our observations that Bent Arrow staff were more likely to support each other in informal ways; for instance, they had frequent opportunities to engage with each other in a rural area owned by the agency ("the land"), where they could live their traditional ways as a group. Frequent turnover of staff can also result in a lack of training for potential leaders because there has been no mentor to teach them effective leadership skills.

Training of management in Aboriginal world view and family life

There seemed to be a lack of understanding between government supervisors, managers, and front-line workers concerning Aboriginal world views and family life. This caused front-line staff to feel a lack of support from supervisors concerning interventions that were oriented to Aboriginal families. One Aboriginal participant explained these feelings when working in a government office: "When I came here, I had a struggle because I didn't feel like my supervisor had necessarily supported my community development approach... I felt like I was not really supported to go and meet with people, nor was collaboration with clients really supported. It felt like it was all theory-driven to some degree and not relationship-building." In comparison, another participant offered this experience at Bent Arrow: "When I came to Bent Arrow, the supervisor had that experience with native communities, so her approach was very community-oriented and about building relationships, making people feel welcome, making people feel like they were being heard and just helping them to get to where they need to go." It was recommended that everyone in human services should be trained in Aboriginal world views and that as many as possible should have some experience working with Aboriginal communities. It was also noted that the current name of the

Ministry of Children and Youth Services in Alberta has left out family in the title, thus reflecting the low priority it places on families.

Supporting creative practice

Some government participants found that their creativity was stifled due to less emphasis on relationship-building, rehabilitation, and supporting families to keep their children at home and greater emphasis on paperwork and forms that identify clients as high-risk. Having supervisors who were flexible and encouraged creativity was a bonus. One participant was grateful for supervisors who were open to new ideas: "...I have had a good number of managers that have been very supportive in pushing the system and being able to be creative." But most participants felt that the lack of communication between higher management and front-line workers was restricting their capacity to meet commitments. According to many of them, the current lack of solid/effective leadership is largely attributable to an emphasis on cost-effectiveness rather than on families, and on filling out forms over casework. In short, when people are freed to do creative work and work is supported by upper management, then effective work can be accomplished that has a positive impact on families.

Promoting teamwork and joint decision-making

Presently, many decisions in government offices are made from above, with little consultation with front-line workers. This is frustrating to workers, as these decisions affect their practice and yet they do not always feel sufficiently consulted. One speaker from the Ministry gave an example of what it is like when decision-making includes everyone involved in the process:

> *... most of the time... the intakes were done at the team table, decision-making was done as a team, service plans were done as a team but it was always interesting that when we were under stress, ...when we were short-staffed or there was a lot going on and there were pressures from the system, we would tend to withdraw and go back to making the decisions on our own too quickly and without thinking. When we lost our team focus we would realise that we weren't involved in that decision and*

> we'd get busted on it. It was a healthy process that made us accountable but kind of spoke to us in how ingrained some of that thinking is.

The speaker also spoke about creativity and taking risks:

> So the longer we're... allowed to be creative and push the boundaries, there's a bit more acceptance as well. In the back of my mind, however, if there is one of those high profile moments and there is a tragedy with one of the youth, we might say, 'We've gone too far, we need to step back and maybe this isn't the practice that we should be doing.'

When people from all levels of the organization are consulted, everyone feels that they are listened to and have an impact on policies and decisions that are made within the organization. This includes consultation with experts from the community and community members themselves in the area where the decision is being made.

Respecting wisdom born out of experience

Some of the highly respected people in Aboriginal communities are elders. They offer words of wisdom and understanding that affect how decisions are made. Similarly, there are also people in human services who have wisdom that comes from experience; they often have insights on the potential effects of policy decisions on the children and the families served. Often these people are front-line workers who have had many years of experience in the field, but who chose not to go into management. Senior managers should take the time to learn from their close connection to what is happening in the field. The breadth of experience of the participants in this research was impressive, yet most felt that their views and wisdom were not being well-utilized.

Question 2. What organizational factors constrain the implementation of effective collaborative practice?

Factors that constrain the implementation of effective collaborative practice were identified as: 1) preoccupation with tragic events; 2) lack of participation of staff in change processes; and 3) lack of senior management being in touch with front-line work.

Preoccupation with tragic incidents

As noted earlier, a series of public inquiries have been critical of the "errors" of child protection systems who did not know about, failed to spot, or omitted to note "warning signs" in the situation. Many inquiries have noted that, in spite of indications that a child was not safe, there were failures to coordinate and collate such information, creating an overall picture leading to mistakes, poor judgments, and increasing suspicion from the public. One participant expressed the fear that is always present in child protection work. While space does not allow for a more complete description of such events in the Canadian context, and indeed in most of the Western world, we assume that individuals who are knowledgeable about child welfare will see the connection between these trends and the current reality of most western English-speaking countries. For those who wish to explore this further, see Lonne, Parton, Thomson, and Harries (2008) and Thoburn (2007). The following illustrates how some of the participants experienced this phenomenon:

> [...] what I'd like to see from policy makers is a non-punitive approach when things don't go right and the analogy I use is an emergency room triage. We have all these files coming in, they're all high-risk kids, and they're all high-risk families. Sometimes things go bad and it's not because we have bad practice, it's not because we have bad policies, it's not because of anything that we've done specifically—it's because it's a bad situation and we're trying to crisis-manage it. When you look at an emergency room in a hospital, there's an assumption that the doctors are treating a patient who is bleeding to death and if that patient dies, the doctor didn't do anything wrong; he's not punished and there's no punitive process in place. There may be a review to see if things can be improved but generally, you don't hear of doctors being punished if a patient dies. In our practice if something goes wrong with the family, everybody looks at the case manager and then their supervisor to see what they didn't do, what policies they didn't adhere to, if the paperwork is up-to-date. There's a very punitive kind of approach when things go bad but we're dealing with high-risk families, we're dealing with high-risk kids and sometimes those

> *risks become insurmountable in certain situations. I would like [...] policy-makers to know that we deal with high-risk people, and that's not always going to turn out well.*

> *We haven't really talked about it as much in this one but about when the mistakes do occur, that's when this will be tested [...] the moment that that first child is hurt out of just the fact that life happens [normal life circumstances], where ... the politicians will do damage control and then that's where everything ... policy gets changed .... that's when they just need to come out and say, "Yeah, this happens and we are going to learn from it and move on"—as opposed to, "Oh my God, optics and policy changes and let's get six more forms out" which they do now—and be like the emergency room, like where that's going to happen because people die. "Unfortunately we did our best and people make choices that we can't always control"— [...] it would be nice if that would be the messaging that would come from the government as opposed to, "We'll look into it and we'll make sure that things are changed." You know, the different optics as opposed to just "Yeah, people make choices sometimes and we can't control that as a government." The tighter the policies become, the harder it is to work in a creative manner.*

Lack of active participation of staff in change processes

Much of the literature on organizational change, of which there has been increased emphasis, has proposed for many years that the active participation of all members of staff in a change process contributes positively to the development and implementation of change. Not surprisingly, such participation promoted improved staff morale, open communication, and lower staff turnover, team problem-solving and improved goal attainment. This worker expressed the feelings of many others, using an automotive metaphor:

> *I think there needs to be more than lip service paid to the fact that these barriers exist. I was thinking about when ... making this a car with the square wheel, we can do that but I think... and*

> this is my own bias, the government's response would be "Well we just need a bigger motor. It doesn't matter if our wheels are all square, we'll just get a bigger, better motor, more cylinders and more this and we'll just force those square, triangular wheels to spin and we'll get to where we want to go," and then when it doesn't happen, "Why didn't we get to point A, our motor's not big enough," and the front-line staff said, "No, our wheels are square. If we had round wheels, we'd go quicker." "No, we need a bigger motor, we need more cylinders, and we need more...." No, our wheels are square and that's kind of ... when I was thinking about the car analogy, that's kind of where I came from. We need more than lip service paid to the fact that we have too much paper, too much intensity, too much work per case and then too many cases on top of that. So not to keep the focus negative, but the barriers, they're real and they need solutions, not lip service, then we can do all of this other stuff around relationships.

Lack of senior management being in tune with front-line work

A strong feeling expressed by one government member was that senior management had

> lost touch with the front lines due to the politics, the policy and even optics we're talking about ...it's not so much about helping families, but how does it look to the public or what is the media saying and what's going on and media control and so when they're so worried about that, they're losing touch with what the actual work that's going on.

In terms of front-line supervision, some supervisors wryly commented about:

> ... running up and down the hallway because of the chaos, the commitments, being pulled fifty different ways, fifty-thousand different committees, the paperwork, the policies, that it's hard to set the tone and to connect with front-line workers again. So those are kind of the two problems. The current reality would

> be that we are maybe lacking effective leadership on both levels due to the external environmental factors and the priorities based on their perception that the families are not the central consideration ... and that creativity and the relationships is not the central focus.

This seems to reflect the transition from previous practices (the subject of so much criticism), which sought to support children and their families, to an approach wherein protection became the primary objective and was to be achieved by closely monitoring risky situations. Increasingly, those who have established their right to determine the solution also determine the part that is expected of front-line staff. Thus:

> The importance of relationship is not given due consideration in policy planning, administration, service delivery or quality assurance. For the current reality, time demands take away from developing relationships, committees take away from caseload, new practice models take away from focus on family; basically, procedural things get in the way. In terms of our objective, that would be to improve relationships; better understanding leads to better planning and better service, a multi-disciplinary approach is of mutual benefit to the department and agency; credibility relieves the fear in the community and makes it a less fearful place.

In a plea for greater understanding and communication, it was suggested:

> Well, I think that our leaders, if they are going to be working in Children's Services, should be required to spend some time each year in a group home or foster home to better know the children that we are serving. I think there needs to be some sort of a mandatory element so that they can more fully understand some of the issues we must address. Even if you have worked in the field previously, when you get away from the clients and the population we serve, you don't know what the issues are. You can imagine if one of the staff were our Minister, the way we serve would be different.

Question 3. How has co-location made a difference with this partnership and is it possible for partnerships to flourish without co-location?

Key factors in effective co-location were: 1) knowing the philosophy of the agencies involved; 2) relationship building; and 3) physical environment.

Knowing the philosophy of the agency

Understanding the organizational contexts of agencies and their similarities and differences can enhance our understanding of successful collaboration between agencies. Horwath and Morrison (2007) provide a framework for collaboration and integration in children's services, identifying issues and ingredients for effective collaboration. This may include a change in physical location so that the partnership can work effectively, as well as a commitment to resources for the partnership. They propose that the processes of the partnership include values, interdisciplinary training, trust, role clarity, and communication. Often in partnerships, people bring their different values and philosophies. This can bring about tensions regarding practice but can also be an avenue for growth. Understanding and talking about these different world views is important, and time needs to be given to reflect on these similarities and differences. "[E]ffective communication is a key component for establishing trust" (p. 12) and without this component a lack of understanding of others' roles or mistrust for other professionals' perspectives can destroy partnerships. These processes were extremely important to explore and this research project allowed staff members the opportunity to explore these components in relation to their work in child and family services. The co-location promoted the kind of dialogue that was necessary for the research.

Relationship building

A number of benefits from the vantage points of front-line, supervisory, and management staff arose during this initiative, including relationship-building. The following serve to illustrate some of them.

> Well, I guess my biggest thing is co-location works, and it works very, very well. A big part of that, of course, is a relationship,

> and I think when you get to know someone over a cup of coffee and food's always involved, it's always a good start. I think it allows us to really approach social work from a grassroots level, multi-disciplinary approach so we aren't the be-all, end-all. Being associated with Bent Arrow ... there's automatically a trust there, built up ... whereas if any of my workers didn't have that rapport, they would have spent so much more time working on that. Because we're one of their programs and perceived that way, the door opens much easier and it allows a connection right out of the gate. So I would say co-location works, it should be promoted. I think it's in the best interests of everybody—clients, government and the agency—to keep promoting that. (Casework Supervisor)

> In terms of Bent Arrow, I feel freer to bring my clients here. I try to introduce my clients to one of the staff here and especially our administrative staff member, who knows many of my clients by name and appearance. This has helped me in my own practice, because when I'm not here they have a face and a name [to connect with]. (Family Enhancement Worker)

Staff spending time with clients as well as with each other enhanced the co-location model.

Physical space

Creating a physical space conducive to acceptance and trust was important. A welcoming atmosphere of an open environment and happy staff members really helped the co-location model to work. One co-researcher states:

> I have some really good working relationships with people that aren't co-located with Bent Arrow but that has taken more time to develop. It's easier to develop when they're just down the hall and we're spending all that time together, breaking bread together, and working side by side together with the families. So that happens very quickly. The other thing co-location's done is that it's really and truly made Bent Arrow a partner

> with the government and the work that Children's Services does. So because I work so closely with Region Six Children's Services, I'm vested in a lot of the decisions and things that are happening with my colleagues that work in the region and so what affects them, affects me and the people that work at Bent Arrow. So that's what I want to share and say is that, you know, we want to move forward, we don't ever want to forget where we've come from and the things that we've learned along the way, but we want to move forward and really keep children and families at the centre of what we do. (Agency Director)

This was compared with the usual physical work setting of government child welfare workers. Bent Arrow was housed in an older building that was not very attractive physically, but that seemed to provide greater opportunities for close contact and humour. While it was somewhat overcrowded, it provided an environment where contact was easily achieved and exuded an atmosphere of relaxed productivity.

> ... Sometimes in a government office, we don't have those opportunities. We're always behind closed doors and the physical space is so different here; it's more inviting and people don't see just a Child Welfare Office. They see the front, they see the programs and they see different people here and I think that this has certainly helped my practice just by being here. (Family Enhancement Worker)

> I don't like the way government offices are set up. I think we need to be very cautious as a society, that we don't destroy our ability to form relationships and our ability to interact with people on every level because that is, in essence, our humanity and if we strip that from ourselves, we [may] lose so much more than what we've already lost. (Family Enhancement Worker)

Co-location projects may not be the answer for all government offices, but certainly the feeling amongst the group was that it was a positive change and a pleasant environment to work in. While one could not assert that collaboration could not occur without co-location, the mix of actors and environment seemed to facilitate a more comfortable relationship than might have been possible otherwise. We have also seen co-location efforts that have failed miserably and some that work well. In the end, it seems more likely that the nature and quality of relationships between the people involved would be the most powerful factor, no matter how these might be achieved. (For further reading concerning the pros and cons of co-location, see Kahn & McDonough III, 1997; Ulrich, 1995; Waldegrave, 2003; Williams, Shore, & Foy, 2006).

Question 4. What beliefs, values and philosophical orientations have affected the way in which child and family services are practiced in this setting?

A key factor in the relationship between beliefs, values, and orientations affecting co-location was a positive workplace environment.

Positive workplace environment

Some interesting dimensions arose in the comparison of organizational factors between such NGOs as the Bent Arrow Healing Society and a government setting. The participants' comments seem to support Wagner's framework on values and frameworks for practice that are peculiar to such different settings. Wagner, van Reyk, and Spence (2001) stress the importance of effective leadership in ensuring the success of any climate/cultural change initiatives, stating that, while poor workplace climate can also be affected by organizational constraints, this can be offset by strong team identification, and skill variety. Workplace stress can be relieved by reducing unhealthy stressors, by giving employees a sense of control and connectedness where they have a sense of support and security, where they are challenged and motivated, and where they can work at a reasonable pace. Greater job autonomy can build trust with employees and in turn also improve workplace climate. In addition, while excessive policy changes and paperwork can be sources of job dissatisfaction, this can be offset by higher levels of self-efficacy to achieve higher levels of innovation.

> *In terms of looking at the objective, I guess if we look at the Bent Arrow site specifically, it's the physical presence, it's the openness, it's the friendliness, it's the "Come on in and have a*

cup of coffee, grab a piece of toast"... this minimizes barriers and fear ... okay, fear of people and of systems. (Family Enhancement Worker)

Part of the benefits of the co-location project is [actually] seeing the families, seeing the people we work with, getting to know them, getting to know the extended families, getting a real sense of what the issues are ... You need to know all of this to be able to create solid case plans. In the co-location projects, you get so much more done so I'm really a big proponent of co-location. Being of different cultures ... is secondary to the fact that we're all human; we all have the same basic needs for belonging, for nurturing and to ensure that this is intact. (Family Enhancement Worker)

When you have workers and supervisors working with community agencies and the actual families under one roof or in one very small area, you get to understand the perspective of the families, the geographic location, the ethnicities that live in that location and if you can get a perspective of where the families are coming from, you... [can] provide better service delivery to those families and probably help deal with their issues better.

It seems clear that the benefits of co-location in such a setting are significant and help to counter some of the more negative aspects attributed to large government systems. It seems to provide a buffer zone from some characteristics of large bureaucratic systems: hierarchy, specialization, rigidity, disconnection from community, communication problems, distance from leadership, and public mistrust.

DISCUSSION

The changes in child welfare over the past twenty years, from rehabilitation and treatment to surveillance and investigation, represents a philosophical shift affecting all those involved in the Western world. A review of the literature about the social and political context in which changes have taken place in child welfare practice supports this trend and helps to explain some of the leadership dilemmas that have increasingly plagued child welfare practice for the past 25 years, especially in the United Kingdom, Canada, the United States, Australia and New Zealand. As broader societal constraints emerge, child welfare systems have become tighter concerning approaches taken in meeting the needs and desires of the families they serve and in meeting social work staff needs for adequate time and space to conduct meaningful work. Many in leadership positions find tension between this philosophical shift and their own social work education.

Related to the foregoing, some interesting dimensions arose in the comparison of organizational factors between the Bent Arrow Healing Society (NGO) and a government setting. All NGO staff members in this project had opportunities to discuss values and frameworks for practice. Weekly meetings were enhanced by the close physical proximity of sitting in a small room together, thus providing continuing opportunities to discuss case progress. Government staff, on the other hand, while desiring such opportunities, tended to discuss practice on the run or through supervision when and if it occurred. Weekly meetings tended to focus on administrative issues. While both groups functioned as a team, government workers identified as a team that opposed their identification with the organization. The sense of team was almost developed in the negative, through the restraining force of shared organizational constraints and not through the driving force of shared values and practices.

In the Bent Arrow NGO, there was considerable local autonomy in the establishment of policy, while the government staff seconded to Bent Arrow and the Southeast Neighbourhood government workers saw themselves as having to implement policies that were developed at corporate offices far removed from their practice settings, and as having little opportunity to contribute to policy development. A more typical response by government staff was to stretch province-wide policies for the benefit of clients. At times, the government workers seemed to experience organizational constraints as if they were clients themselves, feeling unable to influence policy and failing to even try.

Participants in this study proposed that staff turnover would be lower in a work environment that is more supportive of relationship-building between staff members and their clients, and managers and their workers, resulting in improved communication between senior management and the front line. As one participant stated:

> *It is interesting that of all of the people who have maintained themselves as part of this group over the course of the six months, Bent Arrow staff have stayed consistent, the co-located government unit staffs has basically stayed consistent but the staff from the [neighbourhood] government office has all changed in the course of this project. I find a hundred percent job turnover in that office compared with limited or little turnover in the other offices.*

Much attention was paid to present policies stifling good practice and the need for more flexibility. As one government group member states:

> *It's a very interesting dynamic for me because I don't think our policies work at all for these [high-risk] kids, in any way at all. I think our policies cause more dysfunction because we are labelling them high risk and we are trying to, I don't know, nail them down, tighten up what's going on so that they are not at risk, so that they're not harmed, and that may be contributing to their high-risk behaviours.*

The Bent Arrow co-location project was in no small part intended to sensitize mainstream front-line, supervisory, and administrative staff to the intentions of Aboriginal people to achieve greater self-determination and to create helping systems that serve to counter and even reverse the consequences of the present welfare system. Indigenous-serving organizations have a responsibility to uphold the values and culture they aim to strengthen. Indigenous peoples have a long history of being spoken for, and acted upon, without meaningful discussion or collaboration from those who will directly be impacted by the service. If Indigenous human service organizations seek only to maintain the status quo and work from a mainstream perspective, there is the potential to do harm to the Indigenous population they serve. Too often, Indigenous organizations operate from a Western set of values and Western ways of organizing, giving in to dominant norms and values. Some of these conflicting values are an emphasis on the individual versus community orientation, different understandings of work ethic, and differences in family priorities. Providing a space that is focused on Indigenous ways reinforces to Aboriginal clients the value that is placed on being proud of Aboriginal ways of being. By recognizing the colonized systems that are present in all communities, and seeking ways to work differently, organizations can contribute to decolonizing the attitudes and ways within our communities.

Some thought-provoking questions were raised at the end of the research concerning leadership in a climate of security. If leadership and knowledge come from all levels of the organization, then the most senior people (the leaders) need to value input from all levels of the organization. If this were true, the participants suggested, we would have:

- A commitment—make it work at all levels;
- Greater sincerity and genuine interest in each other's point of view;
- Greater willingness to listen to each other;
- A win-win environment—no "cover your a**" mentality;
- Greater respect for wisdom born of experience;
- An increase focus and commitment to the team;
- More inspired leadership despite the chaos and the handcuffs imposed on workers—we know that it is hard to shine in chaos;
- Greater support for "natural" leaders to lead—not only those in the hierarchy;
- More opportunities for all people to shine—including children, families, and communities;
- More joint decision-making.

Front-line staff and their supervisors in this study have asked that their leaders recognize the reality that some negative incidents are inevitable and also that the additional procedural requirements that follow such events have only succeeded in hampering their efforts to help families by reducing their ability to generate more creative and relational approaches that are consistent with practice excellence.

The following proposed actions to improve policy, education, and practice come out of the literature and the research project concerning leadership. This is not to suggest that many of these are not being considered and applied in some ways today. Perhaps they are just a reminder for each of us to contemplate in the midst of the pressured environment of child protection work today.

Proposed actions for improving leadership skills in child welfare, particularly with Aboriginal families

1. **Issue:** Lack of sufficient recognition in many government agencies of the importance of the relationships between social workers, senior management, and supervisors. Many front-line workers have wisdom from experience, and senior management needs to respect this and tap into this resource. Consultation with people at all levels of bureaucracy is extremely important.

    Proposed Action: That senior management spend a certain amount of time in a group home or as a front-line worker so that they keep in touch with what front-line workers are doing and the kinds of issues experienced on a daily basis. They should be in contact with front-line workers on a regular basis to tap into their wisdom of experience.

2. **Issue:** A significant gap, identified in this study, between the aspirations and desires of front-line staff and the constraints of procedurally oriented policy. Front-line workers are frustrated by their inability to engage children and families in a relational and creative fashion. It is the responsibility of leaders to fill this gap.

    Proposed Action: That child welfare program planners, managers, and front-line workers together review policy and procedures with a view to eliminating redundancy and freeing up child welfare workers to practice in a manner that is consistent with social work values such as self-determination, respect for the dignity and worth of the individual, and client empowerment.

3. **Issue**: Continued fears of negative repercussions on the part of front-line staff members when things go badly wrong in a specific case, especially when the media is involved. While senior management claims that the punitive responses of the past are no longer practiced, this has not yet pervaded the belief system of the workers—they are still afraid, as are their supervisors and managers. In the minds of staff, at least, the focus is still on finding and punishing the guilty.

Proposed Actions: While the intentions of senior management are surely sincere, it will take time for a shift in attitude to become credible. This will call for even greater sensitivity in the handling of cases that go wrong and in de-briefing activities. Ongoing dialogue by front-line workers and senior management can create a greater feeling of safety for all staff that counters the fears expressed by staff about their practice reality.

4. **Issue:** Increasing burden for staff caused by the accumulation of "knee-jerk" responses to real or perceived crises of confidence in child welfare explored earlier with high profile cases in the United Kingdom. This is a trend throughout Australia, New Zealand, the United States, Canada, and the UK—a fear-based over-reaction that gives the illusion of correcting problems that are, in effect, too deep to be corrected by procedure alone.

   Proposed Action: Senior management needs to be more realistic about the capacity to predict and prevent the death and/or abuse of a child in care or under the supervision of child welfare and accept that some children will be harmed no matter how good the system is. Workers worry about this as well, but state that over time the accumulation of such responses make their jobs more difficult and can even create more of these kinds of situations occurring as they spend less time with clients and more time with computers.

5. **Issue:** Professional staffs that are largely uninformed about Aboriginal culture, values, and history (Blackstock, 2009). Not surprisingly, they bring in collective biases and stereotypes to their work. The Bent Arrow experience has provided some valuable learning about the benefits of placing non-Aboriginal staffs in a prevailingly Aboriginal work environment that is open and community-oriented and immerses front-line workers into an Aboriginal context.

   Proposed Action: That all staff, from senior management to front-line workers, develop increased cultural competency to support their work with Aboriginal families. Ideally, this can best be ensured by having staff spend time with Aboriginal agencies in order to better understand

> *their similarities and differences, and to ensure that such relationships are nurtured for good partnerships.*

Finally, one related important point concerning education also emerged from the data. While we were impressed with the dedication and competence of the staff who participated in this project, we were struck by some comments that arose informally that were not part of this study, but that call for some acknowledgement of the challenges around social work education and opportunities for developing leadership skills. Many child welfare workers are not social work-trained, and we would be remiss if we did not recommend that provincial and Aboriginal agencies develop a comprehensive plan with their respective faculty of Social Work that would include the following dimensions:

- The inclusion of a child and family services stream at the undergraduate and graduate level;
- A renewed emphasis on social work with Aboriginal people in academic courses and for continuing education;
- A determination of what roles in child welfare require social work preparation and which can be met by other disciplines such as Youth and Child Care;
- The development of standards of practice over time that can be met by qualified staff with a B.S.W. at the front-line level and a clinical M.S.W. for supervisory levels;
- Executive development for senior managers in the macro areas of organizational development, policy and program development, program evaluation, search methods, and state-of-the-art reviews.

CONCLUSIONS

There is a growing trend in the evolution of child welfare practice from a rehabilitation and treatment practice orientation to one of investigation and surveillance. This trend reflects the overall societal attitudes that focus on punishment and cost-effective services. The support for building relationships with families has decreased over time. The study highlights ways that leadership could affect organizational structures and links the way in which leaders run the organization to the promotion of either a trusting and friendly environment or one of mistrust and surveillance.

It was clear that Bent Arrow Traditional Healing Society practiced many of the findings and positive practices identified in our study. The government agencies did some of the suggested practices in our findings, but it was clear that Bent Arrow had incorporated these practices and that they were congruent with Aboriginal world views. The co-location of a government agency within Bent Arrow was a win-win situation, as Aboriginal people determined Aboriginal services and those in the government office learned from this and worked within this Aboriginal system. The participants in the study felt that our findings were useful to any government or non-government agency and should be incorporated within government agencies as well. The actions proposed would benefit all human services organizations. Concerning co-location, government staff had a much more positive image in the community under that umbrella, and was therefore more accepted by both community and families. Most importantly, the relationships between government staff and their Aboriginal colleagues led to substantially improved collaboration and ultimately to improved and more compassionate service to families. The experience of the agencies involved in this study, entitled the Bent Arrow study, could serve as a microcosm of what is happening at a macro level in child welfare service systems across the Western world (Lonne et al., 2008; Thoburn, 2007).

REFERENCES

Batty, D. (2003). Catalogue of cruelty: 1984 Jasmine Beckford. *Society Guardian*. Retrieved from www.guardian.co.uk/society/2003/jan/27/childrensservices.childprotection.

Batty, D. (2003). Catalogue of cruelty: 1973 Maria Colwell. *Society Guardian*. Retrieved from www.guardian.co.uk/society/2003/jan/27/childrensservices.childprotection.

Batty, D. (2003). Catalogue of cruelty: 1984 Tyra Henry. *Society Guardian*. Retrieved from www.guardian.co.uk/society/2003/jan/27/childrensservices.childprotection.

Beckford Report. (1985). *A Child in Trust: the report of the panel of inquiry into the circumstances surrounding the death of Jasmine Beckford*. London: Borough of Brent.

Blackstock, C. (2009). The occasional evil of angels: Learning from the experiences of Aboriginal peoples and social work. *First Peoples Child and Family Review*, 4(1), 28–37.

Briskman, L. (2007). *Social work with indigenous communities*. Annadale, N.S.W: Federation Press.

Chandler, M., & Lalonde, C. (1998). Cultural continuity as a hedge against suicide in Canada's First Nations. *Transcultural Psychiatry, 35*(2), 191–219.

Fals Borda, O. (1988). *Knowledge and people's power: Lessons with peasants in Nicaragua, Mexico and Colombia*. New Delhi, India: Indian Social Institute.

Graveline, F. J. (1998). *Circle works: Transforming Eurocentric consciousness*. Halifax, NS: Fernwood Publishing.

Heinonen, T., & Spearman, L. (2010). *Social work practice: Problem solving and beyond*. (3rd ed.). Toronto, ON: Nelson Education.

Hollis, M., & Howe, D. (1987). Moral risks in social work. *Journal of Applied Philosophy, 4*(2), 123–33.

Horwath, J., & Morrison, T. (2007). Collaboration, integration and change in children's services: Critical issues and key ingredients. *Child Abuse & Neglect, 31*(1), 55–69.

Howe, D. (1992). Child abuse and the bureaucratization of social work. *The Sociological Review, 40*(3), 491–508.

Hyde, C. A. (2004). Multicultural development in human services agencies: Challenges and solutions. *Social Work, 49*(1), 7–16.

Jamous, H., & Peloille, B. (1970). Changes in the French university-hospital system. In J. Jackson (Ed.), *Professions and professionalization* (pp. 109-152). Cambridge, MA: Cambridge University Press.

Jaskyte, K., & Dressler, W. (2005). Organizational culture and innovation in nonprofit human services organizations. *Administration in Social Work, 29*(2), 23–41.

Kahn, K. B., & McDonough III, E.F. (1997). An empirical study of the relationships among co-location, integration, performance and satisfaction. *Journal of Production Innovation Management, 14*(3), 161–178.

Kreitzer, L., & Lafrance, J. (2010). Co-location of a government child welfare unit in a traditional Aboriginal agency: A way forward in working with Aboriginal communities. *First Peoples Child and Family Review, 5*(2), 34–44.

Lafrance, J., & Bastien, B. (2007). Here be dragons! Reconciling Indigenous and Western knowledge to improve Aboriginal child welfare. *First Peoples Child and Family Review, 3*(1),105–126.

Lonne, B., Parton, N., Thomson, J., & Harries, M. (2008). *Reforming child protection*. London: Routledge.

O'Connor, M. C., & Netting, F. E. (2009). *Organization practice: A guide to understanding human service organizations* (2nd ed.). Boston, MA: Allyn and Bacon.

Parton, C., & Parton, N. (1989). Child Protection: The law and dangerousness. In O. Stevenson (Ed.), *Child abuse: Professional practice and public policy* (pp. 54–73). London: Harvester Wheatsheaf.

Parton, N. (1985). *The politics of child abuse*. London: Palgrave MacMillan.

Strier, R., & Binyamin, S. (2010). Developing anti-oppressive services for the poor: A theoretical and organisational rationale. *British Journal of Social Work, 40*, 1908–1926.

Thoburn, J. (2007). *Globalisation and Child Welfare: Some lessons from a cross-national study of children in out-of-home care.* University of East Anglia Social Work Monographs. Retrieved from www.uea.ac.uk/polopoly_fs/1.103398!globalisation%20 1108.pdf

Ulrich, D. (1995). Shared services: From vogue to value. *Human Resource Planning, 18*(3), 12–23.

Wagner, R., van Reyk, P., & Spence, N. (2001). Improving the working environment for workers in children's welfare agencies. *Child & Family Social Work, 6*(2), 161–178.

Waldegrave, C. (2003). *Just therapy—A journey: A collection of papers from the Just Therapy Team, New Zealand.* Adelaide, AU: Dulwich Centre Publications.

Williams, J., Shore, S. E., & Foy, J. M. (2006). Co-location of mental health professionals in primary care settings: Three North Carolina models. *Clinical Pediatrics, 45*(6), 537–543.

CHAPTER 4

Awakening to the Spirit of Family: The Family Group Conference as a Strengths-Based Assessment Process

Donald Keith Robinson

The elder[1] said: "A river runs deep underneath the surface, quiet yet powerful." He was talking about the power of the subconscious mind (he called it "the mind of the mind") and the tendency of people to believe that the conscious rational mind is superior. When learning about the family group conference model, one may be enticed by the protocols (aspects of "how to do it"), the statistics, and the logic models, giving less credence to the trust and relationship-building inherent in the approach. In this chapter, I will attempt to provide the lessons learned about the river that flows underneath the practice of family group conferencing. Based on my experiences as a Family Group Conference (FGC) Coordinator, I will describe how this work changed my social work practice and

---

1   This elder, who prefers to remain anonymous, gave this powerful teaching in a personal spiritual counseling session.

SUGGESTED CITATION: Robinson, D. K. (2012). Awakening the Spirit of Family: The Family Group Conference as a Strengths-Based Assessment Process. In D. Fuchs, S. McKay, & I. Brown (Eds.), *Awakening the Spirit: Moving Forward in Child Welfare: Voices from the Prairies* (pp. 71–92). Regina, SK: Canadian Plains Research Center.

my perceptions of families, child welfare workers, and the agencies who employ them.

The family group conference model is one that promotes family-centered practice, involves the community, and widens the circle to include collaborative relationships with child welfare workers (Pennell, 2009; Burford, 2000; Burford & Hudson, 2000; Routhier, 2002). This chapter will discuss the challenge of working in child welfare, outline the origins of FGC and Aboriginal historical traditional practices, and present the FGC model and its potential for decolonization. As the child welfare system in Manitoba changes and explores differential response models, the FGC model is presented as one way to reform the child welfare system and make an investment in families and communities.

THE CHALLENGE OF WORKING IN CHILD WELFARE

What motivates a person to enter the social work profession? Pennell (2009) notes that most want to create changes to make our communities and societies better places for everyone. Indeed, our profession has dedicated the entirety of social work education to generalist practice based on ethics and a philosophy of social justice. Social workers entering the child welfare field are plunged into a universe where their education often seems contrary to the realities of practice. They deal with parents who place their children at risk; apprehension and placement of children; angry, resistant, and sometimes violent individuals; serious addictions and domestic violence issues; crises, court work, and endless paperwork. Additionally, the worker often has to overcome the family's fears, hostility, and resistance to develop a working relationship. It is widely known that Aboriginal people have a distrust of child welfare agencies due to the "Sixties Scoop" and a history of strained relationships with the social workers involved in these institutions (Bennett, 2009; Desmeules, 2007; Lederman, 1999).

Child welfare workers carry high caseloads along with heavy administrative responsibilities. Bureaucratic procedures are structured with an individual focus and have child welfare workers "following an established method of intervention with clients, codified into the procedures for intake, assessment, and service " (Minuchin, Colapinto & Minuchin, 1998, p. 68). This focus is the outcome of professional training focused on individual rather than family-oriented theory, case material, and techniques. The child welfare worker is expected to follow these procedures and adhere to policy guidelines. Even if the individual worker was motivated toward family-centered practice, the high caseload would limit the time he or she could spend in building relationships with families.

A study of these challenges by Margot Herbert for the Canadian Association of Social Workers (Herbert, 2007) yielded data indicating that social workers in child welfare are highly stressed due to working conditions in these agencies. Some reported that supervisors and managers didn't support their decision-making in high-profile protection cases. In a climate where child protection services are almost always under review, child welfare workers will place the safety of the children first. The attention by media, families, and communities can create a hostile environment and negative view of child welfare and the social workers working in the field. Herbert found that child welfare workers are dedicated to good social work practice, which they defined as:

> creating the capacity and conditions for positive change within families, so that children could maximize their potential within safe and stable environments. Good practice must be based on strong, personal commitment to serve children and families, and dedication to positive outcomes. Good practice implies the creative use of resources to support each family's plan for their children. (230)

Respondents noted that they were frustrated with colleagues who are poor advocates for themselves and the families they work with. Respondents confirmed that caseload size prevents relationship-building activities with children and families. Family group conferencing was identified as an alternative approach that would create the conditions for good practice.

It is evident that social workers in child welfare desire to create changes for children, youth and families, but experience many obstacles within the bureaucracy itself. Furthermore, they have to overcome a legacy of poor child welfare practices that have resulted in what amounts to cultural assimilation and racism (Johnson, 1983; Kimelman, 1985). The positive contributions and the dedication of the many skilled child welfare social work professionals are minimized and often devalued altogether. In spite of the challenges, many child welfare workers have positive relationships with families, leading to reunification and provision of support along the continuum of services. Many child welfare workers also have excellent relationships and knowledge of the mainstream and community services available in the city.

ORIGINS OF THE FAMILY GROUP CONFERENCE MODEL AND ABORIGINAL WORLD VIEWS OF FAMILY

The Family Group Conference (FGC) model has its origins in New Zealand in 1989, when it was enshrined in the Children, Young Persons and Their Families Act (Hudson, Morris, & Maxwell, 1996). The indigenous Maori were able to reclaim traditional decision-making to empower the extended family (the Whanau) whenever their kin had serious problems involving child welfare and/or youth justice. The child welfare system was mandated to refer Maori families to the FGC stream, where they could access these culturally appropriate services. Since it is a legal requirement in New Zealand, the FGC model has incorporated Maori values, beliefs, and practices and has engaged the Maori as equal partners with child welfare. In Canada, the model has been put into practice in Newfoundland, New Brunswick, Ontario, British Columbia, Saskatchewan, and Manitoba. Many other countries have adapted the model for use in child welfare and restorative justice, with the modifications varying depending on the jurisdiction. In most jurisdictions, the model is not a legal requirement and has been introduced as an alternative service. As a result, the FGC model has in some instances been embraced, yet remains on the sidelines (Brown, 2003). There is promising research data showing that where the FGC model has been implemented, families are powerfully affected and child welfare workers enjoy improved relationships with families and more collaborative partnerships with community members (Mirsky, 2003). For this chapter, only FGC applications in child welfare will be discussed.

The Province of Manitoba in partnership with Ma Mawi Wi Chi Itata Centre implemented the Family Group Conference model in Winnipeg to work with Aboriginal families involved with the child welfare system. This pilot project began in 1997 (Routhier, 2002) in Dauphin, Brandon, Lynn Lake, and Winnipeg to develop partnerships with the family, child welfare agencies, community-based organizations, and government. Ma Mawi Wi Chi Itata Centre is a community-based organization formed in 1984 in response to the over-representation of Aboriginal families in child welfare. The organization believed that the FGC model was similar to the way Aboriginal and Metis families and communities took care of each other historically. Aboriginal people have always had traditional kinship systems in place to provide care for children, families, and elders in their communities. Aboriginal families responded to health crises, to the problems of aging, and to death and dying with immediate care and concern for the children, youth, parents, and elders. Through the practice of kinship care, Aboriginal families and communities had a natural child welfare system, health care, care for the elderly, and social assistance for families in crisis (Desmeules, 2006; Robinson, 1998). For Ma Mawi Wi Chi Itata, participating in this pilot project was an opportunity to activate family systems and communities to make decisions about their children who were at risk.

THE FAMILY GROUP CONFERENCE MODEL

The Manitoba model utilized the principles and process developed in New Zealand and began with a partnership with Winnipeg Child and Family Services. This pilot project was an opportunity to transform child welfare practice and involve families in decision-making about their children. The FGC model involves an intensive preparation stage with the family group, child welfare, and all other significant community partners, leading to a conference for family decision-making. This plan, developed in private by the family, becomes the child welfare case management agreement with the family group. Family group conferencing involves holistic work with families, cultural safety and competence, respect for family world,views, family-centered practice, and outreach to extended families utilizing a home-based approach.

The child welfare agency agreed to work with Ma Mawi Wi Chi Itata Centre to refer families and work with the FGC coordinator. The key feature of the project was that the FGC coordinator reported to Ma Mawi Wi Chi Itata and was independent from child welfare. The coordinator, being neutral and working independently of child welfare agencies, is well positioned to develop working relationships with families who may have little trust with child welfare authorities. Families referred would be those with children in care or with children at risk of being placed in care. Also included are families experiencing difficulties with children who may be out of the control of parents,[2] and families who for various reasons have difficulty working with mainstream service providers in following through with case plans and goals. The challenge was to create collaborative relationships with the child welfare team, build trust and relationships with the families referred, and engage the family group in the process. The FGC process requires a tremendous commitment from the child welfare partners and a big investment from the families involved.

The child welfare commitment involves worker and supervisor time, sharing file information, case conference meetings with the coordinator, attendance and participation at the FGC, accepting and incorporating the family plans into their case management. The commitment continues in the review meetings after the FGC. In effect, the child welfare worker is agreeing to a long-term relationship with the family and the community surrounding them.

This tremendous commitment involves letting go of the power of independent case management and trusting the family decision-making. It is also about commitment to cultural safety and cultural competence. It is the social worker's responsibility to include culture as an important part of assessment. Pennell (2009) defines cultural safety as "a context in which family members can speak in their own language, express their values and use their experiences and traditions to resolve issues" (p. 81). She then asserts that what makes the FGC culturally competent is the fact that it changes how child welfare decisions are made and adapts to the families' cultural contexts. Indeed, this is a tremendous commitment (p. 89).

The commitment and investment required of the family group is their time, resources, and energy at all stages of the FGC. The family group is asked to trust this process despite any previous negative experiences with child welfare and authority figures. They then must engage

---

2   The term "parents" will be used to refer to the parent or parents being referred to FGC; of course, sometimes grandparents and other care-givers may be referred for services.

in an introspection process to examine their history and family dynamics and to air "dirty laundry" (family feuds, secrets, and weaknesses). The FGC process requires a heavy emotional investment as the family group struggles through hearing about how addictions, violence, abuse, and neglect have affected the children. Truly transformative work with families requires that the often unspoken rule against airing dirty laundry in public is broken. Usually family problems and secrets are kept hidden and this powerful family rule operates to keep outsiders from knowing the truth. Oftentimes, these truths are not known even within the family group.

As for the investment of time and energy, the family group will ask themselves commitment questions: Am I willing to participate in the FGC? What strengths and resources do I/we have? What can I do to help my relatives? What commitments can I make? How much energy can I honestly invest? What happens if someone fails to follow through on their commitment—who will step in? What needs to be done if the family plan starts to unravel and the children are at risk? Kegan and Laskow Lahey (2001) have developed tools that help people understand their immunity to change. They suggest that a new language—new questions to explore issues that are hidden in complaints, blaming, and lack of accountability—is vital for moving toward commitment and personal responsibility.

All proponents of the FGC model (Burford, 2000; Desmeules, 2006; Marsh & Crow, 1998; Merkel-Hoguin, 2004) agree that adequate preparation is vital: the coordinator works to prepare all the participants to engage successfully in this process. This stage is intensive because these commitment questions are raised and worked through with child welfare workers and with the family. Child welfare workers are challenged to change from their conventional case management approach to family-centered practice. In my experience with several FGC situations, child welfare workers wanted to covert back to conventional case management when the family plans falter. "Social workers often find it easier to take the safe road and control as many elements of the case plan as possible" (Nixon, Merkel-Holguin, Sivak, & Gunderson, 2000). As the coordinator, I had to address these conflicts with the workers and supervisor, reminding them of the purpose and vision of FGC. Addressing the conflict in a respectful way means validating the worker's assessment and safety concerns, while providing assurance that the family group needs to review and revise their plan. Conflict is intrinsic to the process and dialogue between all participants involved is crucial. As the coordinator, I have to confront conflict and facilitate dialogue in order to create meaningful changes to the ways people interact with one another.

As stated previously, the family group often is hostile to the child welfare agency and distrustful of their actions and interventions. In my experience, the family members' stories typically fall into three categories: the scenario of the evil agency worker(s) who apprehended their relative's children without just cause; the scenario of extended family members with concerns about the children's safety and the parents' and/or caregivers' neglectful or abusive behaviours; and finally, the scenario of an extended family who is essentially unaware of the family situation, having few factual details about their relative's crisis, and relying instead on gossip, rumors, and parents'/caregivers' accounts.

In order to address the conflicts in the first scenario, the family group needs factual information about the nature of child welfare involvement. Building collaboration with families involves addressing these complaints (Kegan & Laskow Lahey, 2001) and validating the family's concern and caring for their relatives. Communication with the child welfare worker about the intervention, protection concerns, the available assessment data, and the facts surrounding their ongoing involvement is shared with the family group. In the other two scenarios, the family group is validated for its involvement and concerns and provided with all the child welfare information to proceed with decision-making. As family members are informed, they begin to understand the reasons for child welfare intervention and understand how serious things are for their relatives. Family members usually agree that children need to be safe and that child welfare intervention is necessary when children are in danger.

Identifying the FGC participants is another important dialogue to have with the family group. Marsh and Crow (1998) state that in order "to work with the family, we have to ask who the family is." While this seems like a simple statement, the fact is that family members often disagree about who should be included in the process. Further, many operate on the belief system that you shouldn't burden others with your personal problems: family members have often commented, "I don't want to bother *my relative*; he has his own family to look after." Other times, the FGC has stirred up family feuds and individuals will refuse to participate if so-and-so is there. Understandably, many family groups have simmering conflicts and unresolved past hurts and have an initial resistance to dealing with these issues. For Aboriginal families, many of these hurts have their origins in residential schools or other childhood traumas. Walsh (1998) notes that "when family members try to protect one another from painful or threatening information through silence, secrecy or distortion, such communication blocks create barriers to understanding, informed decision-making and authentic relating...truth telling is vital" (p. 109). The FGC is not a counselling or therapeutic approach; however, the family group needs help to understand how the past affects present relationships. Family members are reminded that the children need their involvement, and they are encouraged to set aside their personal issues for several hours (the length of the FGC). Most people agree that the children's future and well-being is the highest priority. While healing work is not an FGC goal, dealing with these painful issues can result in improved and restored relationships.

In working with the family, we identify all potential participants, and family members are encouraged to do their own locating and inviting of relatives. I have found that this happens naturally as the news travels fast within the family circle. Outreach to relatives living nearby is easier than to relatives living far away. On one occasion, I travelled to a reserve community to spend the day interviewing the family members there. This approach was significantly easier and more effective than telephone interviews or expecting these relatives to come to Winnipeg. In another situation, I visited a father who was incarcerated in a nearby correctional facility in order to gain his perspective in an FGC involving his children. In other situations, the family members are contacted and interviewed by telephone so that their input can be included. Ensuring that everyone knows the purpose and process of FGC is important, as is obtaining their ideas about possible solutions. This information-gathering process is an opportunity to discover what resources and strengths exist within individuals and within the family group as a whole (Desmeules, 2007).

The preparation stage includes discussions about individual members who are still engaged in addictions, family violence, and other dangerous behaviours (Connolly, 2006; Pennell & Burford, 2000). These individuals may need to be excluded from the FGC if they threaten others. In family situations involving domestic violence, the person who is violent may hamper effective decision-making, but his or her views may still be included through other family members. The family group may decide on exclusions and sometimes the coordinator has to make the decision rather than placing the onus on family members, who may feel threatened (Marsh and Crow, 1998, p. 52).

The family group's information needs include details (criteria, waiting times) on existing programs and services that can be readily accessed. This information is made available for study beforehand and at the FGC for discussion and possible inclusion into decision-making. Other professionals (probation officers, school and health officials) involved provide valuable information at the FGC for the family group.

The entire purpose of the conference is to ensure that the children's voice is heard and that they can communicate their thoughts, feelings, and vision to the family group. Consideration is given to child development and age-appropriate involvement, so usually children under 12 years of age are excluded (Pennell & Burford, 2000). It is also difficult and inappropriate to expect young children to remain quiet for the FGC. For these younger children, resource people with arts backgrounds and/or child play therapy are recruited to help them express their voice in drawings or other works of art. The children's work is shared with the family group during the FGC. Children over 12 are invited into the FGC with a support person of their choosing (friend, therapist, family member) so they can remain courageous and feel supported. This is vital because talking about sensitive matters is difficult even for mature adults. Children like to be close to their parents so usually child-care providers are engaged at the FGC site so they can partake in the socializing pre-conference and the meal.

After much planning and anticipation, the family group is ready for the family group conference; the child welfare worker is on hand, as are all the other participants. The FGC starts with an opening ceremony conducted by the spiritual leaders chosen by the family group. Elders, ministers, and family leaders (grandparents, eldest or others) have performed these ceremonies, offering a prayer and opening comments. The opening ceremony provides a space to honor the cultural values and beliefs of the family and an opportunity to present educational topics relevant to the family issues. For example, elder's teachings on family roles, residential school effects, effects of family violence on children, and schizophrenia have been held during this time. After the opening ceremony, these guests usually leave unless they are family members. This honors the family confidentiality as the meeting moves to the purpose of the FGC.

The professionals present all the information to the family group, providing opportunities for questions and clarification. When this process is complete, the family group retires in private to deliberate and make decisions. Private family time is "symbolic of the heart of FGC... it says that families are the leaders" (Mirsky, 2003). The family group develops a comprehensive plan to address the safety and well-being of their own, outlining the responsibilities of every person who commits to an action.

Upon presentation and review, the child welfare worker acknowledges and validates the decision-making as the agreement for their future work together.

FGC: COLLABORATIVE PRACTICE IN CHILD WELFARE

Madsen (2000, p. 4) states that the blind spot of modern society is a failure to collaborate in deep ways and fully utilize all available resources. As an example he cites the university with its various departments, each with its own silo of expert knowledgeable people. In my experience,[3] the child welfare system is similar, with expert knowledge in night duty, intake, abuse, prevention, and the emergency placement of children. In creating silos, the collective knowledge of the group is preserved within teams and departments. Madsen proposes collaborative practices as a way to deconstruct silos and open the channels of communication. The FGC model is a family-centered practice model that brings the extended family, an under-utilized resource, into relationship and collaboration

---

[3] Program Manager, All Nations Child and Family Resource Network, 2006–2008.

with child welfare. The FGC coordinator is the linchpin for the whole program—connecting family members to each other, and the child welfare worker to the family and all other relevant community partners. In my experience, I have found that there are key steps in this dance with the family, including joining the family system, engaging the family group, and building collaborative relationships. A case scenario is presented below to illustrate the process and effectiveness of family group conferencing.

JOINING THE FAMILY SYSTEM

Aboriginal families have good reasons to distrust outsiders, the concept of family group conferencing, and the child welfare system. Relationship-building begins with going to visit families in their homes, on their own turf—involving them, addressing their concerns, and asking questions. Home visits provide an excellent opportunity to learn so much about families (Boyd-Franklin & Bry, 2000; Rabin, Rosenbaum, & Sens, 1982; Schact, Tafoya, & Mirabla, 1989) and meet important members of family (boyfriends, fathers), extended family, and supportive friends. It helps to get a first-hand view of the family's living situation and the realities of poverty, housing conditions, and neighborhood climate. One can observe the family's child-rearing and their cultural practices. Through careful listening and observation, one discovers the family's strengths and their resources. As a guest, visitors must respect the rules, protocols, and cultural norms unique to the family (Comer & Vassar, 2008) and ask what times work best for home visits. Flexibility is the rule, as often the home visits are complicated by surprise visitors dropping in, children's playmates, illnesses, and other family matters. This approach is perfect for connecting with the younger and older members of the family and to get a real glimpse of family life and culture.

ENGAGING THE FAMILY GROUP

Columbo, the rumpled-coat homicide detective in the 1980s television series, was a character whose insatiable curiosity during his investigating of crimes helped him to understand human motivations and inevitably to solve mysteries. I have found that suspending judgments is an essential requirement in asking the questions that matter. Starting from a position of cultural curiosity (Madsen, 2009), asking the right questions and observing provides answers to the family strengths, rules, values, and customs. Asking questions in a respectful way helps one to understand families, their culture, and the environment (home, neighborhood, and community). Utilizing the continuum of traditionalism[4] (see Appendix on p. 92) helps in understanding the position of each person in this spiritual/cultural domain of life. It is important to know the family's spiritual/cultural belief system so those resources can be activated or alternatives explored. This approach transcends the resiliency research that tended to focus on individual resiliency (Walsh 1998) and acknowledges family resiliency. The appreciative inquiry approach (Madsen, 2009; Thomas Prokop, McKay, & Gough, 2007) helps one understand the family dynamics, with attention to the coping skills people used to overcome past problems. It becomes useful for exploring the origins of family violence as a learned behaviour (residential school, institutional care, other). This discussion held with individual members of the family group is communicated with non-judgment and the understanding that people learned violent behaviour and need help.

The FGC process invites fathers and other male relatives into the circle to participate. In working with families, child welfare has often failed to include fathers (Brown, Strega, Dominelli, Walmsley, & Callahan, 2009), leaving mothers with the sole responsibility for caring for children and the blame for problems. Pennell (2009) confirms that "FGC helps to build or re-build connections with fathers, the paternal side of the family and other male relatives" (p. 89).

BRIDGING THE GAP BETWEEN THE FAMILY AND CHILD WELFARE WORKERS

Under the FGC model, respect is communicated for the child welfare worker and the complexity of the work undertaken to protect children. As I worked closely with child welfare, I found that workers are kind,

---

4 Traditionalism is defined as: 1. Adherence to tradition, especially in cultural or religious practice; 2. A system holding that all knowledge is derived from original divine revelation and is transmitted by tradition. This definition is from www.thefreedictionary.com/traditionalism.

caring, and dedicated to the challenging work. I also know that the workers struggle with knowing the abuse that children have endured and they care about the child's future. In the FGC, I have found that workers are often hesitant to present sensitive child abuse information and are concerned and afraid for family members. Workers are assured that families have been prepared and need to know the details of serious neglect and child abuse. The child welfare worker also receives information on the family members and their strengths, and often meets these individuals prior to the FGC. The worker is able to see the family through the family's lens and through their particular world view. Most important, the worker is witness to the power of family decision-making when families make plans. Workers have commented that these plans are comprehensive and better than any case management plan that they could have made. The worker then re-writes case histories to include the extended family, positive stories, and assessment from a family-centered perspective.

FGC DECOLONIZATION STRATEGIES: AWAKENING THE SPIRIT OF FAMILY

Writing about Metis experiences of social work practices, Richardson (2009) states that a decolonizing skill set involves "promoting life, restoring, giving back/re-resourcing, creating a space for people to make their own decisions, supporting, creating safety, connecting and re-connecting, listening, acknowledging, witnessing and truth telling" (p. 116). I believe that the FGC approach utilizes this entire skill set in working with each and every participant. Another important skill is using humor appropriately with families, as I have found Aboriginal people have the most humorous stories to share and they laugh all the time.

An important fact learned about families is that they have often lost the capacity to have their history recognized and validated. Child welfare workers have created a history based on crisis, deficits, and apprehensions, with some families having lengthy casework files (Madsen, 2007). Madsen goes on to say that "the initial focus on the problem, precipitant, and history entrenches us in a problem focus. It promotes selective attention to dysfunction and selective inattention to competence. It organizes us around a search for causality and locates problems primarily in individuals" (Madsen, 2009, p. 104). The FGC is an opportunity for decolonization as the family reclaims their history and their leaders: the grandparents and elders are the holders of the history and the storytellers of the family trials, tribulations, and triumphs. The younger generations—the parents and children—learn these stories of resilience as they sit, meet, eat, plan, and decide together. The social work interview becomes an important decolonization strategy as individuals are honoured as the experts of their lives. In one FGC, I met a mother diagnosed with schizophrenia who had lost custody of her child. In my first home visit, we talked about the FGC process and about her mental health issues. I advised her that I knew very little about schizophrenia and asked her to teach me about how it affected her and about the medication she was taking. She was very helpful in sharing her knowledge and we concluded by agreeing that everyone involved would benefit from an educational seminar with an expert service provider.

As family members sit together, they are listening and hearing what others are thinking and feeling, often for the first time. The FGC provides a pathway for the family to own their own problems and their solutions and to utilize their own resources first, reducing dependency as much as possible. Through their family plans, members have confronted each other and demanded personal responsibility. Private family time is indeed a powerful decolonization tool as family members realize their power to reclaim responsibility for their children. The family groups have requested teachings to learn about residential schools, their history, ceremonies, and elders' teachings.

Upon implementing the FGC model in Nova Scotia, Joan Glode, Mi'kmaw Nation, stated, "(It) fits with First Nations worldviews of respect, sharing resources, mutuality and interdependence, a family coming together and seeking its own solutions—the primary values in Aboriginal society" (Mirsky, 2003). The Mi'kmaw Family and Children's Services, in its evaluation of the model, yielded initial findings that family group conferencing is a practice that is inclusive and culturally respectful, and it builds relationships within families and with child welfare (Glode & Wien, 2006).

A colleague, Wendy Orvis (now deceased), began to include sharing and teaching circles in her work as FGC coordinator when she noticed that families were isolated in their homes and communities. Families gathered together to have sharing and teaching circles where they supported and learned from each other. My colleague viewed these circles as an opportunity to invite new narratives (Madsen, 1999) and for families to celebrate movement away from crisis (Buckley & Dexter, 2006). The sharing/teaching offered opportunities to make friends, cook, eat, and learn together in a safe environment.

Decolonization work in Family Group Conferencing provides individuals and families an opportunity to reclaim identity, history, and cultural practices and to pass them on to the next generation.

FAMILY GROUP CONFERENCING IN ACTION
(name changed to protect confidentiality)

Case Example: Child abuse denied

The mother in this example was referred to FGC after her arrest for physically abusing her two children. Sarah had assaulted her daughters (ages 6 and 8) after the girls woke her up asking for breakfast before going to school. The school contacted child welfare (CW) officials after the girls came to class crying. The child welfare workers who responded took the girls for medical treatment and notified the police. The CW workers also apprehended a younger sibling (age 4) who was at home. After the initial crisis, the police investigated and charged Sarah with the child abuse of her daughters. When interviewed by the police, she claimed that this incident happened due to an alcohol-induced blackout. She had been out the night before at a drinking party and did not remember assaulting her children that morning. The child welfare worker assigned was concerned about the denial of responsibility and consulted with the author about a referral to the FGC program. After this consultation and a discussion between the worker and Sarah about the referral, Sarah agreed to work with Ma Mawi Wi Chi Itata Centre.

The FGC process found that a large extended family was available and willing to participate. The family group was concerned about the children in non-family foster placements and was anxious to proceed with the FGC. The family was prepared beforehand that they would hear about what happened to the children through the school, police, and medical experts reports. Through the course of many meetings, the mother occasionally expressed sadness about her children but still maintained loss of memory for the assaults. The worker expressed fear about presenting the graphic medical information to the family group, and was worried about how they would react. I assured her that this information was absolutely necessary to their conference. The family reacted strongly and wept upon hearing of the assaults with a broom handle. The reports highlighted the extent of the physical abuse, with pictures featuring extensive bruising over much of both girls' upper bodies.

After a break, the family group deliberated in private for three hours and presented the following plan. Sarah's parents and siblings, who knew her all her life, confronted her and challenged her claim to amnesia. Sarah confessed to her family that she was hungover, knew what she was doing, and reacted in a fit of rage. She agreed to plead guilty when she went to court and to begin attending Alcoholics Anonymous meetings. The family members were very angry with her but agreed to support her to eventually regain custody of her children. In the interim, the family group asked for and received custody of the three children, agreeing to allow supervised visits for Sarah in their home. The family wanted Sarah to rebuild her relationship with the children as they would be afraid of her. The family group expressed concern about relapse and wanted Sarah to have at least six months of continuous sobriety before they would review their decision. I was amazed by the power of the family group that day as they demanded accountability and would accept no less. As outsiders (the police, child welfare, myself), we had no connections and little relationship to be able to confront Sarah in the way that family did. They continued to support Sarah as she went to court, worked on her sobriety, visited in the home, and as she eventually regained custody of her children.

CONCLUSION

It has been ten years since I last worked as a Family Group Conference coordinator but I still hold a strong commitment to the principles and process of the model. I have learned much about resiliency from the families that I met in the three years I was in the job. I also learned about the challenges that workers in child welfare face every day and about their caring and dedication to good social work practice. This chapter is really about the river that flows deep beneath the surface, the spirit of family, their pain, and their stories. I was honored to hear all these narratives and be included within the family circles through FGC.

In this chapter, the FGC model has been presented as a way to transform child welfare practice with an examination of the commitment requirements of child welfare workers and of the family groups. In order to succeed, decision-makers at the highest level have to support the model and give sanction and support to the supervisors and front-line staff. FGC work is truly transformative through the fact that families assume responsibility for the safety and well-being of their children. The transformation is evident in the changes of child welfare's social work practices to support family group decision-making. The FGC model isn't a quick fix or a panacea for long-standing problems within the child welfare system; nor is it tinkering with minor changes to established practices. This kind of family-centered practice can succeed only with sustained effort and collaboration between the families, child welfare, and other community organizations or services in the family network.

Family group conferencing awakens the spirit of the family to realize that their children are in danger, that their relatives are in desperate need of help, and that they can provide that help. FGC also awakens the child welfare system to the ways that they can collaborate with families and communities to create a space for family group decision-making. Once this spirit is awakened, the power of the family circle is truly realized as they reclaim traditional parenting and family values, their history, and their decision-making authority for their children. The Cree have a word that means self-government or self-determination: "ti pe ni mi siwin." When the FGC participants experience the river that flows beneath, individuals and families realize they have power to determine their futures. This is true decolonization.

REFERENCES

Bennett, M. (2009). Jumping through hoops: A Manitoba study examining the experiences and reflections of Aboriginal mothers involved with child welfare in Manitoba. In S. McKay, D. Fuchs, & I. Brown (Eds.), *Passion for action in child and family services: Voices from the Prairies* (pp. 69–98). Regina, SK: Canadian Plains Research Center.

Boyd-Franklin, N., & Bry, B. H. (2000). *Reaching out in family therapy: Home-based, school, and community interventions.* New York: Guilford Press.

Brown, L. (2003). Mainstream or margin? The current use of family group conferences in child welfare practice in the UK. *Child and Family Social Work, 8*(4), 331–340.

Brown, L., Strega, S., Dominelli, L., Walmsley, C., & Callahan, M. (2009). Engaging fathers in child welfare practice. In S. Strega and J. Carrière (Eds.), *Walking this path together: Anti-racist and Anti-oppressive child welfare practice* (pp. 238–256). Halifax and Winnipeg: Fernwood Publishing.

Buckley, E., & Dexter, P. (2006). From isolation to community: Collaborating with children and families in times of crisis. *The International Journal of Narrative Therapy and Community Work 2*, 3–12. www.dulwichcentre.com.au.

Burford, G. (2000). Advancing innovations: Family group decision making as community-centered child and family work. *Protecting Children, 16*(3), 4–20.

Burford, G., and Hudson, J. (Eds.). (2000). *Family Group Conferencing: New directions in community-centered child and family practice.* New York: Aldine.

Comer, D. P., & Vassar, D. (2008). Six principles of partnership: Building and sustaining system-wide change. *Protecting Children, 23*(1 & 2), 96–104.

Connolly, M. (2006). Up front and personal: Confronting dynamics in the Family Group Conference. *Family Process, 45*(3), 345–357.

Desmeules, G. (2006). Presentation: Family Group Conferencing—A sacred family circle. The International Healing our Spirit Worldwide Conference. Edmonton, Alberta.

Desmeules, G. (2007). A sacred family circle: A Family Group Conferencing model. In I. Brown, F. Chaze, D. Fuchs, J. Lafrance, S. McKay & S. Thomas Prokop (Eds.), *Putting a human face on child welfare: Voices from the Prairies* (pp. 161–188). Prairie Child Welfare Consortium www.uregina.ca/spr/prairiechild/index.html / Centre of Excellence for Child Welfare www.cecw-cepb.ca.

Glode, J., & Wien, F. (2007). Evaluating the Family Group Conferencing approach in a First Nations context: Some initial findings. In C. Chamberland, S. Léveillé, and N. Trocmé (Eds.), *Des enfants à protéger, des parents à aider : deux univers à rapprocher* (pp. 263–76), Sainte Foye : Presses de l'Université de Quebec.

Herbert, M. (2007). Creating conditions for good practice: A child welfare project sponsored by the Canadian Association of Social Workers. In I. Brown, F. Chaze, D. Fuchs, J. Lafrance, S. McKay & S. Prokop (Eds.), *Putting a human face on child welfare: Voices from the Prairies* (pp. 223–250). Prairie Child Welfare Consortium www.uregina.ca/spr/prairiechild/index.html / Centre of Excellence for Child Welfare www.cecw-cepb.ca.

Hudson, J., Morris, A., & Maxwell, G. (1996). *Family Group Conferences: Perspectives on policy and practice*. New York: Willow Tree Press.

Johnson, P. (1983). *Native children and the child welfare system*. Canadian Council on Social Development.

Kegan, R., & Laskow Lahey, L. (2001). *How we talk can change the way we work: Seven languages for transformation*. San Francisco: Jossey-Bass Publishers.

Kimelman, E. C. (1985). *No quiet place: Review Committee on Indian and Metis adoptions and placements*. Winnipeg: Manitoba Department of Community Services.

Lederman, J. (1999). Trauma and healing in Aboriginal families and communities. *Native Social Work Journal 2*, 59–90.

Madsen, W. C. (1999). Inviting new stories: Narrative ideas in family-centered services. *Journal of Systemic Therapies, 18*(3) 1–22.

Madsen, W. C. (2000). Claus Otto Sharmer conversation with Robert Kegan. Retrieved from www.dialogueonleadership.org.

Madsen, W. C. (2007). Working within traditional structures to support a collaborative clinical practice. *The International Journal of Narrative Therapy and Community Work, 2*, 51–61. www.dulwichcentre.com.au.

Madsen, W. C. (2009). Collaborative helping: A practice framework for family-centered services. *Family Process, 48*(1), 103–116.

Marsh, P., & Crow, G. (1998). *Family Group Conferences in child welfare*. London: Blackwell.

Merkel-Holguin, L. (2004). Sharing power with the people: Family Group Conferencing as a democratic experiment. *Journal of Sociology and Social Welfare, 31*(1), 155–173.

Minuchin, P., Colapinto, J., & Minuchin, S. (1998). *Working with families of the poor*. New York: The Guilford Press.

Mirsky, L. (2003). Family Group Conferencing worldwide: Part one in a series. International Institute for Restorative Practices. Downloaded from www.iirp.edu/article_detail.php?article_id=NDMz

Nixon, P., Merkel-Holguin, L., Sivak, P., & Gunderson, K. (2000). How can Family Group Conferences become family-driven? Some dilemmas and possibilities. *Protecting Children, 16*(3), 22–33.

Pennell, J. (2009). Widening the circle: Countering institutional racism in child welfare. In S. Strega and J. Carrière (Eds.), *Walking this path together: Anti-racist and anti-oppressive child welfare practice* (pp. 78–95). Halifax and Winnipeg: Fernwood Publishing.

Pennell, J., & Burford, G. (2000). Family group decision making: Communities stopping violence. Retrieved from: www.publichealth.gc.ca.

Rabin, C., Rosenbaum, H., & Sens, M. (1982). Home-based marital therapy for multi-problem families. *Journal of Marital and Family Therapy, 8*(4), 451–461.

Richardson, C. (Kinewesquao) (2009). Métis experiences of social work practice. In S. Strega and J. Carrière (Eds.), *Walking this path together: Anti-racist and anti-oppressive child welfare practice* (pp. 110–127). Halifax and Winnipeg: Fernwood Publishing.

Robinson, D. (1998). Family Group Conferences: A new direction in child welfare. *Manitoba Social Worker, 30*, 5–16.

Routhier, G. M. (2002). Family group decision-making: Does the model work for families? *Envision: The Manitoba Journal of Child Welfare, 1*(2), 85–93.

Schact, A. J., Tafoya, N., & Mirabla, K. (1989). Home-based therapy with American Indian families. *American Indian and Alaskan Native Mental Health Research, 3*(2), 27–42.

Thomas Prokop, S., McKay, S., & Gough, P. (2007). An example of appreciative inquiry as a methodology in child welfare research. CECW Information Sheet 51. Toronto, ON, Canada: University of Toronto Faculty of Social Work.

Walsh, F. (1998). *Strengthening Family Resiliency*. New York: The Guilford Press.

APPENDIX ONE: Continuum of Traditionalism[5]

Traditional, Strongly Committed	Bi-Cultural, Moderately Practicing	Acculturated, Marginally Practicing	Acculturated, Non-Practicing	Church-Influenced, Practicing	Recommitted, Strongly Practicing

Traditional, Strongly Committed – Individuals who have always practiced their traditional beliefs and ways, passing the teachings on to the next generation.

Bi-cultural, Moderately Practicing – Individuals who intermittently follow a traditional way of life and attend ceremonies as time and mainstream responsibilities permit.

Acculturated, Marginally Practicing – These individuals are curious and want to learn about the traditional ways and have contact with elders, teachings, and ceremonies.

Acculturated, Non-Practicing – Individuals who have never been exposed to any traditional ways, attended ceremonies, or expressed any curiosity about learning about the subject.

Church-Influenced, Practicing – Individuals who subscribe to a religious denomination and attend all functions as dictated by their church (or as many as time and responsibilities permit).

Recommitted, Strongly Practicing – Individuals who learned later in their journey of life about the traditional ways and were hungry for spiritual teachings.

---

5   This continuum was adapted from a pamphlet developed by the Islamic Social Services, based on my work experiences and the revisions of earlier work by Vern Morrissette, an Aboriginal educator.

CHAPTER 5

Cultural Safety and Child Welfare Systems

Eveline Milliken

INTRODUCTION

I hear conversations in social work agencies and community institutions involving people who work with marginalized others. Those conversations indicate that many social workers and clients alike are not familiar with the concept of cultural safety. As I try to introduce the concept I am often met by a protest from social workers who say: "We have done cultural sensitivity training already." Protests like this reveal many things, not the least of which is the importance of clarifying that cultural safety is not synonymous with so many of those other terms or approaches which attempt to facilitate social work at the boundary of differing cultures and world views. The concept of cultural safety approaches this conversation in quite a different way.

Unfortunately, such protests, however much they give voice to legitimate frustrations, can serve as a "stopper" (Schaef, 1981) to the

---

SUGGESTED CITATION: Milliken, E. (2012). Cultural safety and child welfare systems. In D. Fuchs, S. McKay, & I. Brown (Eds.), *Awakening the Spirit: Moving Forward in Child Welfare: Voices from the Prairies* (pp. 93–116). Regina, SK: Canadian Plains Research Center.

inter-cultural conversation. While it may be a defensive reaction to what feels like criticism of mainstream approaches, if there is to be an "awakening of the spirit" and movement forward in child welfare in the Prairies, the North, or elsewhere in Canada, it is important that the conversation between social service providers, oppressed groups, and marginalized people continues.

This chapter seeks to support that ongoing conversation. First, I will define and describe the concept of cultural safety as it has come to us from Aotearoa/New Zealand.[1] I will contrast cultural safety with other terminology with which it is often confused by first identifying five consequences of the so-called synonyms that can have a limiting effect on the helping relationship, and then by identifying three distinguishing characteristics of cultural safety. With these distinctions in mind, I will return to a basic, problematic dynamic underlying the protests which sometimes are elicited, and describe how that other terminology (with its inherent assumptions) can silence the cross-cultural conversation and prevent effective child welfare delivery. Lastly, I will present several suggestions through which the child-welfare practitioner may begin to move toward "cultural safety." While this list is by no means exhaustive, it is indicative of directions that child welfare practice could move and of possible benefits for child welfare conversations.

CULTURAL SAFETY DEFINED AND DESCRIBED

The joining together of the terms "cultural" and "safety" into a unified concept first took place among Maori healthcare workers in the 1980s (as documented by Castello, 1994; Ramsden, 1997; Fulcher, 1998; and Polaschek, 1998). This phrase was used to describe and analyze crucial experiences that Maori workers recognized were missing for Indigenous persons in the mainstream system of healthcare in Aotearoa/New Zealand. Those writers identified that the healthcare system, thought to be generic and culturally neutral, lacked respect for Maori culture and lacked understanding of traditions and perspectives that were important

---

1   The first inhabitants of the country now known as New Zealand called the land Aotearoa. Out of respect for the Maori tradition, I will use both when referring to this country, except when directly quoting others.

to healing for Maori people. Irihapeti Ramsden is credited with being the mother of this cultural safety movement. In her 2002 dissertation, "Cultural Safety and Nursing Education in Aotearoa and Te Waipounamu," Ramsden outlined the development of the concept of cultural safety in Aotearoa/New Zealand, from the naming of the concept in 1988 to the introduction of cultural safety into the educational curriculum for nurses in 1992.

This concept of cultural safety refers to "actions which recognize, respect and nurture the unique cultural identity needs of marginalized peoples and safely meet their needs, expectations and rights" (Polaschek, 1998, p. 452). Cultural safety is characterized as:

> that state of being in which the individual knows emotionally that her/his personal wellbeing, as well as her/his social and cultural frames of reference, are acknowledged, even if not fully understood. Furthermore, she/he is given active reason to feel hopeful that her/his needs and those of her/his family members and kin will be accorded dignity and respect. (Ramsden, 1997, in Fulcher, 1998, p. 333)

Polaschek (1998) named "cultural safety" as the goal that Indigenous service providers in Aotearoa/New Zealand have for their own people. Ramsden found that feeling safe enough to be oneself (including who one is culturally) was a key determinant of effective participation in health services delivery (Ramsden, 1990).

A variety of subsequent authors (Garrod, 2002; Hughes, 2003; Jeffs, 2001; Joyce, 1996; Sherrard, 1991; and Tupara, 2001) affirmed the relevance of this concept, acknowledging that Indigenous people have been treated with less than appropriate service for years. In an effort to repair the situation within health services, these authors name many experiences in which issues of cultural safety arise. It is evident that the sense of feeling culturally unsafe is not limited to particular policies or practices, but pervades the whole encounter between differing cultures.

Cultural safety is a term that is only beginning to find its way into Canadian social work literature. Victoria Smye's name appears beside a number of Canadian forays into this topic. She recently (Smye, Josewski,

& Kendall, 2010) summarized literature relating to cultural safety in an *Cultural Safety: An Overview for the First Nations, Inuit and Métis Advisory Committee*. Smye indicates the migration of this concept through the literature of a variety of professions. Both Aboriginal Nurses (2009) and the Chiefs of Ontario Office (2008) have spread the word. However it is within titles from nursing journals and publications from Aotearoa/ New Zealand and Australia that the bulk of such references continue to be found.

One might well expect that the concept of cultural safety would be a welcome addition to the vocabulary of the Canadian social worker. With the history of racial friction in North America, whether involving people of Aboriginal, Asian, African, or Eastern European descent, exhibited in the residential school system, head taxes, wartime internment, slavery, and hostility towards displaced peoples, it is not difficult to imagine that cultural safety might be of interest in Canada in general, and in child welfare service in particular. While the research I led, with Aboriginal graduates as co-researchers, focussed on experiences of people who self-identified as Indigenous, it is evident to me that this concept has relevance beyond First Nation's contexts (Milliken, 2008). As I attend conferences and workshops discussing cultural safety, my discussions with members of other groups facing oppression based upon gender, sexual orientation (GLBTT)[2], visible minorities, immigrants, disability community, or with intersecting identities grounded in multiples of these "cultures" suggest that the concept resonates with a wide variety of others as well.

CONTRASTS WITH PRIOR CROSS-CULTURAL TERMINOLOGY

From the beginning, those writing about cultural safety (Fulcher, 1998; Polaschek, 1998; and Ramsden, 1997) distinguished between cultural safety and previous language that intended to exhibit goodwill between New Zealand mainstream service providers and oppressed groups. Canadian attempts likewise were made to move the social work encounter from fearful distrust, misunderstanding, silence, and assimilation, to

---

2   GLBTT is an abbreviation for a range of sexual identities; it stands for Gay, Lesbian, Bi-sexual, Trans-gendered, and Two-spirited.

naming, acknowledging, and attempting to include different cultures. Social work literature in recent decades has been committed to "recognizing" and "respecting" Indigenous and other non-European cultures. Such literature (Asamoah, 1996; Compton & Galaway, 1999; Heinonen & Spearman, 2001; Kadushin & Kadushin, 1997; Al-krenawi & Graham, 2000; Sue, 2005) encouraged social workers to be "culturally aware or sensitive," to use "trans-cultural" or "ethnic-relative" models, to work in "culturally appropriate" or "ethnically sensitive" ways, and most recently, to develop "cultural competence."

Krajewski-Jaime, Brown, Ziefert, and Kaufman (1996) pointed toward "ethno-relativism" as "the ability not only to accept and respect cultural differences, but also the empathetic ability to shift to another cultural worldview" (p. 16). Significantly, they acknowledge that social workers from the dominant culture should recognize that the social work profession and curriculum have had Eurocentric western culture foundations and therefore social workers must seek to challenge themselves to be open to other truths and ways of being.

The National Association of Social Workers (NASW) (2005) set standards for cultural competence to which social workers should aspire. Waites, Macgowan, Pennell, Carleton-LaNey, and Weil (2004) note in their scan of literature that cultural competence is often seen as having the following four components: knowledge of the client's cultural context, including history and world view; practitioner awareness of her or his own assumptions, values, and biases; application of appropriate interventions and skills; and advocating for social change (p. 292).

These various approaches have been important stepping stones, which address both the need for attitudinal shifts and the need for action. The writers creating these concepts were on the way to making a difference. No doubt their hope was that equality would ensue as educators and practitioners struggled with issues of inclusion, respect, sensitivity, and systemic inequality. These efforts signal the good will that social workers from the dominant world view intend and their commitment to connect with members of communities other than their own.

Unfortunately, this terminology is insufficient, for several reasons. First, the breadth of cultural issues and realities faced by helping professionals is huge, and is nigh impossible to encompass. Ethnicity, for example, is a term that refers to a mixture of issues, including religion, values, cultural practice, shared histories, and genealogical ancestry. The multiplicity of cultures causes one to wonder: Can a child-welfare professional be trained well enough to be able to claim competence with respect to all of these aspects of another's culture? Is it possible for a professional to shift sufficiently to a different world view if she/he has not been raised in that other world view? How does an outsider (to a culture) gain even rudimentary knowledge about a second, or third, or nth cultural viewpoint sufficient to make effective cultural bridges on a continuing basis?

The assumption that one can be aware of, sensitive to, or even competent in all of that richness can lead to inappropriate behaviours. One such inappropriate behaviour is co-opting another culture's practices. For example, if one believes that to be culturally appropriate or competent when working with any Aboriginal person means to employ methods used in an Indigenous gathering (e.g., a cleansing smudge or a sharing circle), one might co-opt the practice of smudging. To do so could well be to insert one Aboriginal (high-context) practice into a mainstream (low-context) situation which otherwise remains unchanged, without the cultural context that makes sense of this Indigenous "technique."[3] I have heard persons declare, "Hey cool! I made a 'traditional drum' at a workshop for students in my school, so now I am making drums for all my friends," without recognizing their violation of a cultural boundary. Such actions may be well-meaning, but are an affront to generations of tradition and training in how sacred practices are to be conducted. A lack of such depth of personal knowledge may also lead to stereotyping. With superficial knowledge and experience of a culture, one may easily make assumptions about people's values and beliefs based upon their appearance.

A second shortcoming of the prior language of cultural awareness,

---

3   In low context cultures, legal terms define relationships, and rules are defined by written agreements: job descriptions, terms of reference, rules of order, contracts, and so on. By contrast, in high context cultures, harmonious relationships are seen to be more important than rules. The good of the community supersedes that of the individual. For a thorough discussion of the distinction between high and low context cultures, see *Beyond Culture*, by Hall (1976).

relativity, and competence is the assumption that there is an all-inclusive model of social work that equips social workers to function appropriately across a variety of differing cultures. Such an assumption might well lead the professional to overlook the myriad of differences and inequities that occur between different cultural groups. Aboriginal persons, for example, are no more likely to be all the same than are all Caucasian people. What is a custom and practice for one community may not be significant for another group sharing that ethnicity. Further, not all cultural groups have experienced the same level of oppression. Sensitivity levels to cultural hot-button issues will vary between individuals and groups. It is crucial that child welfare workers and others be aware of the variety of cultures within society, and the diversity within each culture.

Without such awareness, one could readily imagine the following situation arising in a child-welfare encounter: immigrants from one nation in Africa might meet with a child welfare worker who is unaware of the many countries in Africa and their rich histories and unique customs. It is quite likely an expatriate of one such country might become highly offended at having their family's practice and identity lumped together with that of a neighbouring country's tribal violence or ethnic genocide by assuming they are all "African." The bridge of trust between client and child-welfare worker could be weakened or broken, and the client might well storm out of the room, leaving behind a bewildered, frustrated, or angry child-welfare worker.

Thirdly, the previous cross-cultural language lacks operational referents that can be easily identified or measured. The question must be asked: How does one assess a worker's level of cultural awareness, sensitivity, or competence? People may believe they know enough of what is culturally appropriate based on their limited personal exposure to the practices of others. Helping professionals may have "taken the training." They even may have immersed themselves in cultural experience. However, as Robin LaDue (1994) so bluntly declared in the title of an article: "Twenty sweats do not an Indian expert make." To truly know if something is "culturally appropriate," one has to have a wide and deep knowledge of the culture, and not just a superficial acquaintance. Social worker M. Lands (personal communication, May 24, 2002) stated that an appropriate leader or assessor of such competence is "one who thinks in the language and ways of the culture." The prior terminology lacks referents that enable a client (or worker) to assess that the worker has a sufficiently accurate perspective of the client's world view to make the necessary translations for helpful cultural conversation to continue.

Even if one earns continuing education credits, diplomas, or degrees in cross-cultural studies, given the multiplicity of cultures faced by child welfare workers, a host of challenges to this "competence" will arise: How does the child welfare worker know whether she/he continues to be culturally sensitive, appropriate, and competent with respect to every culture in each professional encounter she/he subsequently undertakes? How does that social worker, or a client or supervisor for that matter, measure the degree to which a helping professional is able to comprehend the multiple challenges of another's intersecting cultural identities? How does "awareness" or "competence" or "relativism" enable the child welfare worker, charged with upholding a mandated service, to distinguish between adaptations of that mandate which are culturally necessary, as opposed to personally convenient? Can such a worker actually make a world-view shift and adapt options of response when the presuppositions of another culture are perceived to differ so dramatically from those of the social worker? For example, the high-context, embedded-in-community relationship culture of First Nations peoples is vastly different from the low-context, embedded-in-law culture of European-descended immigrants to Canada. How does the child welfare worker balance the expectations of the "law" as they encounter the priority of Aboriginal extended-family relationships?

Fourthly, the language of cultural or ethnic relativism tends to be read as if all cultures are of equal value, and ignores the differences in power enjoyed by each (Polaschek, 1997, p. 453). Such neutral and evenhanded terms lack "political substance and [are] sociologically naïve" (Dominelli, 1998, p. 13). Consequently, such language may be insufficient to motivate different behaviours or political action if the issue of the imbalance of power between cultures is left unaddressed and unchallenged. As Raven Sinclair (2004) so accurately declared: "As a profession, social work can do many things with 'awareness' of critical issues, such as racism, including nothing" (p. 52).

Fifthly and finally, as one reviews the terminology and approaches described above, it begins to be clear that these have been developed from the perspective of the service provider(s) rather than from those of the service receiver(s). In virtually every case, the terminology of cultural exchange listed above implies that the decision to consider and evaluate culture, difference of power, best practice, competence, and so on, lies within the authority and discretion of the social work system and its social workers. The focus, from "cultural awareness" to "cultural competence" continues to be the practitioner's consciousness and skill-set rather than the definitions, priorities, perceptions, and response of the client. To be sure, the invitation to be "culturally appropriate" and "ethno-relative" encourages social work practitioners to examine their own assumptions and behaviours. However, the focus of what is cross-culturally "acceptable" must move beyond examining "ourselves" to listening to the world of "the other."

Such language as previously used continues to suggest that social work practitioners can stand outside of the relationship and control the designation of what is appropriate. The child welfare practitioner therefore can retreat to the established practice of the agency/institution if she/he feels uncomfortable, let alone unsafe. Therefore, she/he may not, or perhaps cannot, consider the issues from the perspective of the culture of the member of the oppressed group or identify steps that may be more successfully embraced by the client.

DISTINGUISHING QUALITIES OF CULTURAL SAFETY

The concept of "cultural safety" goes beyond the previously used terminology in at least three ways. First, the inclusion of nurturing in the description of cultural safety, provided in Ramsden (1990), Fulcher (1998), and Polaschek (1998), seems to move the child welfare social worker (as well as many other helping professionals) into a different relationship with clients. Respect (and its synonyms: honour, esteem, regard, and consideration) can be offered from a distance. One can verbally state and intellectually believe in concepts like "respect" but, at an unconscious level, remain distant, dominant, and controlling. Nurturing another's culture, on the other hand, requires action and demands a more thorough, ongoing change of attitude and behaviour. Implicit in nurturing is a call to engage and to understand and support the other. To nurture requires hands-on, committed, persistent action and interaction. To participate in nurturing another's cultural safety of course requires recognition of and respect for cultural values. In order to know what needs, expectations, and rights exist, the nurturing one must learn about another's cultural identity, recognize its uniqueness, and respect its worth. Nurturing then goes a step further, to actively support the choices of the other within the context of the latter's culture.

While recognition and respect alone do not necessarily require putting one's self on the line, nurturing does involve risk. As they seek to ensure the sense of cultural safety in another, child welfare workers may well recognize their own discomfort; they may well feel a vulnerability that comes from relinquishing control and moving from a dominant posture into one that is not, thus risking the unknown and the unpredictable. To leave the place of certainty for uncertainty feels, and is, risky. To move from one's own world view into another's is "uncharted territory." This definition of cultural safety (Fulcher, 1998) challenges the profession to give up some established ways of practice that are comfortable to the practitioner.

Second, joining the word "safety" to "culture" makes a connection to the history of oppression and the reality of power differences experienced by clients. Attaching the word "safety" to the discussion of culture sends a strong signal that, in issues of cultural dialogue, the dominant culture is perceived as dangerous and threatening. It invites those who use the term to acknowledge the painful history of colonization, to accept responsibility for the complicity of the social work profession, through action and inaction, in the residential school system, the "Sixties Scoop" policies, and for racist policies and practices used against Aboriginal and other cultures.

The term "safety" generally connotes freedom from harm or danger and, as such, resonates deeply with social workers (see, for example, OED, 1989). "Safety" implies a number of levels of response. It is about commitment that is consistent, congruent, and comprehensive. Social work practitioners understand that for safety to exist between practitioner and client, the social worker must acknowledge reasons why oppressed others might be nervous about trusting social workers. To make a commitment to someone's safety is more than an intellectual exercise or a written institutional policy; it is an all-encompassing, holistic pledge.

These values are intrinsic to social work as it is applied in the dominant Eurocentric culture. In the past, however, safety was separated from the concept of culture in social work education and practice. Safety was assumed to be offered by helpers from the dominant perspective. However, this assumption caused harm by independently assessing safety, as it was then understood, only from the dominant world view. Hence the "benefit" of taking children to residential schools was rationalized by the dominant culture without any notion of the horrible cost of loss of cultural identity, weakened family structures, lack of attention to children's developmental needs, and devastation of Aboriginal communities. "Until the effects of … inequality in power between groups in society are addressed we cannot ensure that the needs of persons from minority cultures will be met" (Polaschek, 1997, p. 252). Minimally, mutual agreement defining "what is safe" is necessary.

Thirdly, what is most strikingly different about the concept of cultural safety is that it provides a practical operational referent: the client's perception of safety is the measure of whether the helping professional is being culturally aware, relevant, appropriate, or competent. The most vulnerable person then decides what is safe, not the worker, the agency, or the statement of policy. The "cultural risk" is felt by the client rather than the professional; "people from one culture believe they are demeaned and disempowered by the actions and delivery systems of people from another culture" (Ramsden and Spoonley, 1993, p.164). It is, therefore, from the client's perspective that the measure of "cultural safety" must be assessed. The most vulnerable persons in the social work encounter need to be able to define for themselves what safety feels like, and it is the goal of the professional who is seeking cultural safety to reduce that cultural risk.

Whether the social service is healthcare, justice, education, or child welfare, by seeking cultural safety one moves from talking in "nice words" about culture to perceiving the inequality expressed when one culture dominates another. In the term "cultural safety," the measurement reference is implied in the term "safety." Safety is a measure assessed only from the perspective of the service receiver from the minority culture, rather than from the perspective of the dominant culture practitioner. The practice of "cultural safety" demands a humble question—"Does this feel safe to you?"—and the subsequent silence in which to hear an answer.

UNDERLYING DIFFICULTIES OF PRIOR CROSS-CULTURAL TERMINOLOGY

These terms and the conversations stopped by the words "we've already had that training" reveal what turns out to be a peculiar and unhelpful assumption: that workers from the dominant cultural group feel entitled to decide what they need to know to work with a group of people to which they do not belong, a group that frequently feels excluded from the mainline culture. When workers in agencies and institutions make such an assumption, they fall into the problem so insightfully described by Simone Weil (cited in Young, 1990, p. 39): *"Someone who does not see a pane of glass does not know they do not see it. Someone who, being placed differently, does see it, does not know the other does not see it."* Such workers believe, from their own point of view, that they are adequately equipped to deal with issues faced by another. However they are blind to the barriers, from the point of view of the other, that actually impede compliance or success.

Given their different "placements" or perspectives, there is often a breakdown of communication that neither is able to identify immediately. The unhelpful or unexpected responses of each of the participants in the helping conversation are often attributed to negative motivations —resistance, laziness, hostility, addiction, on the one hand, or laziness, ignorance, bigotry, racism, on the other. When this happens, as Greene and Watkins (1998) warn us, "far too often, practitioners may perceive norms and cultural patterns that vary as cultural deficits rather than differences they need to understand" (p. 85). This creates frustration and friction between the parties. There isn't interaction with the marginalized other to see if that is so. The dominant group huffs off feeling others are being "ungrateful" or not appreciative of the overtures being made. The client goes away frustrated or feeling helpless that what the child welfare worker is offering is not helpful. More distance is created, not less.

Further, it is unlikely that the marginalized person seeking service is going to correct the insular, echo-chamber reasoning of the service provider. The marginalized often cannot articulate what is missing, and given their vulnerability, even if they could, would they? The outsider-other, who already is feeling powerless, marginalized, and voiceless, frequently can respond only by sitting in silence. It is quite logical for such persons to conclude: "If those who are educated and powerful don't get it, how can we expect those who are struggling with lots of trouble in life to explain and express sufficiently that professionals still aren't getting it?" By assuming "I'm deciding for you what you need to receive from me," those already marginalized persons continue to be disenfranchised.

INTEGRATION OF "CULTURAL SAFETY" IN CHILD WELFARE PRACTICE

What I found in my research into cultural safety with Aboriginal people who came from marginalized groups and who have now been educated in professional social work language was that when we spoke of the concept of cultural safety they essentially said, "That's it." As one participant put it:

> After you came to talk to me, I really thought more about cultural safety.... I think a lot of this has made an impact for me, in terms of how I am dealing with the people I work with; not only the immediate people I'm working with but the clients who come through our doors. (Milliken, 2008, p. 229)

> And I think that if we continue to talk, and to teach, and to educate our people, our young ones, I think it's going to help. I think bringing this kind of research ... is really important. I haven't seen anything to this point about cultural safety to this extent, and I think it's really good. I think... that what comes out of here is going to help a lot

of people, a lot of organizations hopefully. So I'm really
happy to be part of this actually. (Milliken, 2008, p. 229)

They hadn't heard the concept before but when they heard it, said, "Yes, that's what's missing."

What follows are suggestions about how to integrate cultural safety into Canadian child welfare practice. In so doing, I make the assumption that child welfare workers are educated as social workers, and that while these recommendations are directed specifically toward child welfare workers, I believe these suggestions are relevant to good social work practice in all fields, including justice, healthcare, mental health, education, family therapy, and community work. Implementing these directions should lead to improved child welfare conversations.

First, seek to personally integrate the concept of cultural safety in your own child welfare practice. To create culturally safe workplaces for child welfare, social workers must first look at what safety means in their own lives. One cannot be culturally safe by learning it as an ideology that only applies to others, or as an intellectual theory without living it as a practice. Similarly, social workers cannot "do" cultural safety to someone else; one cannot take a workshop, and independently nurture cultural safety without a relationship and partnership with the clients.

In order to move this concept from an intellectual notion to an integrated behaviour, the child welfare worker might well seek similarities and commonalities of values between oneself and the client. While there are differences in roles, the exercise of putting oneself in the shoes of the other person may well change the climate of the conversation. For example, if you had to speak to the client in the language of their culture (not English or French), how successful would you be? Child welfare workers might well think about a family member in their life (a child, a senior, a partner) and ask, "Under what circumstances would they be caused to fail to provide adequate care?" What would it take for you to not provide optimum care for a vulnerable person whom you love? Participants often identify poverty, fear, disability, hostility of others, addictions, depression and other mental health challenges as factors that would affect their ability to be an adequate caregiver. As a result, workshop participants often become reacquainted with reasons for their clients' problematic behaviours. It is then that the social worker can begin to understand some of what it means to seek to nurture clients in their own culture milieu.

Second, the social worker can then, with integrity and integration, invite clients to consider the value of the phrase "cultural safety" for themselves. The concept of cultural safety empowers the client with a measure of control over a stressful situation. She/he is the one who measures in her/his own being her/his own sense of safety. She/he does not need to take courses to understand the variety of meanings within a culture. By virtue of her/his lived experience, she/he is the one who best able to assess how well her/his particular culture or intersecting identities are being recognized in the cross-cultural encounters.

Ask this question of clients: "Are you feeling safe?" Whatever the level of cultural training of the social worker, the language of cultural safety provides the client with a simple means of signalling that there is a problem. Like simply saying, "ouch!"—a phrase like "I feel unsafe" or "I feel culturally unsafe" indicates that there is a problem that needs to be addressed before the agenda of the agency will proceed successfully. A client feeling culturally unsafe will be unlikely to offer the trust and full participation to the problem-solving options under discussion.

Practical follow-up questions could include: "Can you think of anything that would help you to feel safer?" Suggestions that might arise could be "to have an elder or spiritual leader from my culture present"; to include other members of a relevant community (family members, or a same gendered partner not recognized as parent or primary caregiver); to meet in a more neutral place, other than the social work office or the family home; to have more time to put on a head covering; or to have a chaperone. A client might suggest more holistic activities such as walking about the community; doing more group work; observing youth sporting or music-making activities; gathering medicines together. These activities enable taking the time to develop a more nuanced relationship, to nurture the pride of culture, to find opportunities to interact in settings that are more natural than sitting in an office analyzing individual feelings. The client might ask for a different interpreter, revealing that a current translator could be saying things that are demeaning or threatening. It may not be possible or advisable to agree to all requests, but additional support for the helping relationship could no doubt be revealed. (More will be said about this below.)

Third, understand that silence does not mean agreement. Silence may rather be an expression of confusion and an unwillingness to risk losses by questioning the social worker who is in a position to deny services to the client. Silence can be an expression of helplessness, fear, or frustration (Milliken, 2008). The social worker who understands silence as a signal of cultural unsafety might be more disposed to recognize disconnections, explore the meaning of silence, invite clients to assess their sense of safety, and so encourage the continuation of a genuinely helpful conversation.

Fourth, while it is important to respect values, beliefs, customs, and choices, it is also important to move to action and nurture that choice. As Pennell (2005a) notes:

> Issues that bring families to the attention of public authorities are usually extensive and complicated. These kinds of issues require a cooperative effort to identify and assess what is happening, develop a plan of action, carry out the plan, and review and modify the plan as needed (p. 5).

Pennell and Anderson (2005) have explored this shift of the locus of expertise as it occurs through family group conferencing. According to them, the purpose of the many techniques used to create a welcome space is to "move the family to the centre of the planning" (p. xii). As a result, the participants (family members) then "can apply their insider knowledge and long-term commitment to develop a plan that works.... They need to feel 'at home' and to speak in their own words" (Pennell, 2005b, p. 33). When translators are required, the social worker who seeks to be culturally safe will ensure that the presence of a translator does not shift the focus of the conversation to the social worker; instead the center of the conversation remains the family members' circle, with the translator assisting the social worker to comprehend and offer support.

By moving the family to the centre of the conversation, the social worker no longer falls into the problematic dynamic of being the one deciding for others what is culturally safe or appropriate. By augmenting the conversation with participants relevant to the particular culture and client, the social worker avoids the burden of having to be expert in multiple cultures, variations of experience, or intersecting identities. The awareness of cultural safety thus can eliminate obstacles to the helping conversation, and move to decisions that are more fully shared.

Fifth, recognize that there is diversity within similar groups. The culturally safe child welfare worker does not need to be an expert in all those diverse groups. However, that worker might well ask the client, who *is* the ultimate expert in her/his own personal cultural perspective and what are her/his priorities for cultural safety (note that this expertise is in the client's own perspective of culture, not in the client's culture as it is more academically defined).

Sixth, equalize power differences. Greenwood, Wright, and Nielsen (2006) identify that, as researchers, educators, and practitioners working in the area of cultural safety, "cultural safety is absolutely about identity, and this is where we focus our teaching and practice" (p. 214). They further say that the "focus for us was unambiguously on racial politics... cultural safety has become a cloak for considering all forms of oppression and discrimination" (p. 213).

Seek to become and remain aware of your privileges. This is more difficult than it sounds, for privilege is often invisible to those who enjoy it (McIntosh, 1990). We wrongly assume that such freedom is shared by all. Polaschek (1998) asked us to be aware of power relationships on a continuum from social disadvantage to outright racism.

Similarly, social workers are reminded to be aware of cultural differences within groups. Zon et al. (2004) suggest looking at "the societal position of the particular cultural minority group in total, not the social positions of individual members of that group, which will vary from deeply traditional to multimodern ways of life that differ little from the dominant culture" (p. 290). The child welfare worker's experience of racism may be different than the client's. The client may have other intersecting identities that amplify their vulnerability. Asking the question "Are you feeling safe; what can I do to help you feel more culturally safe" begins to give that power to the client.

Seventh, advocate for changes to attend to those inequalities. Recognize that there are societally shaped inequalities based on particular historical, political, and economic realities that cause particular concerns. Polaschek (1998) asked us to commit to understand and work toward de-colonizing approaches that are built into mainstream child welfare systems. Consult with constituents to identify priority issues and work together for change.

Eighth, commit to seek to become a culturally safe organization. With colleagues and administrative teams, study what cultural safety might mean in your own institution or agency. Include client-constituent members in creating that sense of what is culturally safe for them. One of the components of moving toward becoming a more culturally safe organization is to establish strong connections with various cultural groups and leaders. These leaders may become partners in programming, organizational assessment, and clarification of issues that are raised by workers and clients. Seek out those who represent a variety of cultural perspectives. Identify leaders with whom you can work. With such relationships agencies can explore nuances of cultural difference, such as, for example, the difference of meaning for various Muslim groups between a head scarf (hijab) and a face scarf (niqab).

Clearly, an agency response might well be to argue that the language of cultural safety could be used speciously, as a kind of mask, a type of cultural immunity, a free pass that prevents interventions that are needed or mandated. However, from the point of view of a client from a minority culture who carries the memory and scars of other dominant-culture mandated services (like an Aboriginal survivor of the residential school system, for example), the expression of a lack of trust and safety may be a very real issue in the conversation.

Ninth, invite organizations to develop and include culturally safe practices within their own field. Cultural safety or risk can be experienced when people meet someone from another culture in any number of settings, whether social, voluntary, or for profit, in government or non-government organizations. As a consequence, one might expect cultural safety to receive a warm hearing when explored with educational, health, and justice institutions, faith groups, and even business organizations. Groups made up of people with various vulnerable intersecting identities could explore ways of providing greater cultural safety for their constituents.

Tenth, recognize that cultural safety applies to the child welfare social worker also. Researchers in Alice Springs, Australia, found that the concept of cultural safety was valuable not only for the families they worked with, but also for Indigenous child protection workers. Aboriginal workers felt "damned if you do, and damned if you don't." Aboriginal workers described feeling culturally unsafe within the mainstream organizations in which they worked. At the best of times, relations between workers of different cultures can be impeded by the sense of cultural un-safety of a more vulnerable group. However, by definition, there has been an inherent lack of safety within the child welfare system. Overworked child welfare workers and stressed child welfare systems are expected to be involved in and resolve complex situations abandoned by other systems, whether healthcare, education, justice, mental health, or other voluntary services. As a legally mandated service, child welfare systems cannot say "no" to these most painful of circumstances. When child welfare workers are scrutinized by the mass media, politicians, or even social workers from other disciplines, child welfare case workers and managers may feel it best to hunker down and cover their own vulnerability. When the system is under such pressure, due, say, to the death of an infant in care, there may not be the time, flexibility, or inclination to adapt one's own practice to the uncertain possibilities of another's unfamiliar culture. Social workers may well see such options as bizarre and as unhelpful as the make-believe world of Alice's Wonderland. Under such intense scrutiny, workers might revert to low-context, strict adherence to policy approaches. Front-line workers may approach meetings with clients with "by the book" care. To recognize the presence of cultural unsafety may assist in finding language that is useful when relationships with colleagues "go off the rails." When the system is unsafe for visible minority social workers it is unlikely that those employees will be trusted by their kin to make the system safer for their visible minority clients.

The Alice Spring social workers indicated that they face criticism and ostracism from their own community members also. Such workers

> may be seen as collaborators with the state in its on-going destruction of culture and family life; and if they speak out and criticise the current cultural circumstances that block effective intervention, they may be seen as traitors

> to their own culture and strangers to themselves, their families and communities. (Zon et al., 2004, p. 293)

> Regardless of whether they have any input into decisions regarding particular cases, their relationship to the community means that Aboriginal workers are at greater risk of being held accountable by the community for the actions of the department on those cases than are their non-indigenous colleagues. (Zon et al., 2004, p. 295)

The Alice Springs study found cultural safety to be useful in "creating more appropriate workplaces for Aboriginal staff in child protection and for assisting casework approaches and decisions for all staff" (Zon, et al., 2004, p. 288). The Australian experience not only linked Indigenous people with others around the world, and named the importance of the concept within the helper-client conversation; it also illustrated that cultural safety is a concept which resonates within the larger system of child welfare. Clients, front-line child welfare workers and managers whose intersecting identities put them at risk may all feel culturally unsafe. Cultural safety requires the "goal of safeguarding family voice, worker accountability, community involvement, and consensus building" (Pennell, 2005a, p. 5).

CONCLUSION

The term "cultural safety" gives new, functional language to address a frustration that has otherwise been unnamed. While people from groups that have been oppressed may find benefit in the concept, education about cultural safety is intended particularly for social workers from the dominant culture. It is for those people who do not see the pane of glass barriers embedded in many aspects of social work practice. Prior efforts to develop cross-cultural language show an intention to be helpful. However, in the absence of a paradigm shift communicated by the concept of cultural safety, this intention lacks a practical tool through which to achieve this ideal. As a result, marginalization will be maintained by people who are simply doing their jobs. Oppression is not necessarily conscious or intentional but often is embedded structurally in everyday habits, unquestioned norms, and unchallenged assumptions that inhabit institutional rules, and the effects are felt in the consequences of following those rules (Young, 1990, p.41).

If, as social workers we keep presuming to tell people what we think they need, regardless of the culture, the ground, out of which they have grown, rather than listening for solutions clients identify as workable, we will not move forward in child welfare. If we think we educate ourselves by hearing only our own culture's point of view, rather than understanding the painful histories which twist people from their most natural affinity (their children), we will not awaken that shared and mutual healing spirit in our work.

The pursuit of cultural safety can help social workers better understand clients, fellow workers, and agency managers by exploring what makes them feel safer and responding with positive valuation. As Pennell (2005a) so aptly put it: "People with supports, protections, clear limits, real opportunities, and pride in themselves and their heritage are prepared to contribute to their society" (p. 8). In this complex and important work, the circle of care involves safety for all parties: the families, the communities, and the social workers. Cultural safety helps widen the circle and sustain the helping conversation. Cultural safety can help *awaken the spirit* of hope for *moving forward in child welfare*.

REFERENCES

Aboriginal Nurses Association of Canada (ANAC), Canadian Association of Schools of Nursing (CASN), & Canadian Nurses Association (CAN). (2009). *Cultural competence and cultural safety in nursing education: A framework for First Nations, Inuit and Métis nursing*. ANAC.

Al-Krenawi, A., & Graham, J. (February, 2000). Culturally sensitive social work practice with Arab clients in mental health settings. *Health and Social Work, 25*(1), 9–22. Retrieved February 16, 2012, from hsw.oxfordjournals.org/content/25/1/9.full.pdf+html.

Asamoah, Y. (Ed.). (1996). *Innovations in delivering culturally sensitive social work services: Challenges for practice and education*. New York, NY: Haworth Press.

Castello, H. (1994). Barriers to nursing experienced by Maori: A historical overview. *Whitireia Nursing Journal, 1994*(1), 17–24.

Chiefs of Ontario Office (COO). (2008). Aboriginal health human resources initiative, chiefs of Ontario request for proposals, cultural safety: In relation to first Nations health care. Retrieved September 16, 2009, from www.nationtalk.ca.

Compton, B., & Galaway, B. (Eds.). (1999). *Social work processes* (6th ed.). Toronto, ON: Brooks/Cole.

Dominelli, L. (1998). Anti-oppressive practice in context. In R. Adams, L. Dominelli, & M. Payne (Eds.), *Social work: Themes, issues and critical debates* (pp. 3–19). London: MacMillan.

Fulcher, L. (1998). Acknowledging culture in child and youth practices. *Social Work Education, 17*(3), 321–338.

Garrod, A. (2002). Cultural safety: Living with disability. *Whitireia Nursing Journal,* 2002(9), 14–19.

Greene, R., & Watkins, M. (Eds.). (1998). *Serving diverse constituencies: Applying the ecological perspective.* New York: Aldine De Gruyter.

Greenwood, S., Wright, T., & Nielsen, H. (2006). Conversations in context: Cultural safety and reflexivity in child and family health nursing [Highlights from the 7th International Family Nursing Conference: Plenary Address]. *Family Health Nursing,* 2006(12), 201–224.

Hall, E. (1976). *Beyond culture.* Garden City, N.Y.: Anchor Press/Doubleday.

Heinonen, T., & Spearman, L. (2001). *Social work practice: Problem solving and beyond.* Toronto, ON: Brooks/Cole.

Hughes, H. (2003). A cultural safety journey. *Nursing New Zealand, 9*(11), 22–23.

Jeffs, L. (2001). Impact of cultural safety education on clinical practice researched. *Nursing New Zealand, 7*(7), 6.

Joyce, M. (1996). Cultural safety in Aotearoa/New Zealand: An overview. *Whitireia Nursing Journal,* 1996(3), 7–16.

Kadushin, A., & Kadushin, G. (1997). *The social work interview: A guide for human service professionals* (4th ed.). New York, NY: Columbia University Press.

Krajewski-Jaime, E., Brown, K., Ziefert, M., & Kaufman, E. (1996). Utilizing international clinical practice to build inter-cultural sensitivity in social work students. *Journal of Multicultural Social Work, 4*(2), 15–29.

LaDue, R. (1994). Coyote returns: Twenty sweats does not an Indian expert make. *Women and Therapy, 15*(1), 93–111.

McIntosh, P. (1990). White privilege: Unpacking the invisible knapsack [Electronic version] (Excerpt from P. McIntosh (1988), White privilege and male privilege: A personal account of coming to see correspondences through work in women's studies [Working Paper 189, 1988], Wellesley Centers for Women, Wellesley College, Wellesley, MA). *Independent School*, 1990 (Winter). Retrieved August 22, 2007, from seamonkey.ed.asu.edu/~mcisaac/emc598ge/Unpacking.html.

Milliken, E. (2002). Margin or centre: Building a culturally safe context in which Aboriginal students can develop social work practice competencies. Unpublished paper. St. John's, NF: Memorial University of Newfoundland.

Milliken, E. (2008). *Toward cultural safety: An exploration of the concept for social work education with Canadian Aboriginal peoples.* St. John's, NF: Memorial University of Newfoundland.

National Association of Social Workers [NASW]. *NASW standards for cultural competence in social work practice.* Retrieved June 6, 2005, from http://www.socialworkers.org/sections/credentials/cultural_comp.asp.

OED [Oxford English Dictionary] (2nd ed.). (1989). Safety. Oxford: Oxford University Press. [Electronic version]. Retrieved October 28, 2011, from http://www.oed.com.

Pennell, J. (2005a). Widening the circle. In J. Pennell & G. Anderson (Eds.), *Widening the circle: The practice and evaluation of family group conferencing with children, youths, and their families* (pp. 1–8). Washington, DC: NASW Press.

Pennell, J. (2005b). At the conference—Advancing cultural safety. In J. Pennell & G. Anderson (Eds.), *Widening the circle: The practice and evaluation of family group conferencing with children, youths, and their families* (pp. 33–51). Washington, DC: NASW Press.

Pennell, J., & Anderson, G. (Eds.). (2005). *Widening the circle: The practice and evaluation of family group conferencing with children, youths, and their families.* Washington, DC: NASW Press.

Polaschek, N. R. (1998). Cultural safety: A new concept in nursing people of different ethnicities. *Journal of Advanced Nursing, 27*(3), 452–457.

Ramsden, I. (1990). Cultural safety. *The New Zealand Nursing Journal, Kai, Tiaki, 83*(110), 18–19.

Ramsden, I. (1997). Cultural safety: Implementing the concept. In P. Te Whaiti, M. McCarthy, & A. Durie (Eds.), *Mai I rangiatea: Maori wellbeing and development* (pp. 113–125). Auckland, NZ: Auckland University.

Ramsden, I., & Spoonley, P. (1993). The cultural safety debate in nursing education in Aotearoa. *New Zealand Annual Review of Education, 3*, 161–174.

Schaef, A. (1981). *Women's reality: An emerging female system in the white male society.* Minneapolis, MN: Winston.

Sherrard, I. (1991). How can you teach cultural safety? *The New Zealand Nursing Journal, 84*(9), 25–26.

Sinclair, R. (2004, September). Aboriginal social work education in Canada: Decolonizing pedagogy for the seventh generation. *First Peoples Child and Family Review, 1*(1), 49–61.

Smye, V., Josewski, V., & Kendall, E. (2010). *Cultural Safety: An Overview for the First Nations, Inuit and Métis Advisory Committee.* Ottawa ON: Mental Health Commission of Canada.

Sue, D. (2005). *Multicultural social work practice.* Hoboken, NJ: John Wiley and Sons.

Tupara, H. (2001). Meeting the needs of Maori women: The challenge for mid-wifery education. *New Zealand College of Midwives Journal, 25*(October 2001), 6–9.

Waites, C., Macgowan, M., Pennell, J., Carleton-LaNey, I., & Weil, M. (2004). Increasing the cultural responsiveness of family group conferencing. *Social Work, 49*(2), 291–300.

Young, I. (1990). *Justice and the politics of difference.* Princeton, NJ: Princeton University Press.

Zon, A., Lindeman, M., Williams, A., Hayes, C., Ross, D., & Furber, M. (September, 2004). Cultural safety in child protection: Application to the workplace environment and casework practice. *Australian Social Worker, 57*(3), 288–298.

CHAPTER 6

A Conceptual Framework for Child Welfare Service Coordination, Collaboration, and Integration

Alexandra Wright

INTRODUCTION

This chapter focuses on a discussion of child welfare service delivery and presents a conceptual framework that reflects the intersection of the service delivery continuum and the levels of service delivery. The discussion begins with a brief summary of the importance of service integration in the context of services for children, their families, and communities, followed by a presentation of the service delivery conceptual framework. A review of identified challenges to service integration follows, and the chapter concludes with some recommendations to move forward.

The main aim of the chapter is to contribute to the ongoing discussion of how child welfare organizations, and the leaders who are in charge of

---

SUGGESTED CITATION: Wright, A. (2012). A conceptual framework for child welfare service coordination, collaboration, and integration. In D. Fuchs, S. McKay, & I. Brown (Eds.), *Awakening the Spirit: Moving Forward in Child Welfare: Voices from the Prairies* (pp. 117–133). Regina, SK: Canadian Plains Research Center.

these organizations,[1] can improve service planning and delivery to the benefit of children, their families, and communities. While a key premise of the chapter is that integrated services can provide improved conditions for staff working within the child welfare system and, more importantly, improved services for children, families, and communities involved with child welfare services, the author notes that not all organizations may choose to pursue the goal of integrated services, given their internal or external environmental contexts. Authors have noted difficulties with service coordination or integration initiatives (e.g., Farmakopoulou, 2002; Hallett & Birchall, 1992; Reilly, 2001), and Hassett and Austin (1997) provide a useful list of strategic questions for Human Service Organizations [HSOs] prior to implementing service integration that addresses issues such as "Why is reorganization needed?" "How much change is needed?" and "When should changes occur?" (p. 25).

Although the chapter highlights challenges to service integration, the author argues that managers must administer and manage with the support and involvement of an inclusive organizational team (including service users). Whenever possible, such management should be proactive and based on informed choices. The contention in this discussion is that it is the child welfare organizations' managers who must take responsibility and leadership in implementing innovation and change in order to achieve integrated services. Thus, managers of social services organizations must anticipate and respond to change on a regular basis, change that is internal to the organization as well as change that is external to the organization.

REVIEW OF USE OF THE TERMS SERVICE COLLABORATION, COORDINATION, AND INTEGRATION

The interest in service collaboration, coordination, and integration is not new (see, for example, Aiken, Dewar, DiTomaso, Hage, & Zeitz, 1975; Hudson, 1987; and Hassett & Austin, 1997, for a review). However, the terms *service collaboration*, *service coordination*, and *service integration* have been frequently used interchangeably or defined in multiple ways in the

---

1   Although the author notes the role differentiation, for the purpose of this discussion administrators and managers will be referred to as managers.

literature over the past few decades. For example, some of these alternate definitions have included the co-location of services, partnership between organizations (Ferguson, 2004), or the broader community change initiatives (Austin, 1997). They have been used differentially by various authors based on the level of formality between the organizational relationships (Kagan, Goffin, Golub, & Pritchard, 1995; Reilly, 2001), policies and procedures (Konrad, 1996), the focus of the intervention (King & Meyer, 2006; Park & Turnbull, 2003; Scott, 2005; Stroul, 1995), or the "seamlessness" of service provision (Friesen & Briggs, 1995). Definitions of coordination, collaboration, and integration used in this chapter are based on contributions of key authors. For the purpose of clarity, these terms warrant some discussion and definition.

Konrad (1996) presented five levels of integration, in which service coordination, collaboration, and integration reflect a continuum from informal, minimal integration (cooperation and coordination) to fully integrated and formal arrangements (integration) with service policies and procedures. The extent to which services are fully integrated varies, depending on the formality of policies between organizational relationships. Accordingly, cooperation/coordination, collaboration, and integration occur on all levels of service planning and provision: case (direct practice), organizational, and the larger service system.

Scott (2005) concurred with Konrad's perspective of collaboration as occurring within a continuum of services and provided a framework for the analysis of inter-organizational collaboration. The author argued that, due to the complexity of collaborative efforts in human services, challenges to collaboration occur on different levels and distinguish the focus of analysis: the organizational (inter- and intra-), the inter-professional, and the personal (inter- and intra). Hodges, Hernandez, and Nesman (2003) characterized collaboration as a developmental process with five stages, moving from individual action to "increasingly collaborative processes" and climaxing in "true collaboration" that includes professionals and family members (p. 298).

King and Meyer (2006) identified functions and activities of service integration and service coordination for a co-ordinated care outcome in the context of a family-centred approach. In this conceptualization, *service integration* occurs on system and organizational levels of service delivery and includes efforts such as planning or administrative activities to produce a "comprehensive range of service" particular to a specific area (p. 479) with a greater efficiency in service provision. This can occur intra-agency, inter-agency, and inter-sectorial. In contrast, *service coordination* is viewed as a process that occurs on a clinical level, and functions include activities that support families "to navigate the system and obtain services they need" (p. 480).

Park and Turnbull (2003) contributed to the concept of service integration by distinguishing between the interpersonal and the structural. The interpersonal dimension of service integration includes "characteristics of relationships between individuals that enhance or inhibit collaborative efforts" (p. 50), whereas the structural dimension includes inter-organizational or system level elements that support collaboration.

Friesen and Briggs (1995) articulated that "seamless" service delivery, or "smooth transitions from one service to the next" (p. 69) are key elements of service coordination that lead to service integration on three levels. First, on the intra-agency level, uninterrupted service over time, which includes staff and program stability, contributes to seamless service delivery. Second, on an inter-agency level, the coordination of services and resources that minimize disruptions contributes to seamless service delivery. Third, on the direct practice level (child or family specific), seamless service delivery occurs when the system eases "…transitions across developmental stages or statuses" (Friesen & Briggs, 1995, p. 69). This results in service integration, a seamless approach to services across a child's lifetime based on needs. Service integration includes:

> … Interagency agreements designed to facilitate the movement of children and their families among agencies, joint programming aimed at maximizing the efficient use of resources and … the pooling of resources to create flexible funds to increase the individualization of services.
> (Friesen & Poertner, 1995, p. xxiii)

More recently, authors such as Horwath and Morrison (2007) provided a list of necessary elements for collaboration under the headings of pre-disposing factor, mandate, membership and leadership, machinery, and process.

The following section provides a conceptual model of service coordination, collaboration, and integration incorporating these authors' contributions. The proposed conceptual framework builds on the service spectrum concept as identified by Konrad (1996) and, with some modification, the levels of analysis proposed by Scott (2005). It expands these concepts to create a framework of service delivery that defines service coordination, collaboration, and integration in the context of the service delivery level. Thus, the framework provided displays the intersection of the three elements of the service delivery continuum (coordination, collaboration, and integration), with the three service delivery levels (direct practice, organizational, and system- or sector-wide).

DEFINED TERMS IN THIS CONCEPTUAL FRAMEWORK
COORDINATION

The conceptual model presented considers service coordination as the means to ensure the needs of families are met and "that multiple services are delivered in a coordinated manner and that services are adapted to the changing needs of youngsters and their families over time" (Stroul, 1995, p. 5). Service coordination processes are generally coordinated on a more *ad hoc* basis with little view of the overall system and no larger systematic planning approach. Thus, service coordination on a case level can be defined as "working together" (Scott, 2005, p. 132) or as a "…loosely organized attempt by autonomous agencies and programs to work together to change procedures or structures to make all affected programs more successful" (Konrad, 1996, p. 11).

Collaboration

In contrast, service collaboration has a greater emphasis on joint formal policy and practice across different fields and organizations. Service collaboration is defined in a broader sense as: "…all interaction aimed at working together, both informal and formal, which occurs across the boundaries of different organisations and sectors" (Scott, 2005, p. 133), and includes "…the formal joining of structures and processes between organizations" (p. 132). Thus, on a case level, collaboration reflects a "working together" (p. 132) albeit in autonomous organizations: "Still-autonomous agencies and programs work together as a whole with a common goal, product, or outcome" (Konrad, 1996, p. 11).

Integration

Service integration is defined as "functions and activities that are aimed at the formation of a unified and comprehensive range of services" (King & Meyer, 2006, p. 479). Service integration can occur between staff intra- or inter-organizationally, through policies and practice, and on a system level. An added dimension of service integration relates to the seamlessness of service transition for families and children. Thus, joint interagency agreements and services that support children and their families maximize resources to meet identified needs (Friesen & Poertner, 1995, p. xxiii). On a system level, service integration requires the dismantling of structural components that create obstacles to integrated services and the development of strategies to improve service integration through a reduction in service fragmentation, meeting identified service needs, and the availability of a service continuum based on assessed need.

BENEFITS TO SERVICE COORDINATION, COLLABORATION, AND INTEGRATION

Collaborative or integrated services have been found to benefit the service user in children's mental health services (Hodges et al., 2003), families who have children with special needs (Dinnebeil, Hale, & Rule, 1999), and families involved with the child welfare system (Green, Rockhill, & Burrus, 2008). Green et al. found that collaboration between child welfare, treatment, and court systems for families with a substance abuse problem benefitted parents through shared value systems, better communication, and increased support.

Benefits of a collaborative approach to service provision include an improved service experience for both families and professionals who provide services (Larsson, 2000). Larsson reported that families experience inter-organizational teams (teams that span organizational boundaries) as more family-centered, which results in families having a greater sense of control over service provision. The author concluded that inter-organizational teams are able to extend beyond set boundaries and thus are able to work with the system as a whole to the benefit of the service user. Other benefits to service integration include the formation of a shared inter-professional view and team approach (Larsson, 2000), and the provision of a common inter-professional language, policy, and practice (Wright, Hiebert-Murphy, & Trute, 2010). Integrated services can also result in a reduction of duplication, costs, and inappropriate service use (Hassett & Austin, 1997; King & Meyer, 2006).

The need for service coordination has been identified as an issue for on-reserve services for children and their families (Toubeh, 1989; Wright, Hiebert-Murphy, & Gosek, 2005). In a Canadian study examining services to Aboriginal children and youth with behavioural and learning difficulties, community participants found that poor interdisciplinary coordination and the lack of voluntary agencies and support services available to on-reserve residents were perceived as contributing to poor services and unmet needs (Wright et al., 2005). The researchers found that the child welfare agencies reported a general lack of agency and broader community resources necessary to provide sufficient services to children and their families. Findings also identified a lack of coordination among existing service providers and an identified need for collaboration across the country. On a broader organizational level, inter-organizational collaboration can assist with organizational change and innovation (Jaskyte & Lee, 2006) and can allow for a more flexible and creative delivery system (CASW, 2003).

In order to implement change or innovation, such as service integration, a conceptual framework such as the one provided may be useful for child welfare (and other services sectors) organizations' staff to understand and effectively manage service coordination, collaboration, and integration challenges. In addition, the author believes that a greater understanding of service integration may prove helpful for social services organizations' supervisory, front-line, and support staff to understand and effectively implement service integration to benefit children, their families, and communities.

A CONCEPTUAL FRAMEWORK OF SERVICE DELIVERY

Table 6.1 presents a conceptual framework that incorporates a matrix design synthesizing the intersectionality of the service delivery continuum with three service levels. The framework presents examples of service coordination, collaboration, and integration on three different service levels: direct practice, organizational, and system-wide.

There are potentially multiple benefits to the use of the conceptual

Table 6.1. A Conceptual Framework of Service Delivery

	Direct Practice: Service Users/Service Providers	**Organization**	**System**
Coordination	• Distinct organizational policy. • Multiple services with some efforts for joint MOUs, planning, programmes or policies. • Independent organizations working together to improve specific programmes' success and service user access. • Greater reliance on informal relationships.	• Organization-specific policies regarding service eligibility and access • Service user has easier access to programmes based on joint policies/programmes. • Information-sharing and communication between professionals.	• Intra-organizational programs are categorical, targeted, with unique funding and eligibility requirements. • Teams generally not used. • Transitioning between programs is necessary. • Some but limited mechanisms to link programs.	• Distinct jurisdictional boundaries and policies although some ad hoc joint development. • No funding to support coordination. • No systematic linking. • Characterized by service and policy fragmentation. • Service systems operate autonomously.
Collaboration	• Formal and informal efforts that transgress organizational and sector boundaries. • Independent organizations working together with a shared vision or goal. • Greater reliance on formal relationships and planned.	• Inter-organizational professionals working together to benefit service user. • Ad hoc policy and protocols related to case. • Attempts to minimize individual transitions.	• Intra-organizational programs have a common goal with cross-program sharing. • Some formal joining of structures and processes between organizations. • Inter-disciplinary teams have a common goal, language. • Between program/organizational transitions marked by working together.	• System support for inter-organizational efforts for joint service planning and provision. • Resources aimed to minimize disruptions. • Linkages established across professions and sectors.
Integration	• Formal relationships with unified goal that aim for comprehensive and seamless services (through policy and programming) spanning sectors. • Service continuum based on needs. • No service fragmentation or gaps.	• Relationships between professionals unified and focused on child or family specific. • Seamless service delivery experience for service user across stages and changing needs.	• Intra-organizational culture has staff and program stability. • Organization support for inter-professional/disciplinary teams, partners are equal. • Seamlessness in transitions between programs and blended activities. • Unified, comprehensive, organizational policies and practices: Rules and boundaries clearly delineated in formal documents.	• Unified formal policy between jurisdictions, organizations/sectors, working with the same "lens". • Coherent system with mechanisms for joint planning, service development, problem solving, funding and evaluation of service. • Funding to support integrated services.

SERVICE DELIVERY CONTINUUM

framework. First, an important contribution of the framework is that it provides a clear definition of the terms collaboration, coordination, and integration. Given that the literature is replete with these terms and that these terms are associated with multiple meanings, having clarity in definitions is significant. In addition, the conceptual framework intersects the defined terms with the three delivery levels: personal, organizational, and system. By providing clarity in definitions of terms and levels of policy/service, the framework provides a common language with which intra- and inter-organizational participants can speak. Effective teams should be able to communicate with and understand each of their own members. Second, from a managerial viewpoint, the framework can be used to assess and understand where an organization's policies and practices are situated in the framework to provide guidance as to next steps, both within the organization as well as with other service providers. Third, from the perspective of a service provider, the framework has the potential to explain challenges experienced in the field, and to point to possible solutions to overcome them. This framework can be useful for knowledge transfer activities such as training and supervision, and can contribute to organizational evaluation. Ultimately, from the perspective of a service user, the conceptual framework may encourage improved policy and service delivery, decreasing fragmentation, gaps, and disjointed policies and practices.

In summary, there is clear support for service integration in child welfare planning, delivery, implementation, and evaluation. The conceptual framework defines a continuum of service delivery on a case, organizational, and system level. Implementation of such a framework requires that the challenges to service coordination, collaboration, and integration are recognized. Key challenges are described below, along with recommendations for how to move forward in child welfare.

CHALLENGES TO SERVICE COORDINATION, COLLABORATION, AND INTEGRATION

Challenges to service coordination, collaboration, and integration occur intra-organizationally, inter-organizationally, and system-wide. For the sake of clarity, these levels are presented as distinct; however, some elements of these levels may overlap with others. For example, adequate resources for child welfare services impact organizations and the delivery system equally. In addition, inter-professional or inter-disciplinary issues often span intra- and inter-organizational boundaries and are relevant to the system level as well.

Intra-organizational

On an intra-organizational level, the organization's culture and climate can severely affect the capacity for service integration. Glisson and Green (2005) found that an organization with a "defensive culture" can result in service provider apathy as well as opposition to new approaches. Elements of defensive cultures, as these authors described it, include: "requirements for extensive documentation of process, micro-management of all decisions, and conformity to a rigid array of strategies meant to serve as protection against public criticism, administrative sanctions, and litigation" (p. 435). In addition, negative climates are characterized by staff experiencing "emotional exhaustion, role overload, and depersonalization" (p. 435). High caseload numbers negatively impact attempts at service integration (Adams & Nelson, 1997), yet high caseloads, a crisis orientation, low morale, poor supervision, and few opportunities for professional development often characterize the work environment of child welfare service providers (Anderson & Gobeil, 2002; CWLA, 1995). Case managers in defensive organizational environments have been found to use avoidance to service responsibilities (Glisson & James, 1992) and are willing to maintain ineffective behaviours and "defensive cultural norms" in order to survive in the negative workplace (Glisson & Green, 2005, p. 436). Negative organizational climates promote reactivity rather than responsiveness to the needs of children and families. Other variables related to an organization's culture and climate that have been found to negatively impact the ability to provide integrated services include personal factors such as staff holding negative attitudes and a lack of commitment to interagency collaboration, being resistant to change, and having a lack of trust in other professionals (Hassett & Austin, 1997; Martinson, 1982).

Administrative factors also impact the organization's ability to provide integrated services. These include such things as poorly defined responsibilities, no involvement of responsible personnel, a lack of commonly shared or understood procedures or rules for collaboration, no communication system, and little or no administrative support for collaborative activities (Martinson, 1982; Park & Turnbull, 2003).

Inter-organizational

On an inter-organizational level, challenges to service collaboration include a lack of cross-disciplinary training and policies, as well as professionals working from an "expert" position and professional hierarchy (Wright et al., 2010). Child welfare services have been found to be rigid, with a lack of flexibility in service eligibility and services provision (CASW, 2003). In a review of early intervention service integration, Park and Turnbull (2003) identified many system level variables that challenge the ability to implement integrated services: limited federal policy, poor or no funding to support service integration, little state support, a lack of a centralized information system, and no administrative support for collaborative activities. The lack of co-located services with multiple points for intake and assessment can also contribute to difficulties in the provision of integrated services (Law et al., 2003). For workers providing on-reserve services, coordination can be a particular challenge, in part because many of the professionals do not live in the community even though there is often a need for greater networking and collaboration among on-reserve services in order to maximize the services offered. Funding and jurisdictional issues also appear to interfere with opportunities for collaboration and cooperation (Wright et al., 2005).

System level

Social services operate within a "climate of relentless change" (Horwath & Morrison, 2000, p. 245) and child welfare services are under-resourced (CASW, 2003). On a system level, structural components that have been identified as creating obstacles to integrated services include a high demand for services that exceeds availability (Hamilton & Sinclair, 1992); limited, disjointed, or no centralized policies (CASW, 2003; Harbin et al., 2004; Hostler, 1991); and jurisdictional issues (CASW, 2003, Wright et al., 2005). Papin and Houck (2005) noted the difficulty of attaining an integrated and collaborative approach to human service provision due to the design of human services/service organizations in an ad-hoc, "piecemeal" approach:

> ...they were all created at different times, they all have different funding mechanisms, and all are administered by different levels of government or private organizations with different goals, rules, and administrative processes and philosophies. (p. 305)

The authors argue that organizations' leadership often opts to maintain a fragmented service system because it is easier for them to do so.

On an operational level, implementing service integration is not simple. For example, in an analysis of integrated service delivery initiatives across Canada by provincial governments, eight principal challenges were noted by the Public Sector Service Delivery Council (PSSDC): organizational cultural differences; partnerships; resources; technology; resistance to change and change fatigue; leadership; citizen-centred services; and marketing (PSSDC, 2003). The study found nine factors critical for success: leadership, governance and accountability, partnerships, citizen-centred, culture, demonstrating value, marketing, technology, and buy-in.

In Manitoba, the initiative focused on creating an integrated service delivery approach to programs related to family services and housing (partners included child and family service, day care, children's special service, employment and income assistance, housing, and support for adults with disabilities, as well as health authorities in Winnipeg and Manitoba Health). The department used a service integration model composed of five stages depicting levels of service integration (fragmentation, cooperation, coordination, collaboration, and integration). A reorganization of the department resulted, although progression to service integration was reported as reflecting a co-location of services.

MOVING TOWARD A DIFFERENT CHILD WELFARE VISION

A key role of child welfare administrators/managers is to understand and effectively plan for and manage challenges, such as those described above, that arise in service delivery. This calls for competent and knowledgeable child welfare managers (Larsson, 2000), and managers who provide leadership in this area (Austin, 1997; Drabble & Poole, 2011). The conceptual framework provided may be a useful tool for managers to assess, plan, implement, and evaluate the organization's location on the continuum of service and the service level.

In order for managers to move toward an integrated service delivery on an intra-organizational stratum, they must address organizational structures, policies, and practices that hinder approaches to the implementation of service integration. This includes the promotion of a constructive organizational climate and culture (including caseload and workload issues) to encourage and enable the development of staff characteristics that support coordinated, collaborative, and integrated service approaches and responses. Smith and Mogro-Wilson (2008) found that staff perceptions of agency policy were associated with collaborative practice. Clear definitions and distinctions between terms provide a common language within and between organizations (inter-professionally and inter-disciplinary) that directs an understanding of, and solutions to, joint policy and service planning, implementation, and evaluation, whether on a case, organizational, or system level. This includes, when appropriate, the development and engagement with inter-professional teams.

There are no absolutes in terms of the types of services or supports that should be integrated, other than those that impede a comprehensive and seamless service experience based on assessed need. Service integration should occur when service users experience fragmented, disjointed, inaccessible, and interrupted services, with insufficient service quality and quantity. On a practical level, child welfare services, mental health services, addiction services, criminal justice, housing, and education could all strive to provide children and their families with needs-based service delivery through coordinated, collaborative, and ultimately integrated services. The goal of service integration is to reduce fragmented and disjointed policies and practices so that the service user experiences minimal disruptions when in periods of transition, but also in terms of providing the service user accessible services based on assessed need, both in terms of quality and quantity of services.

Consequently, on a system level, managers must advocate for the dismantling of structural components (i.e., jurisdictional disputes) that create obstacles to integrated services and the development of strategies to improve service coordination, collaboration, and integration. The service delivery system requires an overall and consistent service strategy to frame services for children, their families, and communities. As a result, the service delivery system, and the plurality of service providers across various regions should reflect consistent and complementary policy based on joint policy/protocols. Integrated service delivery allows for the incorporation of different service models (i.e., a community caring model, the incorporation of traditional Indigenous knowledge, and services geared toward newcomers). Managers should strive to create policies, procedures, and mechanisms that inter-connect the multiple service providers to create a comprehensive service delivery system that effectively meets needs (Papin & Houck, 2005).

Although there are multiple challenges facing an organization and the larger service delivery system in applying this framework, managers can initiate steps within the organization, between organizations, and with the larger service delivery system to result in improved policies and services for children and their families. Managers can begin to use this framework within the context of the internal organization, using the framework to examine current policies and practices, to determine where the policy or practice fits in the service continuum, and to decide whether modification or change is warranted. Similarly, with inter-agency committees, development of joint protocols or pooled funding may be instigated to create more formalized partnerships that aim to improve access to assessed needs-based services. Within the broader delivery system, managers must engage with funders and political leaders to ensure leadership and support in real terms (Hassett & Austin, 1997). In addition to developing sustained support from government officials, support from the organization's staff is essential for progression to occur. The ultimate goal and benefit should be to meet the needs of the children, families, and communities.

REFERENCES

Adams, P., & Nelson, K. (1997). Reclaiming community: An integrative approach to human services. *Administration in Social Work, 21*, 67–81.

Aiken, M., Dewar, R., DiTomaso, N., Hage, J., & Zeitz, G. (1975). *Coordinating human services*. Washington, DC: Jossey-Bass.

Anderson, M., & Gobeil, S. (2002). *Recruitment and retention in child welfare services: A survey of Child Welfare League of Canada member agencies*. Centre of Excellence for Child Welfare. Retrieved from www.cwlc.ca/files/file/pubs/Recruitment in CW.pdf.

Austin, M. (1997). Service integration: Introduction. *Administration in Social Work, 21,* 1-7.

CASW (Canadian Association of Social Workers). (2003). *Canadian Association of Social Workers child welfare project: Creating conditions for good practice.* Ottawa, ON: Author.

CWLA (Child Welfare League of America). (1995). *Standards of excellence for child welfare services.* Washington, DC: Author.

Dinnebeil, L., Hale, L., & Rule, S. (1999). Early intervention program practices that support collaboration. *Topics in Early Childhood Special Education, 19,* 225–235.

Drabble, L., & Poole, N. (2011). Collaboration between addiction treatment and child welfare fields: Opportunities in a Canadian context. *Journal of Social Work Practice in the Addictions, 11,* 124-129.

Farmakopoulou, N. (2002). Using an integrated theoretical framework for understanding inter-agency collaboration in the special education needs field. *European Journal of Special Needs Education, 17,* 49–59.

Ferguson, C. (2004). Governance of collaborations: A case study. *Administration in Social Work, 28,* 7–28.

Friesen, B. J., & Briggs, H. E. (1995). The organization and structure of service coordination mechanisms. In B. J. Friesen & J. Poertner (Eds.), *From case management to service coordination for children with emotional, behavioral, or mental disorders: Building on family strengths* (pp. 62–94). Baltimore: Paul H. Brookes Publishing Co.

Friesen, B. J., & Poertner, J. (1995). *From case management to service coordination for children with emotional, behavioral, or mental disorders: Building on family strengths.* Baltimore: Paul H. Brookes Publishing Co.

Glisson, C., & Green, P. (2005). The effects of organizational culture and climate on the access to mental health care in child welfare and juvenile justice system. *Administration and Policy in Mental Health and Mental Health Services Research, 33,* 433–448.

Glisson, C., & James, L. (1992). The interorganizational coordination of services to children in state custody. In D. Bargal & H. Schmid (Eds.), *Organizational change and development in human service organizations* (pp. 65–80). New York: Haworth Press.

Green, B., Rockhill, A., & Burrus, S. (2008). The role of interagency collaboration for substance-abusing families involved with child welfare. *Child Welfare, 87,* 29–61.

Hallett, C., & Birchall, E. (1992). *Coordination in child protection: A review of the literature.* Edinburgh, UK: HMSO.

Hamilton, A. C., & Sinclair, C. M. (1992). Manitoba public inquiry into the administration of justice and Aboriginal peoples. *Report of the Aboriginal Justice Inquiry of Manitoba: Child Welfare, Vol. 1.* Retrieved from www.ajic.mb.ca/volume.html.

Harbin, G., Bruder, M. B., Adams, C., Mazzarella, C., Whitbread, K., Gabbard, G., & Staff, I. (2004). Early intervention service coordination policies: National policy infrastructure. *Topics in Early Childhood Special Education, 24,* 89–97.

Hassett, S., & Austin, M. (1997). Service integration: Something old and something new. *Administration in Social Work, 21,* 9–20.

Hodges, S., Hernandez, M., & Nesman, T. (2003). A developmental framework for collaboration in child-serving agencies. *Journal of Child and Family Studies, 12,* 291–305.

Horwath, J., & Morrison, T. (2000). Identifying and implementing pathways for organizational change: Using the framework for the assessment of children in need and their families as a case example. *Child and Family Social Work, 5,* 245–254.

Horwath, J., & Morrison, T. (2007). Collaboration, integration and change in children's services: Critical issues and key ingredients. *Child Abuse and Neglect, 31,* 55–69.

Hostler, S. (1991). Family-centered care. *The Pediatric Clinics of North America, 38,* 1545–1560.

Hudson, B. (1987). Collaboration in social welfare: A framework for analysis. *Policy and Politics, 15,* 175–182.

Jaskyte, K., & Lee, M. (2006). Interorganizational relationships: A source of innovation in nonprofit organizations? *Administration in Social Work, 30*(3), 43–54.

Kagan, S., Goffin, S., Golub, S., & Pritchard, E. (1995). *Toward systemic service integration for young children and their families.* Falls Church, VA: National Center for Service Integration.

King, G., & Meyer, K. (2006). Service integration and co-ordination: A framework of approaches for the delivery of co-ordinated care to children with disabilities and their families. *Child: Care, Health & Development, 32,* 477–492.

Konrad, E. L. (1996). A multidimensional framework for conceptualizing human services integration initiatives. *New Directions for Evaluation, 69,* 5-19.

Larsson, M. (2000). Organising habilitation services: Team structures and family participation. *Child: Care, Health and Development, 26,* 501–514.

Law, M., Hanna, S., King, G., Hurley, P., King, S., Kertoy, M., & Rosenbaum, P. (2003). Factors affecting family-centred service delivery for children with disabilities. *Child: Care, Health & Development, 29,* 357–366.

Martinson, M. (1982). Interagency services: A new era for an old idea. *Exceptional Children, 48,* 389–395.

Papin, T., & Houck, T. (2005). All it takes is leadership. *Child Welfare, 84,* 299-310.

Park, J., & Turnbull, A. (2003). Service integration in early intervention: Determining interpersonal and structural factors for its success. *Infants & Young Children, 16,* 48–58.

PSSDC (Public Sector Service Delivery Council). (2003). *Integrated service delivery: A critical analysis.* Available from www.iccs-isac.org/en/publications/pr.htm.

Reilly, T. (2001). Collaboration in action: An uncertain process. *Administration in Social Work, 25*(1), 53–74.

Scott, D. (2005). Inter-organisational collaboration in family-centred practice: A framework for analysis and action. *Australian Social Work, 58,* 132–141.

Smith, B., & Mogro-Wilson, C. (2008). Inter-agency collaboration. *Administration in Social Work, 32*(2), 5–24.

Stroul, B. (1995). Case management in a system of care. In B. J. Friesen & J. Poertner (Eds.), *From case management to service coordination for children with emotional, behavioral, or mental disorders: Building on family strengths* (pp. 3–25). Baltimore: Paul H. Brookes Publishing Co.

Toubeh, J. (1989). Disability and its prevention in Indian populations: Is it someone else's responsibility? *American Rehabilitation, 15,* 7–11.

Wright, A., Hiebert-Murphy, D., & Gosek, G. (2005). *Final report: Supporting Aboriginal children and youth with learning and/or behavioural disabilities in the care of Aboriginal child welfare agencies.* Faculty of Social Work, University of Manitoba, Winnipeg, Canada.

Wright, A., Hiebert-Murphy, D., & Trute, B. (2010). Professionals' perspectives on organizational factors that support or hinder the successful implementation of family-centered practice. *Journal of Family Social Work, 13,* 114–130.

CHAPTER 7

Fathers in the Frame: Protecting Children by Engaging Fathers when Violence against Mothers Is Present

Carla Navid

BRINGING MEN INTO VIEW

Although all children who come to the attention of child welfare systems have fathers, men often are curiously excluded from these interventions (Strega et al., 2008). In cases of violence against women, fathers who physically assault mothers are virtually invisible in child welfare practice, policy, and discourse. Within the existing child welfare literature, there is an overrepresentation of information on mothers who have found themselves in abusive relationships and a lack of information on the fathers who perpetrate violence. Strega (2004, p. 23) discusses how, through the operation of language, power, and institutional practices, the "reality" of men beating mothers becomes transformed into the "reality" of mothers failing to protect their children. In fact, according to feminist

---

SUGGESTED CITATION: Navid, C. (2012). Fathers in the frame: Protecting children by engaging fathers when violence against mothers is present. In D. Fuchs, S. McKay, & I. Brown (Eds.), *Awakening the Spirit: Moving Forward in Child Welfare: Voices from the Prairies* (pp. 135–156). Regina, SK: Canadian Plains Research Center.

post-structural theorist Chris Weedon (1997, p. 82), language can be where inequality begins. The power of discourse constrains what can be known and what can be said in specific social and historical contexts. Therefore, this invisibility of men automatically focuses our attention on the mother's behaviour and, as a result, removes any responsibility on the part of the perpetrator.

"Fathers in the Frame" (Navid, 2009) uncovers how the various ways in which the child welfare system intervenes in cases of violence against women in Manitoba are shaped by the discourses embedded in the province's child welfare legislation and policy, and also by the ways child welfare workers speak to their practice. Based on the author's graduate thesis in social work, this examination of text (legislation and policy) and talk (how child welfare workers speak to their practice) lends support to the argument that fathers/men need to be included in the frame of our child welfare lens in order to diminish risk and increase safety for mothers and children in cases where violence against women is present. It sets out to confirm the argument that violent men whose partners are involved with the Manitoba child welfare system need to be included as both risks and assets in the frame of our child welfare lens when assessing risk for children in order to realize a feminist perspective in our work with families. A feminist discourse analysis was utilized in this research to uncover the extent to which the notions of "fathers missing in action" and "mothers failing to protect" are dominant themes in the Manitoba child welfare system. Literature and research from within child welfare and feminism, coupled with my own data analysis of interviews with child welfare workers, are used to explore these dominant discourses. This project substantiates how these discourses contribute to the failure of the current system to hold the perpetrator accountable for his violence and how inconsistency can be found in workers' language about this work and the policy that guides their practice.

While I acknowledge that women are also capable of violence, and violence occurs between those of the same gender, these forms will not be examined here as these situations are rarely encountered in child welfare. As the statistics I have cited reflect, violence that transpires within the family is predominantly the violence of men towards women and children. Focusing my attention on men's violence towards women more accurately reflects my own professional experiences as a child welfare worker, sexual assault advocate, and domestic violence counsellor, as well as the data I have encountered as a feminist researcher.

The data tell us that injuries requiring medical attention from physical or sexual assaults between intimate partners occur more than seven times as often to women as to men (Tjaden & Thoennes, 2000, cited in Bancroft & Silverman, 2002). Sexual assault by intimate partners occurs eight times as often to women as to men, and stalking occurs eight times more often to women as opposed to men (Tjaden & Thoennes, 2000, cited in Bancroft & Silverman, 2002). Researchers have concluded that cases of mutual abuse are rare (Berk et al., 1983, cited in Bancroft & Silverman, 2002).

During my own work as a child welfare worker, I often struggled with our approach to mothers who found themselves in a violent relationship, as no clear standard of practice existed. When I first came to this work, I believed someone had to be held responsible for the protection of the children when violence occurs between their parents. I would set out to assess the risk of the male partner to his wife and children. But if Dad turned out to be uncooperative or difficult to access, I would turn my investigative focus on a mother's ability to keep her violent spouse away or ask her to consider leaving the relationship for the sake of her children. In some other circumstances, for example, if a no contact order was in place, I would become frustrated if I discovered that Dad had been around the home. In these instances, I would warn the mother that this was not in the best interests of her children, and if she was going to subject her children to the chance of witnessing more violence, she would not be what child welfare considers a "protective parent." This apparent ease in holding mothers responsible without questioning this practice led me to inquire why child welfare workers seem to so easily accept the position of blaming mothers as the standard of practice and the "common sense" approach.

Over a three-year period (2006–2009), I researched and gathered data while employing a feminist discourse analysis method to examine child welfare policy, legislation, and practice in southwestern Manitoba in cases of violence against women. Analysis focused on documents that inform and shape child welfare practice when violence against women is present: The Manitoba Child and Family Services Act (legislation), and The Safety Assessment and Plan (policy). To further enrich findings, I performed in-depth, open-ended, semi-structured taped interviews with four child welfare workers from southwestern Manitoba. These were transcribed and analyzed. Each participant chose a pseudonym and these were used in the transcripts to protect confidentiality. The rationale for conducting only a small number of interviews was that they were conducted as a supplement to analyzing child welfare documents and in order to make observations about the effects of the discourses. Because of the employment of both interview and textual analysis, a small number of interviewees kept data to a manageable level.

MISSING IN ACTION: FATHER EXCLUSION

Two themes appear prominent in the current child welfare system where violence against women is present: fathers are invisible and mothers are responsible. UK researchers Brigid Daniel and Julie Taylor (1999) have stated that child welfare does not appear to *purposefully* engage with fathers either as risks or as assets. They note the assumption that it is a good idea to take into account fathers when assessing the situation of children at risk or in need, but not necessarily to determine how a father is or might be an asset. It appears from their findings that child welfare social workers and administrators start out with the intent to include fathers, but that this rhetoric rarely matches reality. In other words, a consensus appears to exist in the social work field that including fathers is a good *idea*, but that, in reality, "men in general, and fathers in particular, are not being engaged with purposefully, either as potential risks (to the mother and child) or as potential assets" (p. 210). The result of this "gap between rhetoric and reality" (p. 211) is that the focus of social work intervention remains firmly on the mother. This was confirmed in my own research, as is evident in the transcripts of my interviews of child welfare workers:

> *Any assessment of his parenting? The reason I ask is you had mentioned completing that with Mom so I was wondering if that same process happened with Dad.* [Interviewer]

> *You know what? Not really.* [Social Worker Kate]

Strega (2004) and others have questioned this contradiction and explored possible rationales for why workers may ignore men/fathers:

- Workers can be under-trained in interventions with violent fathers and as a result may lack the confidence, knowledge, and skills to intervene in such cases. As Peled points out, "very little information is available on parenting work with violent men" (2000, p. 32).
- Men are constructed as having rights (to stay in his house, to have access to his children) and women are constructed as having responsibilities (emotional and physical caretaking of men and children). Child welfare workers are hesitant to infringe on men's "rights" but are quick to expect women to fulfill their "their responsibilities" (Pence & Paymar, 1993).
- Workers who work in child welfare see themselves as "copers" and are impatient with the inability of battered mothers to "cope" (Saunders, 1994).
- Social workers, most of whom are women, may be acting out their own failed attempts to resist patriarchy, their own compromised choices; their battered clients are simply the location of these struggles. For example, it continues to be true that while women numerically dominate social work at the practice level, they are usually in the minority in managerial, administrative, and academic positions.

The observations of these researchers parallel my own experience as well as those of my colleagues in the child welfare field. Some of the fathers do not wish to meet with the worker, even when the invitation is given. It is a response that workers readily accept. Some workers admit they do not try to engage fathers at all. They feel that due to caseload pressures, they just cannot spare the extra time it sometimes can take.

> *That's a time issue....because the caseloads are through the roof and the expectations are basically told to you...as long as the kids are safe.* [Social Worker Tammy]

> *It never really crossed my mind to interview him. I think I was just more concerned about her safety so I focused my energy on her and the children.* [Social Worker Kate]

Strega et al. (2008) conducted a quantitative study of child welfare practice in a mid-size Canadian city by random sampling and reviewing case files. File recordings demonstrated that almost half of workers considered fathers to be irrelevant; 20% of fathers were described as risks to both mothers and children while 20% were considered assets. Notably, contact with fathers described as risks to their children was documented in 40% of files, in contrast to contact with fathers described as assets documented in 70% of files (Strega et al, 2008, p. 6). This demonstrates that more reflection is required into child welfare systems assessing how to engage these violent fathers not only as risks but also as potential assets to the family. But regardless if a father is considered a risk or an asset or a combination of both, child welfare social workers must always keep in mind that the priority is to assess the risk they pose to children and their mothers.

Our use of language is also important to how violence against women may be viewed. Strega (2004) points out in her research that men's involvement in the problems of women and children is made invisible simply by the language we use to describe domestic violence. Discourses used in the field when describing violence against women—such as "family violence" or "domestic violence"—inadequately represent the reality of the problem. An additional point she makes is that these terms primarily emphasize physical abuse, not the emotional or sexual abuse that can also be suffered. Gender-neutral terms imply that both mother and father can be perpetrating the abuse when we know that, in the majority of cases, it is violence directed at women by men. Strega goes on to highlight other examples of male invisibility when she notes the "moral panic in both the UK and North America over single motherhood, yet men's primary role in creating single motherhood by their absence as fathers is rarely, if ever noticed" (2004, p. 5). Strega asserts that as a result, the question of "why does she stay" is asked, and not "why does he hit her?" Yet the answer for future analysis may not be as simplistic as shifting the focus to why men batter mothers. Instead, both inquiries can provide child welfare workers with valuable information to assist families and ultimately their children.

Child welfare workers do not deserve all of the criticism, however. The lack of understanding of battering fathers can also be credited to the batterers themselves. Peter Jaffe, in his foreword to *The Batterer as Parent* (Bancroft & Silverman, 2002, p. viii), points out that abusive fathers tend to make themselves "unavailable for participation in services or research studies so they have remained invisible and poorly understood." For example, a majority of the early research into violence against women was completed in battered women's shelters and, as a result, leads us to correlate children's emotional and behavioural difficulties with their mother's physical and psychological well-being without adequate attention to how the conduct of batterers was influencing the behaviour that researchers were observing (Bancroft & Silverman, 2002). One of the main reasons the research began in this way was the easy accessibility of abused women and their children. In addition, women were highly motivated research volunteers because they hoped their participation might bring about change and affect their situations.

There are men who intentionally avoid social workers despite the workers' best efforts. Perhaps these men hold the belief that childcare is only a mother's concern or they find it unpleasant to come face to face with a person who is going to challenge their problem behaviour. Others can be intimidating or threatening in their demeanour, which discourages workers from attempting to work with them. Scourfield (2008) cautions that we cannot dismiss the very real dangers that child welfare workers face with these men. In other words, social workers exclude men because some of the men they encounter are very difficult, though it must be noted that some of the mothers that workers encounter can be equally difficult.

In Scourfield's (2003) research conducted in a Canadian social work agency, he found that perpetrators of violence against women are rarely interviewed by workers. Even when men are parents (i.e., either biological or step fathers), the visible perpetrator within the home and the catalyst for the child welfare intervention, they are usually spared an interview by workers. In my research I found the same to be true. One participant disclosed that in five years of practice she had never included a father or male partner in her assessments—even when he was the known perpetrator in the home. Two participants said they had conducted an initial assessment with a perpetrator, but admitted that this was an exception and did not occur in the majority of investigations. When a man was interviewed, it was usually to assess his level of cooperation (determine risk) or hear his side of the story as it pertained to the investigation. These assessments were limited, as they did not include an assessment of the father's parenting abilities or his willingness to develop new skills (as is most often the case with assessments of mothers). Judith Milner (2007, p. 95) warns that when we rely on "men as threat" constructions to guide child welfare interventions, social work ends up demonizing men who are already socially excluded, with the added result that the women who live with them are also excluded by association.

> *I met with him and did an offender interview; got his side of the story and then gave him some resources and phone numbers to call and that was it.* [Social Worker Tammy]

> *He was interviewed ... but he was a very hostile person. I tried to engage him but he was uncooperative. I finally got him to sit down for the interview ... I did not give him a choice ... Mom had taken off so I needed to assess things because we were concerned if he was violent with Mom.* [Social Worker Barb]

Putting the focus on fathers and exposing men's "missing in action" status may contribute to reducing violence against women in two ways. First, we may encourage workers to learn more about men's contributions and risks to the family and, second, social workers will have an opportunity to learn how to intervene better with families where violence is present.

MOTHERS FAILING TO PROTECT: RESPONSIBILITY CONFIRMED

Gender bias within the child welfare system has been well and consistently documented over several decades (Callahan, 1993; Gordon, 1988; Hutchison, 1992; Mills, 2004). Because women are viewed as being responsible for the care and control of their children, they are also blamed as inadequate and neglectful when something happens to them (Milner, 1993, cited in Tutty & Goard, 2002). Historically, mother-blaming has been a prominent phenomenon: when neglect and/or abuse were identified, women were deemed responsible because they were in charge of children's care (Gordon, 1988).

Eileen Munro (1998) notes that the scrutiny mothers face at the hands of child protection workers is "surprising ... since men are considerably more likely than women to be violent and so, one would think, professionals would give men more, not less, attention than women in assessing danger to children" (cited in Scourfield, 2001, p. 85). Child welfare sees abusive men "as a danger to women and children" and believes they should be removed, but it is seen as the mother's responsibility to ask him to leave, and "not doing so constitutes 'failure to protect,' so it is women's actions and attitudes that are scrutinized" (Scourfield, 2001, p. 85). Based on my own experience, I believe there is a general feeling in the field that women would be better off without these particular men, and little empathy is shown by workers if the mother does not wish him to leave.

> *When I interviewed her, the option of having her partner leave the home or staying in the home ... she couldn't make the decision ... which made us feel that she wouldn't be able to protect, as she was unable to place the children first to make sure they were safe. Again, the concern is that the mother may not be able to have the power to protect her children if she is unable to protect herself.* [Social Worker Kate]

> *You know, if you (mom) loved your kids then you know what you need to do and you are the only one that can do that (end the relationship).* [Social Worker Tammy]

Julia Krane (2003) outlines one of the child welfare work processes central to invisible fathers and responsible mothers: the transformation of mothers into "mother protectors." Women are thrown into the position of choosing between their children and their partners and there is a lot of pressure to choose their children. She points out that turning mothers into protectors may seem beneficial at first and is likely one of the contributing factors as to why this practice is so widely used. With an increased focus on mothers, the child welfare authorities ensure that something is being done about children being abused and that minimum standards are being met. It may also be cost effective, without putting too much of a burden on public funding. But these coerced and cajoled mother protectors are often angry, anxious, frustrated and resentful. Instead of working in unity with child welfare agencies, Krane fears these women try to survive despite them. In the end, she makes a clear point that an adversarial child welfare system can never be for the "best interests of the child" when it is guilty of ignoring the needs of the women whom workers are entrusted to help.

The "failure to protect" concept appears to be applied almost solely to mothers. Consider, for example, the case of Andrea Yates, the Texas mother who killed her five children. Her husband knew of her distressed mental condition (postpartum depression), yet he continued to leave the children alone with her with no support or supervision. Where was the "failure to protect" for the father in this case (Risley-Curtiss & Heffernan, 2003, p. 4)?

CHILD WELFARE PRACTICE AND POLICY

Several findings confirmed my earlier assumption that I would uncover the gap between rhetoric and reality. First, there is no direct mention of domestic violence in the Child and Family Services Act (legislation) despite what the current literature contains. Second, the legislation does not define violence against a child's mother as emotional abuse of a child, again, despite current social work practice and current literature. Third, the term "failure to protect" does not appear anywhere in legislation or in policy (The Manitoba Safety Assessment and Plan). Fourth, the language of intimate partner violence found in the policy focuses on the victim's behaviour (usually the mother) and is gender neutral. Consequently, the gender-specific nature of domestic violence, which is essentially violence against women, remains hidden. For example, current Manitoba legislation uses terminology such as "family violence" to characterize violence that is almost solely against women. In the Child and Family Services Act, the gender-neutral term "person" is used when describing what constitutes a child in need of protection, while in the Safety Assessment, "caregiver" is used when referring to either a victim or a perpetrator of violence. The gendered terms "mother" or "father" are never used and, as a result, the gender specificity of woman abuse remains hidden. Gender-neutral language, in the end, fails to attribute accountability and responsibility for the abuse to the male perpetrator and minimizes the abuse a mother is subjected to. Fearing the removal of her children, an abused woman will likely not disclose the abuse (Tutty & Goard, 2002). Even though this fear is very real, the statistics on what Canadian child welfare agencies in fact do in these cases suggests that women may not have as much to fear as they thought.

According to the findings of the Canadian Incidence Study of Reported Child Abuse and Neglect completed across Canada in 2003, children who are the subject of investigations involving only substantiated exposure to violence against their mother are less likely to be removed from their home than children experiencing other forms of maltreatment. In fact, cases remained open for ongoing services less often for substantiated investigations involving exposure to domestic violence compared to substantiated investigations involving other forms of maltreatment (36% versus 45%) (Trocmé, Fallon, et al., 2005). From this information, it would appear that Canadian child welfare agencies recognize domestic violence as a form of maltreatment but do not consider these families to require ongoing services from child welfare agencies.

What appears to be the largest barrier to effective practice is conceptualizing what is meant by the "emotional abuse" of children. While there appears to be a visceral sense that children who witness the abuse of their mothers are being emotionally maltreated, Manitoba has failed to develop comprehensive statutory definitions that would mandate how Child and Family Services should intervene. As previously noted, domestic violence specifically is not identified in child welfare legislation or policy as being emotionally abusive to children. Emotional abuse is mentioned but not defined within the legislation and policy. One will not find a direct policy statement that mother abuse is emotionally abusive to children, despite this being what I was taught and what I implemented as a child welfare worker. My surprise comes from the contradiction not only between policy and practice and the body of child welfare literature but also how I was supervised and trained as a child welfare worker. Despite domestic violence being presented during supervision and training as emotional abuse of children and equal to other forms of abuse a child may endure, in my experience, domestic violence is not acted upon as often as or in the same way as are more obvious forms of abuse. This lack of clarity respecting emotional abuse speaks to what and who is considered a priority. The current Manitoba child welfare policy proves to be in line with the dominant discourses: mothers themselves are only in need of protection and have rights in their homes when abuse they are subjected to impairs *their* ability to parent. This is further evidence of the gulf between rhetoric and reality.

Finally the fact that there is no legislative mention of "failure to protect," while the practice is *all about* "failure to protect," affirms the argument that a powerful discourse is at work. What I have come to learn with certainty is that a dominant discourse is at work when child welfare practice does not follow legislation or the present social work literature because the dominant discourse is so powerful it does not have to. In other words, child welfare practice does not follow legislation or policy in this instance, as "failure to protect" is not specified in the text. It is not that child welfare workers can proceed as they see fit; in most instances they are unsure how to continue, but "failure to protect" is how they are trained and supervised to proceed.

RESPONSIBILITY AND "MISSING IN ACTION" CONFIRMED

It seemed likely from my discussions with colleagues prior to beginning this research that the results would demonstrate what I had predicted: that in the accounts of child welfare workers, men are not considered either as risks or assets in cases involving woman abuse. I was uncertain, however, whether the gulf would be found in the policy and legislation that guide social work practice or uncovered in how child welfare workers spoke regarding their practice. As it turned out, I found both. Of particular interest, but perhaps not surprisingly, I found that all four study participants were unable to cite any specific policy or law that guided their practice. Three were able to recall where relevant policy was located (for example, the Intake Module under Safety Assessments and Maltreatment Windows). Two participants stated they trusted that the child welfare mandate must include violence against women, their rationale being that child welfare agencies would not be acting upon this information if they were not required to do so. Workers, then, did not view their practice as necessarily being guided by any particular policy, other than the Intake Module that contains the Safety Assessments and Safety Plans that are mandatory for child welfare workers to complete when there is believed to be any risk to a child. In other words, according to the workers themselves, legislation and policy did not define for them what their practice should be. In the absence of specific case direction from law or policy, workers rely on dominant discourses to guide their practice.

Another not-so-unexpected finding was that participants tended to concentrate their interventions on the behaviours of abused mothers since they saw mothers as primarily responsible for protecting their children from violent situations. Only one participant had actually included a father as part of her assessment and planning during a case where domestic violence was cited as a concern. The father in this case was incarcerated, and the worker included assessment of Dad's parenting skills, willingness to change, and interaction with his children as part of the case plan when violence against the mother was present.

> *He (the chaplain) and I were part of it (the visits) and they were very positive. I think the thing that you have to keep in mind is, and it's sometimes a hard thing for us to get our heads around but domestic violence doesn't necessarily equate being a bad dad. And that was what I needed to get my head around because to those kids that was still their dad, and to him that was still his children, and he loved his children and I believe he wanted what was best for his kids. My observation during those visits, they were supervised, was ... I really had only positive things to say about the visits.* [Social Worker Sarah]

Others acknowledged their lack of attention to the visible male perpetrator, even verbalizing how unfair this casework was, but readily accepting this as "just the way it is."

MALE EXCLUSION AND MOTHER RESPONSIBILITY CONFIRMED

As stated earlier, child welfare workers spoke to their practice in a way that reflected and supports the "mothers failing to protect" and "men missing in action" discourses. Workers did question father exclusion, stating they believed they could do a better job of including fathers in case practice. Workers spoke of men having rights and were hesitant to speak directly of men's violence towards women (evidence of gendered power relations) and continually highlighted a mother's responsibility to protect her children.

> [The Mothers think:] *"My kids are safe here, you know, they are not being abused. We have a roof over our heads, clothes on our backs, so suck it up because I'm not going to be able to provide for them on my own."* And I think the pull that the abusing spouse can have on you, they can tell you they are changing and they aren't going to do this anymore then it happens again. Each time you pray to God this is the last time. So you keep going back. [Social Worker Barb]

> *I guess the other thing is that it makes you concerned if someone is abusive to a partner that they are supposed to love, then what would stop them from abusing their child?* [Social Worker Kate]

All saw "putting children first" as a standard expectation of a protective mother, which they prove to workers by ending abusive relationships or asking their male partners to leave. There were no expectations for fathers to stop being violent and therefore "protective." Workers' language validated that they were hesitant to speak directly of men's violence towards women, and if they engaged men it was to assess their risk, not measure their assets. Evidence of the gulf between rhetoric and reality was found in the following ways:

- Workers believed it was a good idea to include men but did not routinely include them.
- Workers acknowledged that they are aware they are practicing in a way that they know is ineffective.
- Workers spoke to feminist practice found in the current anti-oppressive literature but practiced in ways that contradict this (excluding fathers, making mothers responsible).

To summarize, the discourse places emphasis on the mother's responsibility to protect, which leads both to noticing *women's* roles in cases of child maltreatment and to overlooking or ignoring the role that *men* play. These workers were aware that they were not addressing or "noticing" what men were doing in these cases—they were only "noticing" what mothers were doing. As Susan Strega contends, if we as workers are "hesitant to speak directly of men's violence, it is impossible to resist against it" (Strega, 2004, p. 220). Strega further notes that

> a man hitting a woman is persistently constructed as an act without an agent, a woman being battered by a non-existent perpetrator, as illustrated by the existence of the concept of "battered woman" without the existence of a resulting concept of "battering man." We cannot say "battering man," because such a concept does not "make sense." (2004, p. 207)

At the time I met with these child welfare workers, they were dedicated to protecting children and open to sharing reflections of their practice in cases where violence against women was present. They were aware and concerned about the contradictions found in their practice. All were interested in the research and keen for ideas of change. Even though all spoke to the pressures of the work and lack of resources to make this successful, all were eager to understand how practice could be improved. I admire and appreciate their courage to expose their thoughts and actions.

RESISTANCE

Analyzing the accounts of four child welfare social workers provided insight into how law and policy, coupled with child welfare's dominant discourse, form the foundation for how the Manitoba child welfare system intervenes in cases of violence against mothers. By searching for the dominant discourse enacted through the concepts of "invisible fathers" and "mothers failing to protect," this project demonstrated how these concepts contribute to the failure of the current system to hold male perpetrators accountable for their violence. Because discourse determines the ways a topic can be talked about, as well as influences the way ideas are acted upon, how child welfare workers spoke to their practice provided a rich area to explore how men are excluded and how women are made responsible. The analysis confirmed my contention that men must be included in the child welfare frame when assessing risk for children in order to realize a feminist perspective in our work with families and, in the end, improve overall practice with women, men, and children.

This project raises the question: where can one find the possibilities for resistance when it comes to men's violence and control over women? Workers can begin by asking "why does he hit her?" instead of "why does she stay?" They can say the problem is that "men batter women" not "women are battered," and know it as such. That being said, how might this practice look? To move towards a father-inclusive practice, local child welfare policy-makers, administrators, supervisors, and workers must take steps to promote healthy father/child relationships. This can be accomplished by supporting the development of programs that assist men to be good parents, by helping controlling fathers improve their relationships with the mothers of their children, and by improving the child support system (Sylvester & Reich, 2000). But most importantly, it involves helping to prevent fathers from abusing children and mothers. It is essential that research efforts be relocated to investigate fathering from the perspectives of men themselves and, in this case, from the perspectives of violent men.

Increased gender competency in child welfare agencies would also contribute to more socially just child welfare practice. Scourfield (2008) encourages workers to remain even-handed, not painting all men as aggressive and all women as good mothers. He summarizes by noting, "this is not simply a sexist discourse we can wish away" (Scourfield, 2008, p. 6). One way to accomplish this is to change case documentation requirements to ensure that all men involved in the family are included. Secondly, supervisors must teach and model the value of routinely including both parents (and/or a partner that currently lives in the home and has contact with the children) in assessment stages as well as in intervention planning. From an educational perspective, social work programs have a responsibility to remove gender-biased materials from their curriculum and add father-inclusive materials to curricula and in class discussions. In this way, child welfare systems could be empowered to act "less like critical fathers and more like supportive mothers" (Milner, 2007).

Scourfield (2008) contends that in order to accomplish this reform, we need to know what works when intervening with men. He advises that this may mean any number of different approaches. Interventions he recommends on the basis of research include "family group conferences and pro-feminist education for violent men" (Scourfield, 2000, p. 8). In a recent paper, Scourfield (2008) cites Harry Ferguson's argument for observation of the home visits that child welfare workers conduct with their client families. This "liquid social work," as he calls it, envisions researchers going out in the car and into the homes with social workers rather than staying in the office (Ferguson & Hogan, 2004). To be able to observe what actually occurs between workers and their clients would be enormously helpful and insightful in terms of not only the challenges faced by clients, but social work judgements as well.

In terms of the documents, the absence of clear policy and practice guidelines for child welfare workers, as uncovered in this project, contributes to workers not knowing how to respond in these cases. In the UK and Ireland, some social service agencies have taken a more proactive approach in recognizing woman abuse as a problem in its own right that is worthy of intervention. They have developed an overall policy in addition to step-by-step practice guidelines and comprehensive documentation systems.

But what if the policy and practice required to successfully intervene in cases involving violence against women already exists and only needs to be properly utilized to ensure the protection of mothers? Why not use existing legislation that provides child welfare workers the ability to remove the perpetrator from the home instead of removing the children or their mother? A legislative provision that could be of use in situations of mother abuse is the "Application for an Order to not Contact a Child" contained in Manitoba's Child and Family Services Act. In my own experience, this provision is typically used to remove a perpetrator who is living in the home and abusing a child. But it could also be utilized when violence against a child's primary caregiver is occurring. Romona Alaggia et al. (2007, p. 287) points out that Alaska has led the way in designing new legislation that removes the perpetrator, not the victim, from the home.

I also suggest that child welfare agencies could apply the same rigour to contacting men and holding them accountable for violence as that applied when serving men with court papers. In my own practice experience, when it came to serving fathers notice, all avenues had to be exhausted in our attempts to find a father, regardless of his involvement in the child's life. The shift that must take place is to also view men as having responsibilities, including responsibility for addressing and ameliorating the effects of violence they have perpetrated. This said, supervisors and administrators in the field must be brought on board to assist in the development of a feminist shift in practice. A common theme among the social workers I interviewed was that they learned to intervene in violence against women cases from the direction of their immediate supervisors. It would appear that training in the area of violence against women would benefit not only front-line staff, but supervisors and administrators as well. Practice with mothers, fathers, and children where violence against women is present will require more reflection and clinical supervision on the part of social workers who take on this difficult and demanding work (Davies & Collings, 2004). Men must be welcomed into the frame, so we must find ways to engage without condemning. Men who abuse mothers are a population that has little empirical data available, so further research is needed. This is likely to require more resources than the system currently has, meaning that funding allocations must take into account violence against mothers and the men who batter them as a priority for expenditure.

Research shows that mothers contending with violence are grateful for the support and assistance of workers when it is offered. Magen, Conroy, Hess, Panciera and Simon (2001, p. 596) found that mothers appreciate when child welfare workers inquire about current or past domestic violence and felt better protected from their abuser when they disclose the abuse to the child welfare worker. Magen et al. (2001, p. 595) found that addressing violence directly with abused women both enhances the worker's connection with the client and increases the abused woman's confidence to address the abuse. Mills (2000) points out that the interests of abused mothers and their children are best served when contact by child welfare social workers is direct, empowering, and cognizant of the abused mother's predicament. Child welfare workers may be uniquely positioned to intervene in families where domestic violence is occurring, as their interventions appear to be child-oriented and are therefore less likely to raise the perpetrator's suspicions. This sort of intervention can "buy time" to help an abused mother formulate plans.

Ultimately, partnerships need to be established between child welfare systems and those working in the area of violence against women. Ideally, multidisciplinary teams—with members from child welfare, legal, justice, and battered women's shelters—could be devised. These teams could hold abusive men accountable, and work with families in a more holistic way. Interagency initiatives that have proven successful for responding to child sexual abuse and similar models could be applied to domestic violence.

Finally, agencies must recruit social workers who are willing to include fathers. Workers must speak with fathers directly, instead of relying on mothers to persuade men to participate in meetings or expecting mothers to speak to their partner's thoughts or actions. It is unrealistic and socially unjust to expect that a woman in this position will have any influence with a man who is controlling and/or abusive.

A FINAL NOTE

When I first came to child welfare social work, I believed—much the same as the child welfare social workers I interviewed for this study—that if a mother could not leave her relationship with her abuser, she might also be unable to make good decisions for herself and her children, and therefore her parenting may be questionable and would require further assessment. In completing this research, I have come to better understand my own experiences as a child welfare worker, including the realization that child welfare practice and policy are influenced by dominant discourses that see abused mothers not as victims but as abusers. The dilemmas faced by abused mothers are unique to each individual woman's circumstances and are strongly influenced by emotional and cultural concerns that place an abused mother in a difficult position: insist your abusive partner leave, or risk losing your children. The most disturbing realization that came with completing this project is that with the influence of dominant discourses we no longer see abused mothers as victims but as abusers. As Strega (2004, p. 224) points out, "women are transformed into abusers, and the abuse they are guilty of is 'allowing' their children to be exposed to their victimization despite practice efforts of child welfare workers."

Other researchers continue efforts to explore discourses regarding men's violence in child welfare. In Canada, social work theorists such as Strega (2004), Krane and Davies (2000) and Swift (2001) have developed theories as to how violence against women is constructed in child welfare work and suggestions for change in the areas of both policy and practice. Holt (2003) in Ireland along with Daniel and Taylor (1999), Milner (1993), Scourfield (2003), and Featherstone (2001) in the UK continue the same work there. The findings in this project were consistent with recent research projects with a similar focus, all conducted in Canadian child welfare jurisdictions with legislation similar to Manitoba (Alaggia et al., 2007; Nixon, 2001; Strega, 2004). Kendra Nixon's (2001) thesis research into Alberta's child welfare legislation in domestic violence cases revealed that the participants she spoke to believed the most effective way to protect children in these situations was to focus on the mother's behaviour. Ramona Alaggia's (2007) study on what impact child welfare policy has on abused mothers accessing services revealed increased surveillance of mothers and decreased accountability of perpetrators. In response, several jurisdictions across Canada have implemented differentiated response models, including Manitoba and Ontario. Differentiated response (Waldfogel, 1998) is an approach that relies on accurately classifying cases into varying levels of risk wherein children referred to child welfare systems as a result of exposure to domestic violence would be initially screened as low or high risk and referred accordingly. Perhaps one day "fathers included in the frame" will become standard child welfare practice. We must keep in mind that just because it is "the way things are" does not mean it is the way they should be.

REFERENCES

Alaggia, R., Jenney, A., Mazzuca, J., & Redmond, M. (2007). In whose best interest? A Canadian case study of the impact of child welfare policies in cases of domestic violence. *Brief Treatment and Crisis Intervention*, 7(4), 275–290.

Bancroft, L., & Silverman, J. (2002). *The batterer as parent: Addressing the impact of domestic violence on family dynamics*. Thousand Oaks, CA: Sage.

Callahan, M. (1993). Feminist approaches: Women recreate child welfare. In B. Wharf (Ed.), *Rethinking child welfare in Canada* (pp. 172–209). Toronto: McClelland & Stewart.

Daniel, B., & Taylor, J. (1999). The rhetoric vs. the reality: A critical perspective on practice with fathers in child care and protection work. *Child and Family Social Work*, 4, 209–220.

Davies, L., & Collings, S. (2004). Subject-to-subject: Reclaiming the emotional terrain for practice. In L. Davies & P. Leonard (Eds.), *Social work in a corporate era: Practices of power and resistance* (pp. 45–58). Aldershot, UK: Ashgate Publishing.

Featherstone, B. (2001). Putting fathers on the child welfare agenda. *Child and Family Social Work, 6*(2), 179–186.

Ferguson, H., & Hogan, F. (2004). *Strengthening families through fathers: Developing policy and practice in relation to vulnerable fathers and their families.* Waterford Institute of Technology, Centre for Social and Family Research: Waterford.

Gordon, L. (1988). *Heroes of their own lives: The politics and history of family violence.* New York: Penguin Books.

Holt, S. (2003). Child protection social work and men's abuse of women: An Irish study. *Child and Family Social Work, 8,* 53–65.

Hutchison, E. D. (1992). Child welfare as a woman's issue. *Families in Society: The Journal of Contemporary Human Services, 73*(2), 67–78.

Jaffe, P. (2002). Foreword. In L. Bancroft & J. Silverman, *The batterer as parent: Addressing the impact of domestic violence on family dynamics* (pp. ix-xii). Thousand Oaks, CA: Sage.

Krane, J. (2003). *What's mother got to do with it? Protecting children from sexual abuse.* Toronto: University of Toronto Press.

Krane, J., & Davies, L. (2000). Mothering and child protection: rethinking risk assessment. *Child and Family Social Work, 5*(1), 35–45.

Magen, R., Conroy, K., Hess, P., Panciera, A., & Simon, B. (2001). Identifying domestic violence in child abuse and neglect investigations. *Journal of Interpersonal Violence, 16*(6), 580–601.

Manitoba Child and Family Services Act, S.S. 1989–90, c. C-7.2.

Mills, L. (2000). Woman abuse and child protection: A tumultuous marriage (Part 1). *Children and Youth Services Review, 22*(3–4), 199–205.

Mills, S. (2004). *Discourse.* London: Routledge.

Milner, J. (1993). A disappearing act: The differing career paths of fathers and mothers in child protection investigations. *Critical Social Policy, 13*(48), 48–63.

Milner, J. (2007). *Working with violence: Policies and practices in risk assessment and management.* Basingstoke, England: Palgrave Macmillan.

Munro, E. (1998). Improving social workers' knowledge base in child protection work. *British Journal of Social Work, 28,* 89–105.

Navid, C. (2009). Fathers in the frame: Helping children by including fathers/men in cases of violence against women. Unpublished MSW thesis, University of Manitoba.

Nixon, K. (2001). Domestic violence and child welfare policy: An examination of Alberta's child welfare legislation and the impact on child welfare practice. Unpublished MSW thesis, University of Calgary.

Peled, E. (2000). Parenting by men who abuse women: Issues and dilemmas. *British Journal of Social Work, 30*(1), 25–36.

Pence, E., & Paymar, M. (1993). *Education groups for men who batter: The Duluth model.* New York: Springer.

Risley-Curtiss, C., & Heffernan, K. (2003). Gender biases in child welfare. *Affilia, 18*(4), 395–410.

Saunders, D. (1994). Child custody decisions in families experiencing woman abuse. *Social Work, 39*(1), 51–59.

Scourfield, J. (2001). Constructing men in child protection work. *Men and Masculinities, 4*(1), 70–89.

Scourfield, J. (2003). *Gender and child protection.* Houndsmills, UK: Palgrave MacMillan.

Scourfield, J. (2008). *Gender, place and identity.* New York: Routledge.

Strega, S. (2004). The case of the missing perpetrator: A cross-national investigation of child welfare policy, practice and discourse in cases where men beat mothers. Ph.D. thesis, University of Southampton.

Strega, S., Fleet, C., Brown, L., Dominelli, L., Callahan, M., & Walmsley, C. (2008). Connecting father absence and mother blame in child welfare policies and practices. *Children and Youth Services Review, 30*(7), 705–716.

Swift, K. (2001). The case for opposition: An examination of contemporary child welfare policy directions. *Canadian Review of Social Policy, 47*(1), 59–76.

Sylvester, K., & Reich, K. (2000). *Restoring fathers to families and communities: Six steps for policy makers.* Washington, DC: Social Policy and Action Network.

Trocmè, N., Fallon, B., MacLaurin, B., Daciuk, J., Felstiner, C., & Black, T. (2005). *Canadian Incidence Study of Reported Child Abuse and Neglect—2003: Major Findings.* Ottawa: Minister Public Works and Government Services Canada.

Tutty, L., & Goard, C. (2002). Woman abuse in Canada: An overview. In L. Tutty and C. Goard (Eds.), *Reclaiming self: Issues and resources for women abused by intimate partners* (pp. 10–24). Halifax: Fernwood Publishing.

Waldfogel, J. (1998). *The future of child protection: How to break the cycle of abuse and neglect.* Cambridge: Harvard University Press.

Weedon, C. (1997). *Feminist practice and poststructuralist theory.* Oxford: Blackwell.

CHAPTER 8

Hitting the Target: Transitioning Youth with High-Risk Behaviours

Kathryn A. Levine and Rick Rennpferd

INTRODUCTION

The transition from the child and adolescent service system to adult services for individuals with intellectual disabilities (ID) and high-risk (challenging) behaviours has been identified as an area of concern for policy-makers, service providers, educators, researchers, and family members alike in recent years who have identified the following challenges/questions. What are the program standards and service development needs of young people with ID and challenging behaviours? Which government department is responsible for ensuring the provision of specialized service/intervention for this population? Who is responsible for the coordination of specialized service provision? Who is responsible for service provision/implementation?

SUGGESTED CITATION: Levine, K. A., & Rennpferd, R. (2012). Hitting the target: Transitioning youth with high-risk behaviours. In D. Fuchs, S. McKay, & I. Brown (Eds.), *Awakening the Spirit: Moving Forward in Child Welfare: Voices from the Prairies* (pp. 157–177). Regina, SK: Canadian Plains Research Center.

This chapter explores the context for understanding the transition process for adolescents (ages 12 to 19) with intellectual disabilities (ID) and high-risk behaviours, with an emphasis on sexual offending behaviours. It also identifies factors that facilitate and impede such a transition. It relates a case example to illustrate an unsuccessful transition, and concludes with describing the main implications for service provision and risk reduction for this population.

Challenging behaviours have been defined as "culturally abnormal behaviour(s) of such intensity, frequency or duration that the physical safety of the person or others is likely to be placed in serious jeopardy, or behaviour which is likely to seriously limit use of, or result in the person being denied access to, ordinary community facilities" (Emerson, 2001, p. 3). This definition is particularly relevant for this discussion, as it emphasizes that these behaviours represent challenges to services, rather than problems that are solely located within the individual. For related definitions, see Box 1.

Adolescents with ID and high-risk behaviours present an increasing demand on the social service system. Given that these individuals are frequently identified

Box 1. Definitions

Developmental disability is defined by the Developmental Disabilities Association (U.S.) as "a state of functioning that begins in childhood and is characterized by significant limitations in both intellectual capacity and adaptive skills" (2010). The *Diagnostic and Statistics Manual – IV-TR* defines developmental, cognitive, or intellectual disabilities as "severe, life-long disabilities that may be attributed to mental and/or physical impairments, manifested before the age of 18 that results in the individual having an IQ score of less than 70 with concurrent deficits or impairments in present adaptive functioning" (DSM-IV-TR, 2000). The term encompasses neurological impairment due to prenatal exposure to alcohol and narcotics, as well as diagnoses related to genetic factors including autism spectrum disorders, Down syndrome and cerebral palsy. Intellectual or cognitive disabilities (ID) involve significant limitations both in intellectual functioning and adaptive behaviours, including many social and practical skills of everyday living. In Canada, it has been estimated that approximately 2.5% of individuals have developmental disabilities (Yu & Atkinson, 1993), and about 30% of children under the age of 18 require some form of assistance with activities of daily living (Canadian Institute of Child Health, 2000; Cossette & Duclos, 2002; Statistics Canada, 2006).

and supported within the child welfare, childhood disability, and education systems—which typically end or change substantially around the age of majority—it becomes essential for clinicians to knowledgeably address the transition from adolescent to adult services, a crucial yet frequently problematic period of life. A critical issue is that new lifestyle needs arise as youth begin to enter their adult stages of life, such as residential support, counselling and community living support, vocational support, and recreational activities (I. Brown, 2007).

There is a general expectation that individuals must accommodate to the myriad changes in the support systems, rather than the systems—including child welfare, disability support, adult services, and criminal justice—responding flexibly to their needs. This shift in service accessibility thus increases the risk for sexual offending as the individuals move from systems that are generally better resourced than the adult social support system; the adult system has not only fewer services but significantly more individuals who require them, resulting in the situation where demand exceeds supply (Vaughn, 2003). If we want to understand this particular stage of vulnerability, it is essential to explore the systemic challenges in order to suggest strategies that aim to lessen the inherent difficulties experienced by this population as they begin their journey into adulthood.

Prevalence rates for people with ID and high-risk behaviours vary because of differences in research methodologies, populations, and definitions. However, it is estimated that, within the adult population, 10% to 40% of individuals who display sexual offending behaviours have some form of learning or developmental disability (Craig & Hutchison, 2005; Langevin & Curnoe, 2008; Lindsay, Smith, Law, Quinn, Anderson, Smith, & Allan, 2004). It is likely that, for many of these individuals, these behaviours were present prior to them achieving the age of majority, yet they might not have been identified as areas of concern by service providers.

Sexual offenses by adolescents are under-reported, but there is evidence to suggest that 20% of sexual assaults, and 30% to 50% of all child sexual abuse, can be attributed to adolescent perpetrators (Matsuda et al., cited in Charles & McDonald, 2005). Moreover, several studies concur that adolescent sexual offenders, similar to the adult population, also have higher incidences of learning difficulties (Awad & Saunders, cited in Charles & McDonald, 2005). General estimates of the numbers of adolescent offenders with ID range from 4% to 40% (Veneziano & Veneziano, 2002). Canadian studies have found varying degrees of ID in adolescents who display sexual offending behaviours, ranging from 24% to 36% (Emerson, 2005; Stermac & Mathews, 1987).

Adolescents who engage in sexual offending behaviours are a heterogeneous group with diverse victim preferences, levels of risk, levels of intellectual functioning, psychosocial deficits, strengths, and assets, and are qualitatively different from adults who commit sex offenses (Lambrick & Glaser, 2004). These differences extend to adolescents with ID. Those within the "borderline" intellectual disability range are at an increased risk of committing sexual and other criminal offences, but those with an IQ less than 50 rarely offend (Simpson & Hogg, 2001). This presents a challenge to the service system, as clusters of high functioning domains in adolescents can frequently lead service providers to overestimate competencies in all domains such as interpersonal skills, healthy sexual adjustment, emotion regulation, and problem-solving capacities.

It is also difficult to assess the prevalence of adolescents with ID who are in conflict with the law due to sexual offending behaviours. There are varying definitions of what constitutes the "adolescent" stage (developmental or chronological?), assessments of intellectual and/or adaptive functioning are inconsistent, and there is an absence of agreement about what constitutes offending behaviours (Tudway & Darmoody, 2005). A central question is whether or not behaviours need to meet the legal Criminal Code definition, or if they should be based on social definitions that include challenging or high-risk "behaviours of concern" such as self-injury, self-stimulation, physical and verbal aggression, sexually inappropriate behaviour, and property destruction (Doyle, 2004).

There is a significant body of research that highlights the risk factors for sexual offending in individuals with ID. Childhood abuse (including sexually harmful behaviour, physical abuse, and emotional maltreatment) and non-accidental injury have been found to be significant predictors for sexual offending behaviour in later life (Lindsay, Law, Quinn, Smart, & Smith, 2001; Lindsay, Steele, Law, Quinn, & Allan, 2006; Vizard, Hickey, & McCrory, 2007). Other risk factors include: the absence of social skills and training on appropriate/safe sexual behaviour, minimal sexual knowledge, a history of sexual or physical abuse, exposure to violence and/or pornography, poverty, pervasive use of restriction in daily life, limited or no available sexual partners, and difficulty projecting consequences of behaviours (Sequeira & Hollins, 2003; Søndenaa, Rasmussen, & Nøttestad, 2008). Thus, when children and adolescents with ID enter the child welfare system as a result of having been physically, sexually, or emotionally harmed, it is critical to develop long-term treatment plans that will include resolution of their personal abuse histories, as well as pro-active interventions that will focus on the development of social skills, problem-solving capacities, and healthy relationships.

A final perspective on intellectual disability, challenging behaviours, and transitioning is that racial/ethnic minorities, including First Nations youth, are overrepresented at most stages of the juvenile justice system and among the population of youth with disabilities. Yet, there is little evidence that juvenile justice systems are providing appropriate disability-related programming for this population, or that they have developed culturally appropriate approaches for these youth.

CURRENT DISABILITY PHILOSOPHY AND OUR APPROACH TO ADOLESCENT OFFENDERS

The transition from adolescence to adulthood is generally represented by psychological and physical changes as adolescents/young adults begin the process of developing their own identities and distancing themselves from their families of origin physically, psychologically, emotionally, and relationally. This particular developmental period invites adolescents/young adults to focus upon completing their education, contemplate the idea of independent living, and explore issues related to sexuality and intimate relationships (I. Brown, 2007).

Notwithstanding the potential difficulties this stage engenders for many adolescents, this transition is especially complicated for adolescents with intellectual disabilities who are at risk of engaging in sexual offending behaviours. Like their non-disabled peers, adolescents with ID are waiting for independence. However, unlike their non-disabled peers, they have few opportunities to experience discernable rites of passage other than the chronological attainment of age 18; for example, in most parts of Canada, persons with ID frequently do not graduate from high school until age 21 (Spero, 2003). Moreover, due to their challenging behaviours, this group is likely to have been limited in terms of peer relationships and opportunities to understand and explore their sexuality in healthy, developmentally appropriate ways. As well, it is this same group of behaviours that can restrict their educational and vocational opportunities, and in the absence of effective transition planning, these individuals move from being monitored by the child welfare system to the adult system where "independence" is represented by a decrease in support services.

Adolescents with ID and sexual offending behaviours present a complex challenge to the system and service providers. Given this, it is important to begin from the position that acknowledges the conceptual paradox of ID and sexual offending. As West (2007) has pointed out,

> Our response to those who sexually abuse is characterized by contradiction: the desire to reform contends with the urge to punish; attempts to understand and care are at odds with condemnation of the offending; concerns for public safety vie with requirements for the offender to become more independent and self-monitoring. (p. 254)

The service system response typically is isomorphic to these societal contradictions. At a macro level, there continues to be a pervasive system of discrimination that oppresses people who have mental, emotional, and physical disabilities. This context of "ableism" operates at individual, institutional, and social/cultural levels. The foundation of this particular frame of thinking is grounded within prejudice, discrimination, and bias. When individuals with intellectual disabilities have engaged in sexual offending behaviours, or are at risk of doing so, this in turn justifies even greater public contempt and "less-than" status (McDonald, Keys, & Balcazar, 2007). In conjunction with the ongoing but unjustified myth that individuals with ID are "over-sexed, promiscuous, sexually indiscriminate, and dangerous" (Griffiths, 2007, p. 574) and thus should not be in the presence of children, service providers are subject to the emotional extremes that place the rights and responsibilities of child and community protection against the needs and citizenship rights of the adolescent offender.

Moreover, at the micro level of practice, it is clear that in this particular area the varying components of the social service system are strictly geared toward fragmented and reactive responses rather than proactive. Child welfare responses are frequently limited to immediate removal of the individual from the home/placement, often to a more restrictive setting. Education systems have disallowed individuals from classrooms, citing safety as a concern. Although the youth criminal justice system is predicated on the belief of rehabilitation, the system as it is designed separates the residential or institutional dimensions from the community treatment dimensions. What is generally absent in this position is the idea that adolescent sexual offenders themselves are vulnerable, particularly in criminal justice settings, and may often need to be protected and provided with support through intervention, rather than punished. In fact, the literature generally concludes that intensive treatment for youth with ID and high-risk behaviours results in lower rates of recidivism, compared to youth who were incarcerated with minimal therapeutic intervention (Edwards & Beech, 2004).

THE SOCIAL SERVICES MAZE

In Canada, unlike many states in the United States and many other countries, the Youth Criminal Justice Act focuses on rehabilitation rather than punishment. Police officers can redirect youth and their families to community-based services rather than laying a charge. This generally results in youth under the age of 18 with intellectual disabilities who exhibit high-risk behaviours being diverted toward child and family service intervention rather than criminal court. Although this is perceived as a more helpful intervention than incarceration, it presents its own set of challenges. Unfortunately, moving into the child welfare system does not necessarily result in positive experiences for these youth and can, in fact, exacerbate already difficult situations. Therefore, when the time comes for transition planning, these youth may be dealing with additional challenges.

The Manitoba Child and Family Services Act[1] makes no mention of children with ID, except that parents of children living with a mental disability may enter into a Voluntary Placement Agreement with a child welfare agency if they are not in a position to provide appropriate care and control. However, once in care of the agency, there are no mandated provisions as to the type, nature, or accessibility of services that children

---

1 See http://web2.gov.mb.ca/laws/statutes/ccsm/c080e.php.

or adolescents with ID should receive. Moreover, moving into care can increase the risk of victimization for these children, further complicating an already difficult situation.

Despite the child welfare system acting as the point of entry, child and family service workers are simply not trained to assess risk and need in this population. For example, schools of social work in Canada are not mandated to include curriculum content on disability beyond "an understanding of theories relevant to disability" (CASWE, 2008, p. 9) and may not necessarily include content on ID, particularly content on ID and challenging behaviours. Even though children with ID are at higher risk of neglect and abuse (Govindshenoy & Spencer, 2007; Sobsey, 2002), there remains limited knowledge of cognitive disability and a significant lack of disability competence (including traumatic brain injury, FASD, and mental health issues) within the child welfare field (Fuchs, Burnside, Marchenski, & Mudry, 2007; Lightfoot & LaLiberte, 2006). This includes limited recognition of how ID may affect behaviours and how best to maintain safety and protection for the child as well as others. Given that youth with ID who have been abused themselves are subsequently at higher risk of exhibiting offending behaviours (Simpson & Hogg, 2001), it should be incumbent upon child welfare workers to anticipate the potential for this to occur within this group. While it is critical that abuse victims are not further stigmatized as potential offenders, it is also important that child welfare workers, as professionals, recognize that this population requires specific, proactive, prevention services. For example, some adolescents' offending behaviours appear to be compensatory in nature and, therefore, they may be more drawn to younger children, whom they may perceive to be less threatening. If workers are not aware of the potential risk that is created when children/adolescents with ID who were physically or sexually abused themselves are placed in homes with younger children, they may inadvertently be creating the context for further safety and protection issues.

Challenging behaviours are a leading cause of placement breakdown. Once youth are in care, they undergo frequent transitions from one residential setting to another, including multiple attempts at foster placements. The reality for many of these adolescents is that they are removed to residential or institutional group settings as they generally do not do well in foster care (Pithouse, Hill-Tout, & Lowe, 2002). This absence of training for child welfare workers in the area of intellectual disability and challenging behaviours extends to foster and residential care providers. Many youth service providers are not trained in these areas, and are not aware of the needs and risks of youths with intellectual disabilities (J. Brown, 2007).

Within this framework, service providers and support persons need to be aware of risk situations, and ensure that intervention is directed toward the individual. Dynamic risk factors include pro-offending attitudes, deviant sexual dynamics, hostility, absence of social supports, and minimal capacity for emotional self-regulation (Keeling, Beech, & Rose, 2007). When identified early, these factors are amenable to change via appropriate and targeted therapeutic intervention. Unfortunately, common practice tends to ignore these behaviours until such time as an incident occurs. Therefore, intervention is frequently based on reducing liability—resulting in 2-on-1 supervision models in restrictive residential and institutional settings, rather than therapeutic interventions designed to address the challenging behaviours. "Best-practice" interventions include strategies for assisting adolescents to focus on learning and using skills for managing and reducing sexual arousal and deviancy, challenging cognitive distortions, developing pro-social skills and competencies, enhancing empathic responding, developing and using relapse prevention plans, developmentally appropriate sexual education, and communicating about emotional experiences (Shenk & Brown, 2007). Few agencies are both equipped and willing to work with the complex constellations of risks and needs that intellectually disabled youth present (Emerson, 2005). The result is that child-focused systems generally perpetuate dependence and discourage reasonable risk-taking that would create the context in which the adolescent may become motivated to make choices and changes themselves (Boer, Tough, & Haaven, 2004). Although this may mitigate the risk of potential offending behaviours, it does not create the context in which the adolescent can address his high-risk behaviours and accompanying emotions in a therapeutic and meaningful way.

When examining the transition process for high-risk adolescents with intellectual disabilities, it seems clear that professionals from a range of disciplines could potentially be involved. In Manitoba, for example, this list may include such professionals as a child and family services worker, juvenile probation officer, children's special services worker, adult supported living worker, public trustee representative, foster care provider, residential program coordinator, school representative, family members and/or advocates, supported workplace mentor, primary healthcare provider, psychiatrist, and mental health worker. For Aboriginal and First Nations individuals, the list may be expanded to include band representatives and community elders. Although at one level, this may suggest that this population is well-resourced, an alternative perspective is that the diverse and often contradictory mandates of our service systems complicate the objective of facilitating the transition of adolescents to adult services. An effective response for individuals with ID becomes exceptionally difficult due to their inherent cognitive impairments, the contradictory position of these individuals as both victims and offenders, the fragmented nature of the service systems, and limited public resources.

At the point of transition, the absence of awareness about other service systems that have relevance for this group, including the vocational rehabilitation, supported employment, or mental health systems, impedes child welfare workers' abilities to link young adults with disabilities to services that are essential for their post–child welfare transition outcomes. In Manitoba, standards of practice suggest that a five-year period is required for notification when a high-needs adolescent is requiring adult services. That is, the adult service system will be notified when the adolescent enters his/her first year of secondary school, though most continue until age 21 (Healthy Child Manitoba, 2008). It is the responsibility of the child welfare worker to notify the family regarding transition planning, complete referrals to adult systems, attend transition meetings, and link the adolescent and family to the appropriate adult service system. However, in practice, adolescents with ID and challenging behaviours are frequently not identified to the adult system until just prior to their eighteenth birthdates, leaving minimal time to plan and allocate financial resources to the systems. As indicated by one study that tracked this issue, despite clear guidelines, professionals conceded that adequate transition planning was random and inconsistent, and adult service workers were assigned at a significantly later date in the process than recommended (Abbott & Heslop, 2009). One factor that exacerbates this problem is that an adolescent may have two or more child welfare workers over the span of a few years. Given the current context of significant turnover of child and family service workers in Manitoba and other provinces, including Saskatchewan and Ontario (with a turnover rate of 12% in 2008) (Bourassa, 2010; Csiernik, Smith, Dewar, Dromgole, & O'Neill, 2010; Schibler & Newton, 2006), it is unlikely that the worker who is ultimately responsible for transition will have the historical knowledge, information, and longer-term relationship with the adolescent to ensure that the best interests of the youth are met with appropriate levels of advocacy.

When defined as a "youth," these individuals are accessible to therapeutic intervention. However, at the point of transition, there are significant limitations in the existing service system, including availability of services, funding, and residential placements. Young people who are dealing with numerous vulnerabilities are thus required to undergo a paradigm shift away from the child welfare system, where treatment for the challenging behaviours takes the form of monitoring and intense supervision and thus creates dependence on a system. The difficulty is that this same system treats individuals with ID over the age of 18 as autonomous adults.

BARRIERS TO EFFECTIVE TRANSITIONS

Despite the growing awareness that an emphasis on early identification, assessment, and treatment is a priority with these youth, significant obstacles to effective transition remain. These include:

Different models of professional practice. As indicated above, there are numerous service providers who potentially have a role in transition planning for these youth. Not surprisingly, there are different belief systems between and among the professionals regarding explanatory models and, subsequently, different ideas about service priorities and appropriate interventions. Service providers who view the behaviour as a result of the individuals having been abused themselves as children would emphasize therapeutic interventions designed to address the feelings around being victimized. Those who connect high-risk behaviours to multiple socio-economic disadvantages and/or family circumstances may prioritize addressing the social, rather than psychological, issues. Those who perceive that individuals with ID should strive toward independence may pursue less-supervised residential settings, while those who perceive the individual as incapable of changing behaviour may opt for more-restricted settings.

Absence of consistent standards for assessment and treatment. There are few clear guidelines that outline the parameters for "successful" intervention with individuals with high-risk behaviours. First, mandated treatment can only occur in the presence of a criminal conviction, eliminating any efforts at prevention. Second, there are disparities in the sentences that are imposed, ranging from minimal periods of probation to incarceration. Although the therapeutic literature recommends a minimum period of 3 years' probation in order to address the typical issues of denial and minimization, and to challenge and change beliefs, this is not routinely adhered to in practice (Lindsay, Neilson, Morrison, & Smith, 1998). Moreover, the type and range of interventions varies with this population, and there remain few longitudinal outcome studies that demonstrate which approaches are effective.

Collaboration. Adolescents who have multiple risk factors for challenging behaviours are generally involved with multiple service providers. Effective transition strategies for these youth are therefore dependent upon the development of collaborative partnerships that are clearly highly desired by service providers, yet not easily achieved. As a result, these individuals frequently fall in the divisions within existing service configurations and structures. Calley (2007) summarized the recommended treatment issues for juvenile sexual offenders. Although not specifically designed for youth with ID, they are equally applicable to this population. These include the identification and remediation of family issues, the development of pro-social relationship skills, and identification and expression of feelings and the development of empathy. Unfortunately, the current social service system is not sufficiently resourced to deliver services beyond basic needs for many adolescents such as food, shelter, and education (Bourassa, 2010; Schibler & McEwan-Morris, 2006). The unique needs expressed by adolescents with high-risk behaviours clearly require assistance from a number of organizations simultaneously or in an appropriate sequence to improve the likelihood of positive outcomes and enhanced quality of life.

HOW NOT TO TRANSITION SUCCESSFULLY: A CASE STUDY

Daniel is 18.5 years old and is currently homeless. He occasionally has access to emergency shelters, but his aggressive behaviour toward others constrains the ability of shelter staff to provide him with accommodation. He has been through 12 adult placements so far. At age 13, he was formally diagnosed with Alcohol-Related Neurological Disorder in addition to having intellectual disabilities — his IQ was assessed at approximately 71. This is congruent with the literature that suggests individuals with borderline IQs are at greatest risk of sexual offending, compared to individuals with significantly lower IQs.

Daniel was born at 38 weeks gestation and was noted to be of low birth weight. It was recorded at the time that Daniel's mother had abused alcohol while pregnant with Daniel. When he was one year old, he had been apprehended from his family due to significant parental alcohol abuse and violence and was subsequently placed in a foster home outside of his home community. While in the care of the foster family, he was sexually and physically victimized by one of the family members. No charges were ever laid, nor was Daniel provided with any type of emotional/therapeutic support.

Although the research literature overwhelmingly concludes that the most important goal when working with adolescent sexual offenders is resolving their personal histories of victimization, this was not deemed a priority by the child welfare authorities. Not only was there a lack of attention to the trauma caused by Daniel's removal from his family, but also his intellectual disabilities were cited as a reason *not* to engage in therapy regarding his victimization. Concerns were expressed that further trauma would occur by the discussion of this difficult time in his life and that, generally, it was best to "forget" about it.

Daniel was removed from the foster home, which signified the first of what would eventually become 50 documented placements as a child and adolescent. Referrals to agencies who work with individuals with high-risk behaviours are generally based on residential priorities, rather than on substantive assessment and planning with a view to developing an appropriate resource. Consequently, Daniel was often placed at a resource that would accept him, regardless of whether it "fit" his presenting needs at the time. These placements ranged from foster homes to crisis stabilization units to temporary places of safety, as well as the Manitoba Youth Centre. Discharge planning consisted of identifying a resource that would accept Daniel, albeit in the absence of any therapeutic or psychological support.

Treatment planning primarily focused upon close monitoring of his behaviour and limiting opportunities for Daniel to interact with others. Although eligible for educational support up until the age of 21, the school system refused to provide any academic programming based on the perception of Daniel being a risk to other students. Throughout his childhood and adolescence, he exhibited increasingly disturbing behaviour ranging from arson, to repeated animal abuse, and assault with a weapon—all known outcomes of having been a victim of sexual assault. In addition, he was charged with several break and enters and other crimes against property. Although Daniel demonstrates a high level of street awareness, his adaptive functioning is quite delayed, and he has difficulty with personal hygiene, social interactions, decision-making, and problem-solving skills. Although there have been attempts to support him in learning these skills, he has not remained in a single placement sufficiently long enough to consolidate his learning. He has never been identified as needing counselling for his personal trauma history, and his capacity to trust has been seriously compromised by a seemingly endless revolving door of service providers. He perceives the slightest criticism or direction as a personal attack, and has stated that he is not "retarded."

Daniel has no family system, as he has not had contact with his family since the first foster placement, nor have there been any attempts by the agencies in charge of Daniel to reconnect him with his extended family. These decisions were, once again, based on the perception that contact with his family would increase his acting-out behaviours, and he should simply "forget" about his past. Moreover, the absence of family support was not sufficient for care providers to invite/encourage/facilitate connections with other non-professional networks, again predicated on the perspective that closeness would be perceived as potentially problematic for Daniel.

A frequent occurrence is that documentation of the individual's history is typically sparse regarding needs and successes. As well, details of past placements are often unavailable and accurate records have not been well-maintained. From his involvement with numerous systems, one might anticipate that Daniel's history would be well-documented; the opposite is actually the case. The absence of documentation regarding Daniel's history seems at times to have been deliberate and, consequently, agencies were not provided with all the relevant information on Daniel's history on some occasions. As a result, one agency pulled service without notice, resulting in Daniel's current homelessness. Placement disruptions often reflect inadequate information provided to staff, poor preparation for placements, and limited participation in planning and reviews (Pithouse & Lowe, 2008). Clearly, at a point in time when vulnerable clients require the most support, precipitous discharge is often the result.

Perceptions of Daniel range from acknowledging his vulnerability to perceiving him as a significant danger to others. At this stage in his life, not only is he reacting to the original incident that was the catalyst for entering the child welfare system, but also he is now reacting to the cumulative losses, trauma, psychological harm, and attachment disruptions that have come from 50+ placements, in the absence of any therapeutic support, psycho-educational information on sexuality and healthy relationships, vocational training, and social network connections. Despite the aggression, lack of empathy, violence, and unpredictable emotional responses, Daniel has strengths. He has musical ability and computer skills, and can be quite charming. He demonstrates a remarkable resilience and ability to survive. However, given the service gaps he has experienced, his potential quality of life has been significantly and permanently impaired.

CONCLUSION

Service providers in the field of practice with individuals with intellectual disabilities and high-risk behaviours undeniably face numerous challenges given the complexity of these situations. Although traditional social work values promote the empowerment of individuals, the practice context remains limited in its ability or desire to translate empowerment principles into appropriate clinical interventions for this population. As indicated by Daniel's story, there were numerous opportunities for social service practitioners to intervene in a manner that would address Daniel's unique and admittedly significant needs. However, the service system has not yet undergone the radical changes that are required in order to effectively work with this population.

Daniel's story brings to light important implications for practice. First, too often, the philosophical differences in mandates places workers on opposite sides of the "protect versus punish" debate, with subsequent differences in response. Workers from different agencies differ in the thoroughness of their assessments and in the appropriateness of their proposed interventions, their knowledge of disability-related issues, and in their readiness to make referrals to other agencies. Clearly, there is a need to build upon the capacity of child welfare workers to acknowledge the inherent risks associated with children and adolescents with ID, both as victims and, subsequently, as potential offenders. This requires disability-specific training for child welfare workers, but also appropriate clinical supervision and support. These are not new recommendations, as previous authors have noted these gaps (Fuchs et al., 2007).

Second, there is a need for service development in the area of children with ID. Given the issues identified in this chapter, it is recommended that child welfare policy needs to develop clear and appropriate standards of service for young people with ID and challenging behaviours. Currently, under the Manitoba Child and Family Services Act, there are no specific service mandates for children/adolescents with ID. There is a need for explicit recognition of the risk factors for future challenging or high-risk behaviours, and for understanding how these might be mitigated through targeted assessment and intervention planning. It seems reasonable to suggest that when a child or adolescent with ID enters a system of care as a result of abuse or other trauma, they must be provided with therapeutic opportunities to heal from their experiences, as are children/adolescents who do not have ID. Therefore, it is the child welfare system that has the responsibility of ensuring that the emotional and psychological needs of this group are addressed in a meaningful and thoughtful manner. Many of the challenges that arise in transition-planning are a function of "intervention" being synonymous with restricted monitoring, so that when individuals enter the adult service system and are considered independent adults, they are likely not equipped with the necessary skills and abilities that will assist them in being successful. As such, the child welfare system has the responsibility to provide children in care with the necessary skills to successfully transition to the adult system. Unfortunately, there is limited knowledge in the child welfare system of how to effectively support youth with ID and challenging behaviours, beyond physical and, at times, geographical restriction. Thus, transition becomes an end-point, rather than a process of building on an individual's successes.

Third, it is important for child welfare workers to ensure the coordination and provision of specialized services and intervention while in the care of child welfare. Unfortunately, given the complexity of this area of practice, there are few agencies/service providers that have the willingness and expertise to work with this population. There is a significant need to develop the capacity for service providers to engage in emotionally supportive, long-term, and constructive counselling with this group, not only as a basic citizenship right, but as an effective way of reducing future risk. Early intervention within the child welfare system has the potential to significantly reduce the difficulties that this group encounters when transitioned to the adult service system.

Perhaps most important, the current system of patchwork policies that focus exclusively on education, justice, child welfare, and disability services need to broaden and share their mandates for responsibility for youth with ID and high-risk behaviours in order for these individuals to effectively transition at the age of majority.

REFERENCES

Abbott, D., & Heslop, P. (2009). Out of sight, out of mind?: Transition for young people with learning difficulties in out-of-area residential special schools and colleges. *British Journal of Special Education, 36*(1), 45–54.

Boer, D., Tough, S., & Haaven, J. (2004). Assessment of risk manageability of intellectually disabled sex offenders. *Journal of Applied Research in Intellectual Disabilities, 17,* 275–283.

Bourassa, C. (2010). Summary Review of the Manitoba Child Welfare System for the Saskatchewan Child Welfare Review Report. Final Submission. Submitted to the Saskatchewan Child Welfare Review Panel, August 18, 2010.

Brown, I. (2007). The transition from school to adult life. In I. Brown & M. Percy (Eds.), *A comprehensive guide to intellectual & developmental disabilities* (pp. 511–525). Baltimore: Paul H. Brookes Publishing.

Brown, J. (2007). Fostering children with disabilities: A concept map of parent needs. *Children and Youth Services Review, 29*(9), 1235–1248.

Calley, N. G. (2007). Integrating theory and research: The development of a research-based treatment program for juvenile male sex offenders. *Journal of Counseling & Development, 85*(2), 131–142.

Canadian Association of Social Work Education (CASWE). (2008). Standards for accreditation. CASWE: Ottawa, ON: Author.

Canadian Institute of Child Health. (2000). *The health of Canada's children: A CICH profile: Children and youth with disabilities.* Ottawa, ON: Author.

Charles, G., & McDonald, M. (2005). Adolescent sexual offenders: An overview. *CYC Online: Readings for child and youth care people, 78.* Retrieved from www.cyc-net.org/cyc-online/cycol-0905-charles.html.

Cossette, L., & Duclos, E. (2002). *A profile of disability in Canada, 2001.* Statistics Canada Catalogue no. 89-577-XIE.

Craig, L., & Hutchison, R. (2005). Sexual offenders with learning disabilities: Risk, recidivism and treatment. *Journal of Sexual Aggression, 11*(3), 289–304.

Csiernik, R., Smith, C., Dewar, J., Dromgole, L., & O'Neill, A. (2010). Supporting new workers in a child welfare agency: An exploratory study. *Journal of Workplace Behavioral Health, 25*(3), 218–232.

Developmental Disabilities Association. (2010). *What is a developmental disability?* Retrieved from www.develop.bc.ca/about/development-disabilities.html.

Diagnostic and Statistical Manual of Mental Disorders – 4th Ed. (DSM-IV-TR). (2000). Retrieved from online.statref.com.proxy1.lib.umanitoba.ca/Document.

Doyle, D. (2004). The differences between sex offending and challenging behaviour in people with an intellectual disability. *Journal of Intellectual and Developmental Disability, 29*(2), 107–118.

Edwards, R., & Beech, A. (2004). Treatment programmes for adolescents who commit sexual offences: Dropout and recidivism. *Journal of Sexual Aggression, 10*(1), 101–115.

Emerson, E. (2001). *Challenging behaviour: Analysis and intervention in people with severe intellectual disabilities.* Cambridge, MA: Cambridge University Press.

Emerson, J. (2005). *Service issues for adolescents who sexually offend.* IMPAC (Inter-Ministerial Provincial Advisory Committee) report to Ontario's provincial advocate. Retrieved from provincialadvocate.on.ca/documents/fr/IMPAC%20Report%20Final%20Version%20June%202005.pdf.

Fuchs, D., Burnside, L., Marchenski, S., & Mudry, A. (2007). Children with disabilities involved with the child welfare system in Manitoba: current and future challenges. In I. Brown, F. Chaze, D. Fuchs, J. Lafrance, S. McKay, & S. Thomas Prokop (Eds.). *Putting a human face on child welfare: Voices from the prairies* (pp. 127–145). Regina, SK: Prairie Child Welfare Consortium / Centre of Excellence for Child Welfare.

Govindshenoy, M., & Spencer, N. (2007). Abuse of the disabled child: A systematic review of population-based studies. *Child: Care, Health and Development, 33*(5), 552–558.

Griffiths, D. (2007). Sexuality and people who have intellectual disabilities. In I. Brown & M. Percy (Eds.), *A comprehensive guide to intellectual & developmental disabilities* (pp. 573–583). Baltimore: Paul H. Brookes Publishing.

Healthy Child Manitoba. (2008). *Bridging to adulthood: A protocol for transitioning students with exceptional needs from school to community*. Healthy Child Manitoba, Winnipeg, Manitoba.

Keeling, J., Beech, A., & Rose, J. (2007). Assessment of intellectually disabled sexual offenders: The current position. *Aggression and Violent Behavior, 12*(2), 229–241.

Lambrick, F., & Glaser, W. (2004). Sex offenders with an intellectual disability. *Sexual Abuse: A Journal of Research and Treatment, 16*(4), 381–392.

Langevin, R., & Curnoe, S. (2008). Are the mentally retarded and learning disordered overrepresented among sex offenders and paraphilics? *International Journal of Offender Therapy and Comparative Criminology, 52*(4), 401–415.

Lightfoot, E., & LaLiberte, T. (2006). Approaches to child welfare case management for cases involving people with disabilities. *Child Abuse & Neglect, 30*(4), 381–391.

Lindsay, W., Law, J., Quinn, K., Smart, N., & Smith, A. (2001). A comparison of physical and sexual abuse: Histories of sexual and non-sexual offenders with intellectual disability. *Child Abuse and Neglect, 25*(7), 989–995.

Lindsay, W., Neilson, C., Morrison, F., & Smith, A. (1998). The treatment of six men with a learning disability convicted of offences against children. *British Journal of Clinical Psychology, 37,* 83–98.

Lindsay, W., Smith, A., Law, J., Quinn, K., Anderson, A., Smith, A., & Allan, R. (2004). Sexual and nonsexual offenders with intellectual and learning disabilities: A comparison of characteristics, referral patterns, and outcome. *Journal of Interpersonal Violence, 19*(8), 875–890.

Lindsay, W. R., Steele, L., Smith, A., Quinn, K., & Allan, R. (2006). A community forensic intellectual disability service: Twelve year follow up of referrals, analysis of referral patterns and assessment of harm reduction. *Legal and Criminological Psychology, 11*(1), 113–130.

McDonald, K., Keys, C., & Balcazar, E. (2007). Disability, race/ethnicity and gender: Themes of cultural oppression, acts of individual resistance. *American Journal of Community Psychology, 39*(1–2), 145–161.

Pithouse, A., Hill-Tout, J., & Lowe, K. (2002). Training foster carers in challenging behaviour: A case study in disappointment? *Child and Family Social Work, 7*(3), 203–214.

Pithouse, A., & Lowe, K. (2008). Children in foster care with challenging behaviour in Wales (UK): Key themes and issues for practice and research. *Families in Society, 89*(1), 109–118.

Schibler, B., & McEwan-Morris, A. (2006). Strengthening our youth: Their journey to competence and independence. Retrieved November 10, 2011, from www.childrensadvocate.mb.ca/wp-content/uploads/Strengthening-Our-Youth-Final-2006.pdf.

Schibler, B., & Newton, J. (2006). Honouring their spirits, the child death review: A report to the Minister of Family Services & Housing, Province of Manitoba. Final Report. Office of the Children's Advocate, Manitoba.

Sequeira, H., & Hollins, S. (2003). Clinical effects of sexual abuse on people with learning disability. *The British Journal of Psychiatry, 182*, 13–19.

Shenk, C., & Brown, A. (2007). Cognitive-behavioral treatment of an adolescent sexual offender with an intellectual disability: A novel application of exposure and response prevention. *Clinical Case Studies, 6*(4), 307–324.

Simpson, M., & Hogg, J. (2001). Patterns of offending among people with intellectual disability: A systematic review. Part I: Methodology and prevalence data. *Journal of Intellectual Disability Research, 45*(5), 384–396.

Sobsey, D. (2002). Exceptionality, education, and maltreatment. *Exceptionality, 10*(1), 29–46.

Søndenaa, E., Rasmussen, K., & Nøttestad, J. (2008). Forensic issues in intellectual disability: Sex offenders. *Current Opinion in Psychiatry, 21*(5), 449–453.

Spero, L. (2003). The transition for school to the community: A parent's perspective. In I. Brown & M. Percy (Eds.), *Developmental disabilities in Ontario* (2nd ed.) (pp. 603–612). Toronto, ON: Ontario Association on Developmental Disabilities.

Statistics Canada. (2006). *Participation and Activity Limitation Survey 2006: Analytical paper.* Health Statistics Division, Ottawa, Ontario.

Stermac, L., & Mathews, F. (1987). *Adolescent sex offenders.* Toronto, ON: Central Toronto Youth Services.

Tudway, J., & Darmoody, M. (2005). Clinical assessment of adult sexual offenders with learning disabilities. *Journal of Sexual Aggression, 11*(3), 277–288.

West, B. (2007). Using the Good Way model to work positively with adults and youth with intellectual difficulties and sexually abusive behaviour. *Journal of Sexual Aggression, 13*(3), 253–266.

Vaughn, P. (2003). Secure care and treatment needs of individuals with learning disability and severe challenging behaviour. *British Journal of Learning Disabilities, 31*(3), 113–117.

Veneziano, C., & Veneziano, L. (2002). Adolescent sex offenders: A review of the literature. *Trauma Violence Abuse, 3*(4), 247–260.

Vizard, E., Hickey, N., & McCrory, E. (2007). Developmental trajectories associated with juvenile sexually abusive behaviour and emerging severe personality disorder in childhood: 3-year study. *The British Journal of Psychiatry, 190,* 27–32.

Yu, D., & Atkinson, L. (1993). Developmental disability with and without psychiatric involvement: Prevalence estimates for Ontario. *Journal on Developmental Disabilities, 2*(1), 92–99.

CHAPTER 9

Fetal Alcohol Spectrum Disorder Communities of Practice in Alberta: Innovations in Child Welfare Practice

Dorothy Badry, William Pelech, and Sandra Stoddard

Children with Fetal Alcohol Spectrum Disorder (FASD)[1] have neurological abnormalities related to organic brain injury caused by prenatal alcohol exposure (PAE) (Streissguth, 1997). The term Fetal Alcohol Syndrome (FAS) is primarily used in literature that predates 2002 (Jones & Smith, 1973; Jones, Smith, Ulleland, & Streissguth, 1973), while literature post-2001 often refers to the term FASD (Streissguth and O'Malley, 2001). The distinction between the two terms is that FAS was the first descriptive diagnosis of children who had medically identifiable disabilities related to PAE (Jones & Smith, 1973). Alcohol acts as a teratogen or toxin that disrupts cell development in utero and has different effects throughout the pregnancy. In 2001, Streissguth and O'Malley suggested

---

1 See Appendix on page 212 for a list of acronyms used in this chapter.

SUGGESTED CITATION: Badry, D., Pelech, W., and Stoddard, S. (2012). Fetal Alcohol Spectrum Disorder Communities of Practice in Alberta: Innovations in child welfare practice. In D. Fuchs, S. McKay, & I. Brown (Eds.), *Awakening the Spirit: Moving Forward in Child Welfare: Voices from the Prairies* (pp. 179–212). Regina, SK: Canadian Plains Research Center.

the term FASD both as a means to encapsulate the multiplicity of conditions caused by PAE and to suggest that there is a spectrum of affects and medical problems that result.

The problems of children and adults with FASD are not only medical, but social. We now know that prenatal alcohol exposure can contribute to a variety of disabilities including cognitive, behavioural, and neurological deficits, and is broadly identified as a permanent, organic brain injury (Chudley et al., 2005). Diagnostic guidelines for FASD within Canada were published by Chudley and colleagues (2005) and have served as a foundation for establishing and understanding the meaning of a diagnosis for children and families. Andrew (2010) indicated that the 4-Digit Code (Astley, 2004, 2010; Astley & Clarren, 2000), a key diagnostic tool that examines four features critical to diagnosis—growth, face [facial features], brain function, and alcohol exposure—is used by most clinics in Western Canada.

There was no textbook on child welfare practice with this population in the 1980s and 1990s, and no textbook approach to child welfare intervention exists at this point for the population of children in care with FASD. Such children exhibit a variety of behavioural, learning, and other needs that can be very intensive (Badry, 2009; Badry, Pelech, & Norman, 2005; Vig, Chinitz, & Shulman, 2005). They frequently have histories of early exposure to trauma, often end up in permanent care of the state, and account for high costs associated with their long-term care (Fuchs, Burnside, DeRiviere et al., 2009; Fuchs, Burnside, Marchenski et al., 2009).

The high needs of children with FASD in the care of the child welfare system demand competence in casework and excellence in practice. To this end, Alberta Children and Youth Services (ACYS) initiated an evaluation project in 2009-2010, entitled FASD Communities of Practice (CoP), that built on the promise of earlier research. Both children who are diagnosed with FASD and those suspected to have FASD were considered important to include in the FASD CoP. The principal guideline for the development of specific practice interventions of CoP was that the interventions directly address the identified high needs of the children with FASD.

The CoP applied specific FASD practice interventions (formerly identified as practice standards) that were developed in Region 1 (South West Child and Family Services Authority [CFSA]) in 2002 and are described in more detail below. A relationship between CFSA and the Faculty of Social Work, University of Calgary, was forged in 2003, beginning with a request from the region for support with research that would evaluate the effectiveness of particular interventions for children with FASD. The FASD Practice Standards Evaluation Project Final Report was completed in 2005 after two years working with the region (Badry, 2009; Badry, Pelech, & Norman, 2005). This small project, involving 63 children, evolved into a larger project funded for $100,000 from the Alberta Centre for Child, Family and Community Research (ACCFCR) in 2009-2010. The concept of being a *good guardian* for children in care with FASD was a foundational value of this research.

EARLY WORK CRITICAL TO THE CURRENT PROJECT

Project Beginnings

This project, which had humble beginnings in Lethbridge, Alberta, in 2002, illustrates that care and concern for vulnerable children with FASD can result in research and the development of an FASD CoP. A committed and dedicated group of child welfare caseworkers, foster care workers, and supervisors determined that the work being done with children with FASD in their community required specialized practice. A focussed practice on children in care with FASD did not exist as such at the time, although serious concerns were identified for the needs of children and families, and children often became permanent wards of the state. Donna Debolt (BSW, RSW), a social worker with the Alberta government for 25 years, had a passionate interest in FASD. Along with her colleagues in Lethbridge, she began to develop a focussed practice on FASD within the CFSA. They held the first conference on FASD in Alberta in 1992, with 740 people in attendance from across Canada and the United States. Dr. Sterling Clarren, current CEO of the Canada Northwest FASD Research Network, became involved early in initial training activities within Canada.

Debolt and her colleague Mary Berube (MSW, RSW) developed training workshops for caseworkers throughout Alberta. They consistently delivered this training to a great many people between 1996 and 2003, training approximately 10,000 individuals. Much of the training developed was drawn from casework practice and the challenges that emerged from lived experiences of children with FASD. This truly was pioneering work, driven by the intensive needs of children whose difficulties went far beyond existing casework responses. The primary goals of the training by Debolt and Berube were to support effective child welfare casework that appreciated the complexity of children with FASD, to gain an understanding of the family history of addiction and trauma, and to develop an appreciation of the burden experienced by caregivers and foster parents.

The Canadian response to FASD has largely been driven by the community-based research agenda of the Canada Northwest FASD Research Network, which began in 2005. This agenda has resulted in the development of five Network Action Teams (NATs) in the areas of a) research in diagnostics, b) intervention on FASD, c) evaluating FASD-specific public health and education materials, d) prevention from a women's determinants of health perspective, and e) evaluation of FASD mentoring programs (CanFASD Northwest, n.d.). The availability of a research network with a specific focus on FASD has been critically important to developing an understanding of the complexity of the problems associated with diagnosis and treatment, and has highlighted the need for biomedical and social science research on this topic.

Alberta Government Support for FASD

The Alberta government demonstrated support for understanding the complex needs of children with FASD and their families who are in contact with various ministries by establishing the Alberta FASD Cross Ministry Committee (FASD-CMC) in 2002. This committee is an interdisciplinary group of senior bureaucrats who meet on a regular basis to examine program and care needs for persons in Alberta with FASD and to develop a coordinated response. The FASD-CMC is made up of: Alberta Children and Youth Services (co-chair/administrative lead), Alberta Health and Wellness (co-chair), Alberta Aboriginal Relations, Alberta Advanced Education and Technology, Alberta Seniors and Community Supports, Alberta Education, Alberta Employment and Immigration, Alberta Justice and Attorney General, Alberta Solicitor General and Public Security, Alberta Gaming and Liquor Commission, and Alberta Housing and Urban Affairs. The FASD-CMC also receives support from the Public Health Agency of Canada, First Nations and Inuit Health, Alberta Health Services, and Safe Communities Secretariat.

The FASD-CMC developed a comprehensive 10-year strategic plan in 2008 that spans several service categories: awareness and prevention, diagnosis and treatment, supports for individuals and caregivers, training and education, strategic planning, stakeholder engagement, and research and evaluation. This strategic plan outlines shared goals, and sets out a range of multi-level policy and practice strategies that are designed to reflect the needs of individual communities, families, and individuals. One of the strategies in this community-based approach was to provide support for the CoP project reported in this chapter, which, in turn, endeavors to support and evaluate the best practices set out in the strategic plan.

Development of the Project

As is evident in the above section, there has been a strong commitment within Alberta to move forward with initiatives in support of education, training, and understanding of FASD. This movement goes back to one of the first Alberta training conferences held in Lethbridge, Alberta, by the CFSA in 1992. It was broadly determined within child welfare that training opportunities that acknowledged the unique needs of children with FASD were required (see Box 1). This viewpoint emerged from clinical experience with children in care who had been prenatally exposed to alcohol, and from casework with the families of origin. There was a growing recognition that traditional models of casework for children in care were not working for children with FASD. This was considered to be due to concerns such as behavioural problems, placement disruption and breakdown, and high needs of children for constant supervision and structure. It grew increasingly clear to those on the front line of child protection—foster parents, management, and consultants from other disciplines such as psychology and medicine—that a practice model was required that specifically addressed the needs of affected children.

When encountering children with complex and challenging needs, good guardians develop a range of services and supports that address the needs of their children. When responding to the needs of children with FASD, good guardians may need to develop new standards of care that exceed prevailing practice standards. Such was the case with the CFSA which, in 2003, pioneered the development, implementation, and evaluation of new practice standards. In a roundtable meeting of stakeholders

Box 1. The Need for Specific Interventions for Children with FASD

The complexity of FASD is not just in relation to the diagnosis. FASD becomes a complex matter because of issues related to addiction, traumatic histories of women, poverty, and other social problems related to alcohol-exposed pregnancies and the consequent diagnosis of this disabling bio-psychosocial and neurological disorder. Children with FASD require specific and specialized interventions for the following reasons:

- **Children with FASD have greater needs than most children.** Vig, Chinitz, and Shulman (2005) completed a study that examined young children in care with complex needs and multiple vulnerabilities, and suggested that 80% may have had prenatal exposure to alcohol. Factors cited in removal of children from parental (biological) care broadly includes "neglect" and "parental incapacity" (p. 147).

- **Children with FASD are sometimes living with families where there is abuse and trauma.** Streissguth (1997) identified stable foster care placement as a mediating factor for children removed from home environments where they were frequently traumatized and at risk of abuse from actively alcoholic parents.

- **The literature is sparse on specific ways of caring for children with FASD.** There exists a well-developed body of knowledge on caring for children with disabilities, but this needs to be adapted to care of children with FASD.

- **Family reunification may not occur for children with FASD.** Romney, Litrownik, Newton, & Lau (2006) suggested from their research on children with disabilities in care, that family reunification is less likely and permanent care more likely. This may apply to children with FASD to an even greater degree.

- **Stable foster care appears to be a good care alternative.** Aronson (in Streissguth & Kanter, 1997) suggested that "even though early fostering did not appear to eliminate the harmful effects of exposure to alcohol *in utero,* foster care seems to be the most favourable alternative for children whose biological mothers, despite vigorous attempts at psychological support, continue to abuse alcohol and have severe personal psychological problems. Children prenatally exposed to alcohol who remain in biological families ... remain at continued risk" (p. 24). For children with FASD, stability and structure are hallmarks of good care.

- **The needs of foster caregivers of children with FASD require special attention.** One of the primary concerns in foster care is addressing the needs of foster caregivers. Twigg (2009) identified the following requirements for foster caregivers: need for support; need for recognition; need for addressing financial concerns; and need for training (timely, consistent and relevant to meeting needs of children). Carmichael Olson, Oti, Gelo, & Beck (2009) contended that severe gaps in knowledge and research related to family issues and stress on caregivers are a concern, but that higher quality of caregiving achieves better outcomes for children with FASD. Brown and Rodger (2009) have identified needs of caregivers in the areas of gaining access to obtaining specialized professional services, supports related to the financial costs associated with fostering a child with a disability, support in relation to educational placements and services, supportive responses related to the child's behavioural concerns and issues, opportunities to engage in self-care, support dealing with multiple roles, and in working with the health care system and needs of children.

- **Early intervention may result in improvements.** Koponen, Kalland and Autti-Rämö (2009) specifically examined the caregiving environment required to meet the needs of children with FASD, and discovered that children who came into care at earlier ages (prior to age three) had fewer neuropsychological challenges than those who came into care at later ages. This suggests that early removal of children from chaotic and stressful environments and placing them in a stable care environment may have a mediating effect. This research suggests that early, long-term placement outside of homes where children with FASD are at risk for neglect, abuse, and trauma may have better outcomes in relation to social-behavioural problems.

and service providers involved with child welfare in 2001, concerns were raised about the intense needs of children with FASD in permanent care. The discussions of this group focussed on the construct of being a "good guardian" for children whose care needs exceeded current practice standards. It was recognized that the guardianship of children with FASD was complex, and required additional intervention and support by caseworkers. An underlying concern was the improvement of outcomes for children with FASD in care.

Case management standards were originally drafted in 2002 in the following areas: screening for FASD, child assessment, determining parenting ability, service plans, service plan reviews, home visits, case manager contact with children in care and foster parents, child and family awareness of FASD, permanency planning, transition planning to adulthood, FASD training for child welfare staff, and workload standards for caseworkers. Additionally, program standards were created in relation to kinship care, foster care, residential care, adoptive services, private guardianship and family preservation, and youth mentoring services. Policy regarding the application of the standards was developed in early 2003.

In spring 2003, members of the Project Steering Committee and researchers from the Faculty of Social Work at the University of Calgary met to discuss the design of an evaluation project. It was determined by the Steering Committee that both qualitative and quantitative approaches would be built into the research design. The central study focus would be the experience of implementing the standards. This information was considered to be very important in terms of understanding the approach to casework for children with FASD involved with child protection services and living in foster care. Interviews and focus groups would capture the experiences of caseworkers and foster parents in relation to the standards. The opportunity to discuss the experience of the standards was important within the research design, as the voices of caseworkers and foster parents were considered to be critical.

At that time, a unit within the CFSA was designated for selection of children suspected or diagnosed with FASD as potential study participants. This unit was made up predominantly of Aboriginal children. Ethically, the CFSA was precluded from limiting access to enhanced services and support to children affected by FASD within its service area. As a consequence, neither a randomized sample, nor a comparison group could be made available from within the unit. It was decided by the Steering Committee that a comparison group was essential, but that it could be drawn from another area. The Native Services Unit in Calgary was approached, and it agreed to participate in this study by facilitating random selection of children for a comparison group. To promote greater comparability, school-age children were selected for both the pilot and Calgary-based comparative groups. Children within the two groups were matched as closely as possible on gender, age, diagnostic criteria, and legal status (i.e., Permanent Guardianship Order, Temporary Guardianship Order). Thus, a quasi-experimental matched comparison group design was adopted for the purposes of this inquiry.

A total of 33 children were included in the pilot group, and 30 children were selected for inclusion with the comparison group. Children entered the pilot from July 1 to December 31, 2003, but, since the implementation of the practice standards was to span a one-year period, data collection for each child continued over a one-year period ending in December 2004. Thus, this pilot project ran from July 2003 to December 2004.

The focus of this research was to evaluate compliance with the standards and to capture the experiences of caseworkers and foster parents who applied the standards. Researchers gathered quantitative data relating to the degree to which staff achieved the standards outlined by policy and, with the help of caregivers, data relating to risk behaviours (e.g., unauthorized absences, self-harm, criminal behaviour, substance abuse, acting out, etc.), caregiver placement satisfaction, and placement change. In addition, qualitative data relating to the implementation of the standards was gathered through individual interviews with caseworkers and foster care workers, and through focus groups with staff and caregivers.

There was a strong sense of vision and leadership within the region regarding the development and implementation of the standards pilot project. A sense of hope was instilled through the direction of providing specific supports to children with FASD as determined within the standards. Throughout the project, a sense of enthusiasm was evident in face-to-face meetings, phone conversations, and dialogues with workers. There was a great deal of collective wisdom and knowledge with the groups of caseworkers and foster parents, who applied their experience to the implementation of the standards. A strong sense of commitment to the goal of better meeting the needs of children was clear. It must be kept in mind that the focus of this research was twofold: it focussed both on evaluating the experience of implementing the standards and on the broader issue of compliance with, and impact of, the standards. The experiences of caseworkers and foster parents were reported after an analysis of the data from the interviews and focus groups that identified areas of consensus and conflict within the broad themes that emerged.

The research project certainly noted several limitations in the implementation of the standards but, somewhat surprisingly, it found significant favourable changes in outcomes relating to improved placement stability and caregiver relationships, as well as reduced risk behaviours. Although the pilot group experienced higher rates of placement change before and during implementation of the practice standards, there was a significant decrease in their placement changes as the project continued, resulting in a convergence of mean placement changes over time. Consistent patterns of reduced risk behaviours and school absences were observed with the implementation of the practice standards. Training opportunities were valued, and these were viewed as supporting caseworkers and foster parents in working with children and meeting their needs more effectively. Caseworkers and foster parents were invested in the application of the standards, and they valued the experience and the opportunity to reflect on their practice. The standards stated that there should be a maximum of two children with FASD in a home, and this was a source of conflict for some foster families. The use of respite decreased during the study and, through the focus groups, it was determined that despite the existence of a standard recommending 48 hours of respite per month, foster families largely wanted to determine the level of respite required. For some families, regular respite on a monthly basis worked well, but some families with younger children actually preferred less respite. However, as children with FASD reach adolescence the need for respite became more clearly articulated by foster parents. Finally, family visitation was a major area of conflict and tension, and was considered to be the biggest factor in the "disruption" of the life of the child by foster families. The disruption was primarily related to the child having challenges in adjusting between visits with the biological family and foster family. Despite the importance of these connections, it must be recognized that there is inherent stress that needs to be managed for children with FASD. In sum, these preliminary findings were promising, particularly in light of the relative low sample size of the project. Such promise supported the expansion of this pilot project to several regions of Alberta.

The initial FASD Practice Standards Evaluation Project Final Report (Badry, Pelech, & Norman, 2005) was carefully reviewed and it was determined by ACYS that further work and research related to children in care with FASD was required. Given that the initial research project discovered that focused practice for children with FASD resulted in several positive outcomes for children, caregivers, and caseworkers, a subsequent review of this research in 2008 led to initiating a second, much larger study involving five regions of ACYS. (See Box 2 for an expanded rationale for conducting the larger study, and Box 3 for a map showing the five regions.)

Box 2. Additional Reasons for Conducting the Study

- Many of the needs and characteristics of children with FASD are known from previous research, but there has been very little research that examines the impact of best practices in foster care, such as those articulated in Alberta's enhanced case-management practice standards.

- As guardians, child welfare workers and foster parents share primary responsibility for the needs of children in care.

- There is evidence that children with FASD who are in care experience significantly higher rates of placement disruption (Habbick, Nanson, Snyder, Casey, & Schulman, 1996). Placement instability has been linked to negative emotional outcomes for foster children as well as the decision by parents to leave the system. It has also been linked to the likelihood of later problematic outcomes, especially mental health problems, school difficulties, trouble with the law, and alcohol or drug problems (Streissguth & O' Malley, 2001; Streissguth & Kanter, 1997). Thus, service practice that promotes placement stability may contribute to more positive outcomes for children with FASD.

- There is a need for evaluation research results that can inform practice and policy through exploring how each of the standards influences child and service outcomes. Applications to Alberta's Ministry of Children's Services and child welfare services providers in other jurisdictions should help to support decision-making, develop resource allocation for FASD, and lead to improved policy for FASD services.

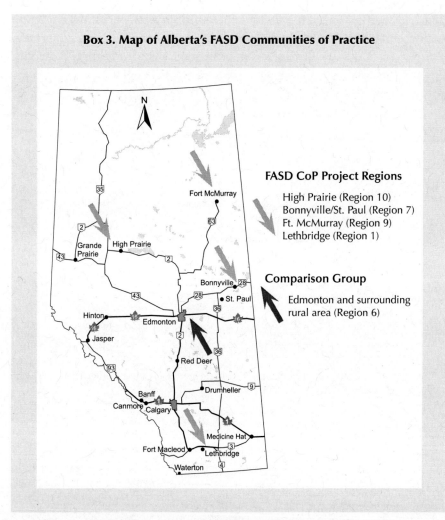

Box 3. Map of Alberta's FASD Communities of Practice

Joining the original region, Region 1 (Southwest Alberta CFSA), four additional regions implemented the FASD Communities of Practice: Region 7 (North Central CFSA), Region 9 (Northeast CFSA), Region 10 (Métis Settlements CFSA), and Region 6 (Edmonton and Area CFSA). Region 6 was then selected as the comparison group due to its size and diversity of population, as it encompasses urban and rural and has a large First Nations population. Geographically, the distribution of the regions covers a large part of the province and the population of children are primarily Aboriginal. Approximately 70% of the children selected for the study from the four study regions (1, 7, 9 & 10) were Aboriginal, while 90% of children selected from the comparison region (6) are Aboriginal. The large majority of children were under permanent guardianship status, with a mean age of 11.7 years in the study regions and 10.7 years in the comparison group. In the present study, the numbers of children of Indigenous ancestry involved in the study raises a concern for this community.

THE CURRENT RESEARCH PROJECT

Alberta is currently seen as a leader in its response to FASD across ministries and sectors of the helping professions. The current research project offered a unique and innovative opportunity to develop relationships across CFSAs and with key stakeholders in relation to direct practice and perceived benefits for children with FASD who may require more intensive and longer-term supports than children who do not have a diagnosis of FASD.

The following questions guided this research project:
1. What particular experiences of those involved with CoP provided guidelines and standards for the care of children with FASD in need of child protection services?
2. To what extent was there compliance with the standards in terms of: a) training for workers and caregivers, b) screening and assessment for FASD, c) home visits and contact with child and foster parents, d) workload standards, e) number of children with FASD in foster homes, f) respite care, g) permanency and transitional planning, and h) completion and review of service plans?
3. Did the application of the standards reduce risk behaviours such as leaving placements, criminal behaviour, drug and alcohol use, school absence and self-harming behaviour?
4. Did the provision of respite reduce placement breakdown and reduce placement changes?
5. Did the application of the standards impact the quality of caregiver-child relationships? and
6. Did application of the standards minimize life disruptions for children in care?

From these, and the results of the pilot study, four hypotheses were developed for testing:
1. There will be a significantly lower number of placement disruptions and risk behaviours for children in the pilot group than for those in the comparison group;
2. The quality of relationships with caregivers in the pilot group will be significantly better than with caregivers in the comparison group;
3. The use of respite care will be negatively associated with indicators of placement disruption and risk behaviours; and,
4. Worker contact with foster homes will be positively related to measures of the quality of relationships with caregivers.

Method

This evaluation project parallels the research design adopted for the original Region 1 study described above. There were two components to the current project:
1. Formative evaluation, involving focus group discussions with staff and foster parents in pilot regions at the beginning, midpoint, and end of pilot implementation, as well as case reviews to determine the level of compliance with the practice standards; and
2. Summative evaluation, involving comparison of outcomes related to residential placement stability, quality of relationships with caregivers and teachers, and risk behaviours.

For the purposes of hypothesis testing and summative evaluation, a quasi-experimental matched comparison group design was adopted.

Participants

The sample included 229 children in care across 5 regions who had been diagnosed with, or were suspected of having, FASD. As there were insufficient cases to perform random sampling, purposive sampling was utilized to select children within the regions for participation. The treatment group included 101 children served by Regions 1, 7, 9, and 10, and the comparison group included 128 children served by Region 6. Region 6 was selected for the comparison group because they offered a consistent profile to the other regions, including rural communities falling within that region. The children in the two groups were matched as closely as possible for age, gender, legal status, number of years in foster care, and diagnostic classification (i.e., diagnosed with or suspected of having FASD). Approximately two-thirds of the cases in the pilot sample came from two of the regions. An important matching criterion was the diagnostic classification of children included in the study. There was a slightly higher proportion of children with a diagnosis in the comparison region, although analysis revealed a non-significant difference between the study and comparison groups with respect to FASD diagnosis ($\chi^2(1, N=229)=.42, p=.51$).

An important aspect in confirming the validity of the research findings and the equivalency of groups was the administration of the Personal Behavior Checklist (PBCL-36), a tool that has shown to be effective in suggesting the need for a diagnostic assessment for FASD (Streissguth, Bookstein, Barr, Press, & Sampson, 1998). The PBCL-36 was administered to all children lacking a diagnosis (suspected of having FASD). Data collection of the PBCL-36 is incomplete in the comparison group (Region 6), but completion of the PBCL-36 by 70 caregivers found a mean score comparable to a prediction study involving adults conducted by Streissguth et al. (1998).

Another important matching criterion was the age of children included in the project. Age is important insofar as analysis of age as at 1 April 2009 for each child revealed that the mean age for children included in the study group was 11.7 years ($N=101$, $SD=4.6$ years). Mean age for children included in the comparison group was slightly younger at 10.7 years ($N=128$, $SD=3.8$ years). These differences were not statistically significant ($t(227)=1.8, p=.072$).

Consistent with general population trends for those diagnosed with FASD, more male children were included in the samples of both groups. Chi-square analysis revealed non-significant differences between the study and comparison groups with respect to gender ($\chi^2(1, N=229)=.40, p=.40$). Additionally, both groups were quite similar in that a large majority of children included in both groups were in care under Permanent Guardianship Order (PGO) status. A significant difference ($\chi^2(2, N=229)=8.41, p=.015$) arose due to a greater number of children under Temporary Guardianship Order (TGO) status in the comparison group. Finally, the groups were compared in terms of the types of placements in which children in the groups were residing. A large majority of children in both groups were at least initially placed in foster homes at the beginning of the study. Perhaps somewhat unexpectedly, given Region 10's emphasis on kinship care, the comparison group had a slightly higher proportion of children placed in kinship care. However, overall, there were no significant statistical differences between the groups in terms of the types of placements ($\chi^2(3, N=229)=5.1, p=.162$).

Procedures

The procedures for this project paralleled those used in the original Region 1 study (Badry, Pelech, & Norman, 2005) and included three components. First, focus group discussions were held with staff and foster parents in pilot regions at the beginning, midpoint, and end of pilot implementation, In addition, case reviews determined the level of compliance with the practice standards. Data from the Intervention Services Information System (ISIS) and case files were gathered, including information related to placement stability and risk behaviours for two years prior to the implementation of the practice standards, one year after implementation, and at the end of two years. Second, for the purposes of hypothesis testing, a quasi-experimental matched comparison group design was used, involving a study group that implemented the practice standards and a comparison group that did not. Children included in the study were matched based upon age, gender, Child and Youth Information Module status (CYIM-electronic information system), number of years in foster care, and diagnostic classification (i.e., diagnosed or suspected). Third, a Community of Practice (CoP)—comprised of caseworkers, supervisors with Alberta Children and Youth Services from the study group, foster care parents, Alberta FASD Service Networks, Community Seniors and Supports, Métis Settlements, the Prairie Child Welfare Consortium, Research and Innovation Branch, and University researchers—was established to support the implementation of the research project and ensure ongoing collaborative partnerships with key stakeholders (see Box 4 for a fuller explanation of Communities of Practice).

This project tracked the implementation of the standards for a period of 12 months although, because children entered the project over a three-month period, the actual project spanned 15 months. The research team included three researchers from the Faculty of Social Work, University of

Box 4. What is a Community of Practice?

Developing a Community of Practice (CoP) for a complex social and medical phenomenon such as FASD warrants some explanation. The construct of a CoP emerges primarily from the discipline of education, suggesting collaborative practice that attends to socio-cultural dimensions of the environment while appreciating diversity and differing needs of children (Matusov, DePalma, & Drye, 2007). Zorfass and Rivero (2005) noted that collaboration is a key construct in communities of practice. Collaboration includes paying attention to interactions within environments, observing, and becoming aware of practices that work. Thompson (2007) noted how collaboration through peer interactions in classrooms facilitated learning and developing leadership skills to respond to the needs of children with disabilities. Standal and Jespersen (2008) identified the need for a feedback loop for rehabilitation professionals by individuals with disabilities who are trying to "make sense" of their situations. The concept that individuals can offer information to support their own learning needs is critical to what works best.

In searching the terms *community of practice* and *child welfare*, it is clear that there is little exploration of this concept beyond the field of education. Thus, the application of the construct of a CoP to child welfare practice is new. Still, child welfare practices such as collaborative care, attention to socio-cultural issues, and responding to specific and differing needs of individuals suggest that elements of CoP are inherent, and that CoP should be a viable systemic response to the needs of complex populations such as children with FASD.

A CoP represents a group of professionals, informally bound to one another through exposure to a common class of problems and common pursuit of solutions. CoPs are associated with knowledge management as a way of developing social capital, nurturing new knowledge, stimulating innovation, and sharing knowledge. CoPs knit people together with peers, and their outputs include leading practices, guidelines/standards, knowledge repositories, problem and solution discussions, and common use of tools, processes, and strategies.

continued ▶

The CoP for the FASD Study

The FASD CoP was formed to focus on improving outcomes for children and youth with FASD or suspected FASD, requiring intensive interventions beyond regular caseload practice time allotments and more face-to-face contact. These children generally have permanent guardianship status, have been in long-term foster care placements, and have limited to no contact with their families of origin.

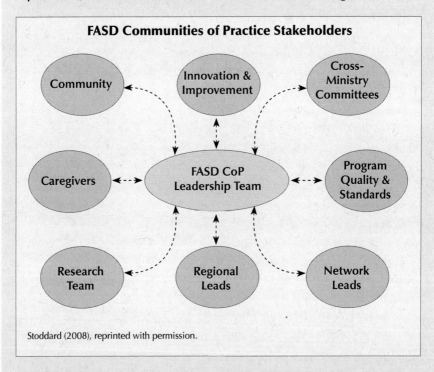

Stoddard (2008), reprinted with permission.

The CoP has developed a charter to guide the practice of professionals involved in responding to the needs of children involved in the project. It states:

The purpose/mission of the FASD Community of Practice is to bring together multiple stakeholders who share a passion for improving outcomes for children and youth diagnosed with or suspected of having FASD. The community will collaboratively implement promising practices in FASD

continued ▶

CHAPTER 9: FASD Communities of Practice in Alberta

and evaluate their impact. The community will deepen their understanding and build expertise in the area of FASD by sharing experiences, learning best practices, testing new ideas and acting on the new knowledge created. By interacting on an ongoing basis, the community will develop a shared language and understanding regarding prenatal alcohol exposure that will result in improved service delivery, improved diagnostic opportunities, and intervention for those children, youth, adults and families already affected. (FASD CoP Team, FASD Community of Practice Charter, 2009, p. 4)

The following figure shows the process and goals of the FASD CoP.

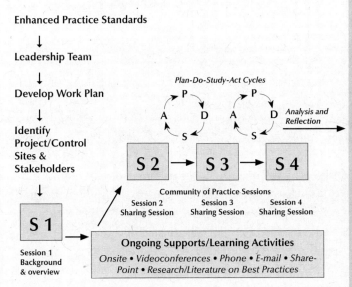

Modified from 2002 Institute for Healthcare Improvement. Stoddard (2008), reprinted with permission.

Calgary (Dorothy Badry, William Pelech, and Bruce MacLaurin), as well as six part-time research assistants (one university-based research assistant, and five regional research assistants).

RESULTS

Qualitative Findings

Focus groups with caseworkers and foster parents regarding their experience of working with the FASD practice standards within the context of a CoP were held midway through the project and close to the end of the project. At the time of writing, the midway focus groups have been completed and analyzed. Although findings at this stage of the research are preliminary, key themes emerged from the first series of focus groups with foster parents and caseworkers that are important to highlight. Key themes focus on the importance of communication, as fostered by increased contact between the caseworkers and children. Increased contact with children by caseworkers has been interpreted by foster parents as contributing to a deeper sense of being part of a team for the child or children in their home. Further, the appreciation of the needs of foster parents and their commitment to the children in their care has grown, and there has been an increased acknowledgement of the burden that is placed on foster caregivers who care for children with FASD. The opportunity to have regular training and case conferences has also fostered better communication and assisted rural foster parents to feel less isolated. One caseworker said involvement in this project made it easier for foster parents to share their struggles with caseworkers. One example of the deepening understanding of the experience of long-term foster parents is highlighted in the following quote from a caseworker: [the foster parent] "has psychologically adopted the child and is the only parent the child has known."

The use of respite on a regular basis is considered to be an important construct in maintaining and supporting placements. Foster parents showed a trend toward decreased use of respite in the past and in this current study. Information from the focus groups has shed some light on the concerns associated with respite. When children with FASD go to respite care, it disrupts their routine and the structure of their lives. Although the opportunity for respite is important for foster parents, the foster parents noted that children in their care struggle with their readjustment to their foster home after respite, and this can be disruptive to their home life. This may indeed contribute to less use of respite, as children who go to respite need to "recover" from this experience. One foster parent reported that respite providers often have more resources and opportunities to engage children in activities that do not typically take place in their homes. Thus, when the children return to their foster homes, they are sometimes upset that they cannot engage in these activities and, at times, this can be a source of conflict.

Shifting perceptions of the casework needs of children with FASD

> He's done nothing he is supposed to and [his worker] said when he turns 18 we are [closing his file]. Then you remember he has an organic brain disability – a reminder... it just kind of jerked [me] back and say, let's start over – that is good...Using hand over hand is necessary. If you let go of his hand he will fall.

This quote is reflective of a shift in practice, where the caseworker had a moment of insight and recognized that a particular response such as *cutting kids off* who were viewed as non-compliant requires some re-thinking. This awareness was a direct result of the training offered on FASD in the region, training that helped to shift the perceptions and thinking of the worker about decisions made in relation to the needs of children. In a similar fashion, another caseworker stated,

> Let's stop setting youth up for things they can't do ... [In] thinking about some of the decisions that were made for children who have FASD ... what were we thinking?... we kept running down [a] futile road with this kid ... when you know better ... we do not ask them to do something they are incapable of doing. You are not going to put a plan in place that isn't going to work ... and waste energy and resources.

These resources are monetary and related to time and hours of effort put into casework that may be going in a direction that will not work for a youth with FASD. These brief examples highlight the benefits of FASD-specific training, the insights gathered through dialogue and awareness developed in training, and a deeper connection to training, including the translation of knowledge to practice.

Quantitative Findings

An important aspect of an inquiry that examines the impact of any practice intervention is the gauging of the extent to which the proposed intervention has actually been implemented. In the case of this inquiry, the assessment of the extent of compliance with the practice standards is essential. It is also important to note that this project was underway at the point of writing this chapter. Summarized below are interim findings relating to 1) compliance, and 2) early trends in risk behaviours.

Compliance

Child assessment. As it is impractical to summarize all of the standards and aspects of compliance that were examined, we will summarize the major elements contained in the standards. The standards provided for comprehensive assessments, including family, social, medical, cognitive-behavioural, psychiatric and neuro-psychological assessments. Family and social assessments were completed or in progress in 25.9% (24 of 93) of cases, and were missing or deemed not applicable in 65.6% (61 of 93) of cases. At the time of reporting, 67% (67 out of 100) of children had completed medical assessments, and 22% were in progress (22 out of 100). Also, 71.2% (69 out of 97) of children had cognitive behavioural assessments completed (55.7%) or in progress (15.5%). The rates of completed psychiatric assessments were lower than the above assessments, where 43.2% (42 of 97) of psychiatric assessments were completed or in progress, while psychiatric assessments were missing or incomplete in 56.7% (55 of 97) of cases. Impressively, at the time of reporting, nearly half (48.5% or 49 of 101) of children included in this project had neuro-psychological assessments completed or in progress.

Concurrent plans and conferences. Evidence of service plan completion was present in case files for over 90% (77 of 85) of the children. Five other standards were outlined for concurrent plan development. First, concurrent plans were to reflect the parents' assessed strengths and weaknesses in terms of the special needs of children with FASD. Of the 97 case files reviewed, approximately half (53.2%) incorporated this assessment in the concurrent plan. Perhaps indicative of the relevance or appropriateness of the two remaining criteria, nearly all concurrent plans addressed placement and permanency planning issues (90 or 92.8%), while few provided evidence of addressing of family planning issues (20 or 31.2%). Approximately half (44 or 53.7%) of the files reviewed reflected the family visitation plan in the concurrent plan.

This standard required that concurrent plans be reviewed through a formal conferencing process at least twice per year. Over 8 to 10 months, it would be expected that one or two concurrent plan reviews would have been completed in order to meet this standard. This standard seemed to have been met in a majority of cases, in that for over three-quarters of the cases (77.4%) at least one concurrent plan review had been completed.

Family visitation planning. There was also a standard requiring that case managers prepare family visitation checklists and family visitation plans for all children in care prior to any visits occurring with natural family and significant others. Less than half (45 of 96 or 46.9%) of the case files reviewed included completed family visitation plans. Accordingly, a somewhat smaller proportion—43.9% (43 of 98)—included completed checklists.

Caseworker contact with child and caregiver. The practice standards require monthly face-to-face caseworker contact with the child and caregiver. At this point in the project, of the 103 case files in the four study regions, only 12 (11.7%) met the standard of a minimum of one contact per month with the child (see Figure 1). However, an examination of the mean contacts over the first seven months of the project suggests that one reason that the caseworkers did not strictly meet this standard might be the impact of holidays over the summer months. When the distribution of monthly contacts was considered, over half or 56.3% (58 out of 103) of the children in the project were visited by caseworkers at least once per month in 5 of the 7 months from April to October 2009. Tracking all worker contacts, including contacts by caseworkers and foster home workers, there was a trend where after an increase in contacts during April and May 2009, worker contacts decreased, reaching a low in August of 2.4 mean contacts. Besides vacations, staff attrition, hiring freezes, and budgetary constraints might have played a role in decreasing contacts.

Respite. Another major pillar of the practice standards was the provision of 48 hours per month of respite for caregivers in foster homes. Among the 43 cases reporting respite hours, we noted that less than

Figure 1. Mean number of caseworker face-to-face contacts with children.

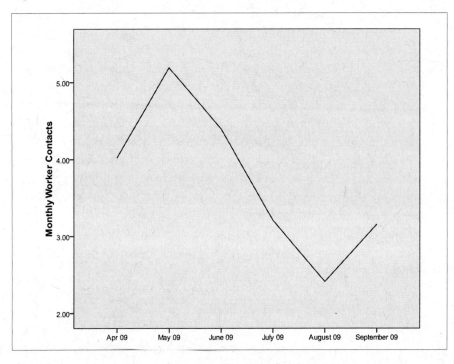

half (21 or 48.8%) met the strict standard for a minimum of 48 hours of respite. The overall monthly average respite hours provided to foster homes in the four study regions was 51.64 hours, which exceeds the standard of 48 hours per month. However, as Figure 2 indicates, after a dramatic increase in provision of respite early in the project, reaching its maximum in July 2009, use of respite hours declined sharply in August and September 2009.

Early trends in risk behaviours

Three categories of outcome variables were measured, including indicators of: a) risk behaviours: occurrences of unauthorized absences (AWOLs), substance abuse, criminal behaviour, inappropriate sexual behaviour, and acting out; b) school-related behaviour: school absences and ratings of the quality of interactions at school; and c) caregiver-related variables: ratings of interactions at home, caregiver strain, and placement

Figure 2. Mean number of monthly respite hours for foster families.

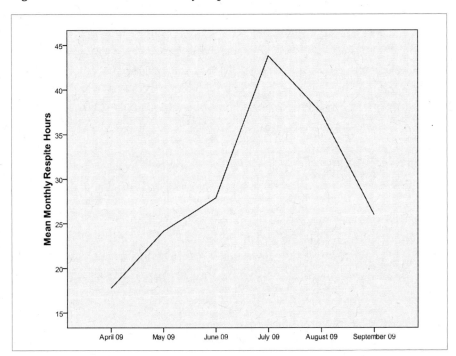

satisfaction. Given that data collection in the comparison group was delayed, and insufficient data was provided before 30 September, no data for the comparison group is presented here and no comparative analysis is available at this time.

Risk behaviours. There was a clear downward trend in mean occurrences of unauthorized absences, although this finding must be considered cautiously as there was a wide distribution of occurrences between cases. A different pattern arises for occurrences of substance abuse, criminal behaviour, and inappropriate sexual behaviour. For these three indicators, there were relatively few occurrences during this period and a general increase in mean occurrences, particularly over the summer months. There was a general decrease in the mean of acting out behaviour reported over this period. Acting out behaviour includes aggressive behaviours such as hitting, pushing, shoving, throwing objects, or kicking that is directed by the child toward others. In terms of overall risk behaviour, there was a general decrease in the mean number of risk behaviours during the first six months of the implementation of the interventions (see Figure 3).

School absences and interactions. Absences from school were recorded for unexcused absences and absences due to illness. In general, mean school absences show a pattern of increase followed by some decrease in September. Caregivers were also asked to report on a five-point scale the child's quality of interactions at school. At the time of reporting, there was a general increase in rating by caregivers during this period (see Figure 4).

Caregivers' ratings of interactions at home, placement satisfaction & strain. Caregivers were asked to report on a five-point scale the quality of interactions occurring with their child at home. There was a general increase in these caregiver ratings during this period (see Figure 5).

Caregivers were also asked to rate their satisfaction with the overall situation concerning the placement of their child in their home each day on a five-point scale. Caregivers' ratings mirror their ratings of the

Figure 3. Mean number of all risk behaviours of children by month.

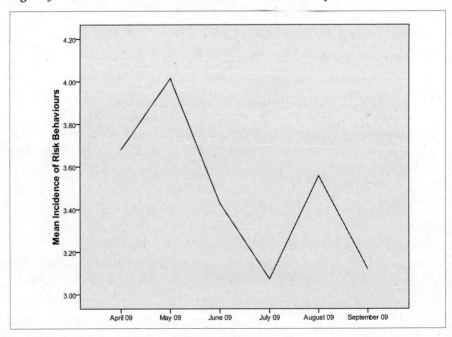

Figure 4. Caregiver's mean ratings of child's quality of interactions at school.

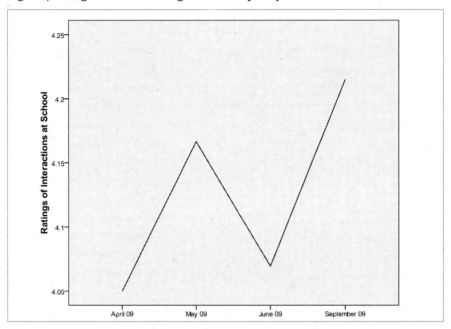

Figure 5. Caregiver's ratings of child's interactions at home.

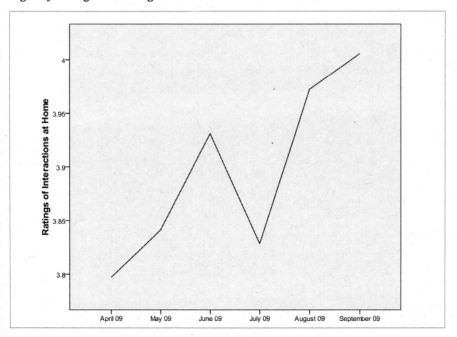

quality of interactions at home, with general improvement from *satisfied* towards *very satisfied* during this period. As above, the overall mean ratings showed a slight decrease for the month of June with a return to rising satisfaction for subsequent months (see Figure 6).

Caregivers were asked to complete a self-report measure of strain. The Caregiver Strain Questionnaire (Brannan, Heflinger, & Bickman, 1997) is a 21-item scale intended to assess perceived strain experienced by caregivers. Each item is rated on a Likert scale from 1=*not at all* to 5=*very much*, with a total maximum score of 105. All items are positively scored such that the higher the score the higher the perceived strain. Caregiver strain appeared to initially increase from May to June and then declined through July and August, perhaps indicative of the impact of vacation time for caregivers. Reported strain by caregivers increased in September, coinciding with the child's return to school (see Figure 7).

In sum, similar to the findings of the original pilot study in 2005, early findings related to risk behaviours, interactions at home, and caregiver

Figure 6. Mean caregiver ratings of placement satisfaction.

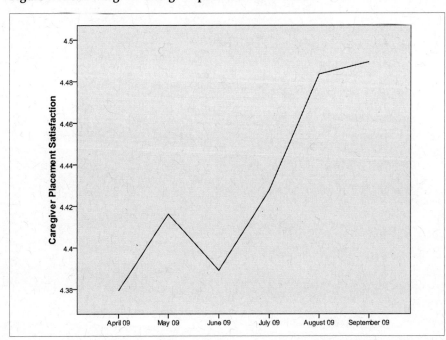

Figure 7. Mean caregiver ratings of perceived strain.

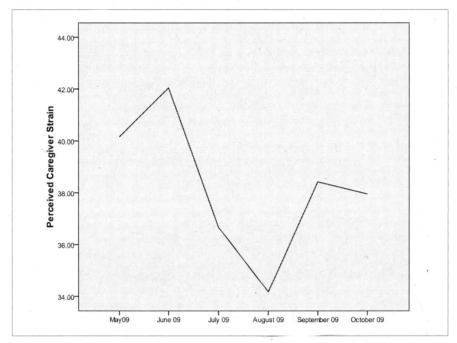

satisfaction are promising. These might be especially promising given that there was a challenging practice environment during the project: budget constraints, hiring freezes, and staff attrition. These factors might have influenced the less than optimal compliance with the practice standards. On the other hand, as noted by project staff at a debriefing meeting, the various challenges created obstacles for full compliance with the practice standards but implementation of the standards has resulted in more supports than were offered prior to the project.

CONCLUSION

This research project, the FASD CoP, was the result of a series of projects and sources of support that span several years involving partners who sincerely care about better outcomes for children in care with FASD. These projects arose from an understanding that many children with FASD are cared for by foster families or kinship care families, since they have high needs for protection due to the problems inherent in their families of origin, including substance abuse, addiction, and trauma-filled lives. From this understanding emerged an appreciation that children with FASD have complex needs throughout their lifespan, and that supporting and mediating these challenges in early life with solid interventions would be beneficial to them and lead to positive outcomes in their lives.

Effective intervention for this high needs population is complicated by the social phenomenon of FASD. Because FASD is preventable, it is often met with moral judgment, shame to family members, and blaming of birth mothers. Such reactions do not fully take into account the complex set of difficulties—such as abuse and trauma—that lead to women engaging in alcohol misuse while they are pregnant. An understanding of the social phenomenon of FASD is essential to a fuller understanding of FASD as a disability. Both can influence positive service responses to children with FASD and their families.

Although children with FASD in care present many challenges to the child welfare system, they also present many opportunities to the professional community to develop models of excellence and best practices that respond to their physical, spiritual, and emotional needs. Involvement in this project resulted in some steps toward this goal. Appreciating what it takes to be a long-term foster parent of a child or youth with FASD is one such step. Having more contact with children, and thus more contact with foster parents who feel better connected and a greater sense of team, is another.

We believe it is important to develop models of practice that respond to the complex needs of children with FASD through innovations emerging from wisdom and experience. By developing a Community of Practice for children and families struggling with FASD we are discovering that focused efforts of this nature have a positive impact on children, caseworkers, and foster caregivers. The FASD Community of Practice will serve to advance knowledge relating to practice for children with FASD through leading edge research.

ACKNOWLEDGEMENTS

This project was funded by The Alberta Centre for Child, Family and Community Research (ACCFCR) and their support of this work was deeply appreciated. The FASD Community of Practice was a collaborative effort between the University of Calgary, Faculty of Social Work, and partners working under the broad umbrella of the Alberta Ministry of Children and Youth Services working in teams and units identified below. A collaborative partnership made this work possible with all involved having a common interest in the well-being of children and youth in Alberta. Dr. Dorothy Badry and Dr. William Pelech (co-principal investigators) would like to thank, in particular, the following individuals working for the Government of Alberta Children and Youth Services as contributors: Sandra Stoddard (senior manager, Innovation and Improvement Research and Innovation Branch); Denise Milne (senior manager, FASD/Children's Mental Health/Community Partnerships); Larry Gazzola and Eoin Rouine (Innovation and Improvement Unit, Research and Innovation); Dude Johnson, Darla Yanchuk, Shawn Miller, Tiara Samson, Julie Mann, and Mark Weninger (CoP research assistants); caseworkers, supervisors and managers, and staff of Regions 1, 6, 7, 9 and 10 of Children and Youth Services and The Alberta FASD Cross Ministry Committee for all their support. Other contributors include Donna Debolt, project lead consultant and FASD expert, offering training and consultation throughout project; and Gabrielle Daoust, lead research assistant with the FASD CoP for the University of Calgary, Faculty of Social Work.

REFERENCES

Andrew, G. (2010). Diagnosis of FASD: An overview. In E. Riley, S. Clarren, J. Weinberg, & E. Jonsson (Eds.), *Fetal Alcohol Spectrum Disorder: Clinical features and treatment* (pp. 127–148). Weinhem, Germany: Wiley-VCH.

Astley, S. J. (2004). *Diagnostic guide for Fetal Alcohol Spectrum Disorder: The 4-Digit Diagnostic Code* (3rd ed.). University of Washington, Seattle. Available from http://depts.washington.edu/fasdpn.

Astley, S. J. (2010). Profile of the first 1,400 patients receiving diagnostic evaluations for fetal alcohol spectrum disorder at the Washington State fetal alcohol spectrum disorder diagnostic and prevention network. *Canadian Journal of Clinical Pharmacology, 17*(1), 132–164.

Astley, S. J., & Clarren, S. K. (2000). Diagnosing the full spectrum of fetal alcohol exposed individuals: Introducing the 4-digit diagnostic code. *Alcohol, 35*(4), 400–410.

Badry, D. (2009). Fetal Alcohol Spectrum Disorder Standards: Supporting children in the care of children's services. *First Peoples Child & Family Review, 4*(1), 47–56.

Badry, D., Pelech, W., & Norman, D. (2005). *Fetal Alcohol Spectrum Disorder practice standards evaluation project final report.* Centre for Social Work Research & Development, Faculty of Social Work, University of Calgary. Also available from http://www.fasdconnections.ca/id112.htm.

Brannan, A. M., Heflinger, C. A., & Bickman, L. (1997). The Caregiver Strain Questionnaire: Measuring the impact of living with a child with serious emotional disturbance. *Journal of Emotional and Behavioral Disorders, 5*(4), 212–222.

Brown, J. D., & Rodger, S. (2009). Children with disabilities: Problems faced by foster parents. *Children and Youth Services Review, 31*(1), 40–46.

CanFASD Northwest. (n.d.). *Network action teams.* Retrieved from http://www.canfasd.ca/networkActionTeams/overview.aspx.

Carmichael Olson, H., Oti, R., Gelo, J., & Beck, S. (2009). "Family matters": Fetal Alcohol Spectrum Disorders and the family. *Developmental Disabilities Research Reviews, 15*, 235–249.

Chudley, A. E., Conry, J., Cook, J. L., Loock, C., Rosales, T., & LeBlanc, N. (2005). Fetal alcohol spectrum disorder: Canadian guidelines for diagnosis. *Canadian Medical Association Journal, 172* (5 supplement), 1-21.

FASD CoP Team. (2009). *FASD Community of Practice Charter.* Edmonton, AB: Children and Youth Services, Government of Alberta.

Fuchs, D., Burnside, L., DeRiviere, L., Brownell, M., Marchenski, S., Mudry, A., & Dahl, M. (2009). *The economic impact of children in care with FASD and parental alcohol issues Phase II: Costs and service utilization of health care, special education, and child care.* Available from Canadian Child Welfare Research Portal: http://www.cecw-cepb.ca/.

Fuchs, D., Burnside, L., Marchenski, S., & Mudry, A. (2009). Children with FASD involved with the Manitoba child welfare system: The need for passionate action. In S. McKay, D. Fuchs, & I. Brown (Eds.), *Passion for action in child and family services: Voices from the prairies* (pp. 185–206). Regina, SK: Canadian Plains Research Center.

Habbick, B. F., Nanson, J. L., Snyder, R. E., Casey, R. E., & Schulman, A. L. (1996). Foetal alcohol syndrome in Saskatchewan: Unchanged incidence in a 20-year period. *Canadian Journal of Public Health, 87*(3), 204–207.

Jones K. L., & Smith, D. W. (1973). Recognition of the fetal alcohol syndrome in early infancy. *Lancet, 302*(7836), 999–1001.

Jones, K. L., Smith, D. W., Ulleland, C.N., & Streissguth, A. P. (1973). Pattern of malformations in offspring of chronic alcoholic mothers. *Lancet,* 1(7815), 1267–1271.

Koponen, A., Kalland, M., & Autti-Rämö, I. (2009). Caregiving environment and socio-emotional development of foster-placed FASD-children. *Children and Youth Services Review, 31*(9) 1049–1056.

Matusov, E., DePalma, R., & Drye, S. (2007). Whose development? Salvaging the concept of development within a sociocultural approach to education. *Educational Theory, 57*(4), 403–421.

Romney, S. C., Litrownik, A. J., Newton, R. R., & Lau, A. (2006). The relationship between child disability and living arrangement in child welfare. *Child Welfare, 85*(6), 965–984.

Standal, O. F., & Jespersen, E. (2008). Peers as resources for learning: A situated learning approach to adapted physical activity in rehabilitation. *Adapted Physical Activity Quarterly, 25*(3), 208–227.

Stoddard, S. (2008). FASD Community of Practice Stakeholders [chart]. *FASD Community of Practice Charter.* Edmonton, AB: Children and Youth Services, Government of Alberta.

Streissguth, A. P. (1997). *Fetal Alcohol Syndrome: A guide for families and communities.* Baltimore: Paul H. Brookes Publishing Co.

Streissguth, A. P., Bookstein, F. L., Barr, H. M., Press, S., & Sampson, P. D. (1998). A Fetal Alcohol Behavior Scale. *Alcoholism: Clinical and Experimental Research, 22*(2), 325–333.

Streissguth, A. P., & Kanter, J. (Eds.). (1997). *The challenge of Fetal Alcohol Syndrome: Overcoming secondary disabilities.* Seattle, WA: University of Washington Press.

Streissguth, A. P., & O'Malley, K. (2001). Neuropsychiatric implications and long-term consequences of fetal alcohol spectrum disorders. Retrieved from *MEDLINE* ISSN: 1084-3612.

Thompson, S. A. (2007). A community just for practice: A case of an inclusive/special education course. *Canadian Journal of Education, 30*(1), 171–192.

Twigg, R. (2009). Passion for those who care: What foster carers need. In S. McKay, D. Fuchs, & I. Brown, (Eds.), *Passion for action in child and family services: Voices from the Prairies* (pp. 165–184). Regina, SK: Canadian Plains Research Center.

Vig, S., Chinitz, S., & Shulman, L. (2005). Young children in foster care: Multiple vulnerabilities and complex service needs. *Infants & Young Children, 18*(2), 147–160.

Zorfass, J., & Rivero, H. K. (2005). Collaboration is key: How a community of practice promotes technology integration. *Journal of Special Education Technology, 20*(3), 51–60.

APPENDIX. Acronyms and Links

Acronyms of Agencies and Key Terms

ACYS – Alberta Children and Youth Services

CFSA – Children and Family Services Authority

CYIM – Child and Youth Information Module (electronic information system for children and youth in care and/or involved with Alberta Children and Youth Services)

FAS – Fetal Alcohol Syndrome

FASD – Fetal Alcohol Spectrum Disorder

FASD CoP – Fetal Alcohol Spectrum Disorder Community of Practice

PAE – Prenatal Alcohol Exposure

PBCL-36 – Personal Behavior Checklist

PGO – Permanent Guardianship Order

TGO – Temporary Guardianship Order

Links

Alberta Centre for Child, Family and Community Research (ACCFCR) – Project Funder: www.research4children.com/

Alberta FASD Service Networks: www.fasd-cmc.alberta.ca/fasd-service-networks/

Canadian Diagnostic Guidelines for FASD: www.cmaj.ca/cgi/content/full/172/5_suppl/S1

FASD 10-Year Strategic Plan: Government of Alberta: www.fasd-cmc.alberta.ca/uploads/1004/fasd10yrplanfinal86321.pdf

CHAPTER 10

Awakening the Caring Spirit for Children and Youth with FASD: Social and Economic Costs to the Child Welfare System in Manitoba

*Don Fuchs, Linda Burnside,
Shelagh Marchenski, and Andria Mudry*

Fetal Alcohol Spectrum Disorder (FASD) is a serious social and health issue for the child welfare, health care, and education sectors in North America with significant social and economic costs. Meeting the needs of children with disabilities creates substantial challenges for child welfare agencies. Fetal alcohol spectrum disorder is a preventable condition, since it is caused by maternal alcohol consumption during pregnancy.

Children with a diagnosis of FASD[1] present at child welfare agencies, as well as the health and education sectors, with an array of complex and

---

1   The term FASD refers to Fetal Alcohol Spectrum Disorder, which includes Fetal Alcohol Syndrome (FAS) and Fetal Alcohol Effects (FAE). The terms are often used interchangeably. Canadian guidelines for diagnosis were published in 2005 (Chudley, Conry, Cook, Loock, Rosales, & LeBlanc, 2005).

SUGGESTED CITATION: Fuchs, D., Burnside, L., Marchenski, S., & Mudry, A. (2012). Awakening the caring spirit for children and youth with FASD: Social and economic costs to the child welfare system in Manitoba. In D. Fuchs, S. McKay, & I. Brown (Eds.), *Awakening the Spirit: Moving Forward in Child Welfare: Voices from the Prairies* (pp. 213–232). Regina, SK: Canadian Plains Research Center.

variable needs as a consequence of a range of detrimental health outcomes. The syndrome includes physical characteristics, inhibited growth, and neurodevelopment problems, as well as behavioural and cognitive difficulties that are inconsistent with developmental levels. Given the significant proportion of FASD-affected children in care, as well as the nature of their needs, it is imperative that agencies, governments, and communities understand the service demands of this population.

The recognition that FASD is a contributing factor to large social and economic costs is helping to advance research on this important issue. The field of cost analysis in FASD research has expanded over the past two decades and there are wide variations of methodological approaches. However there is limited Canadian research that investigates the economic impact of FASD in the child welfare, health care, and education sectors. Moreover, the current body of research makes no meaningful link to the notion that substantial health and educational resources may be consumed each year by children with no FASD diagnosis, but who are affected by parents who misuse alcohol—both prenatal and postnatal misuse.

This chapter presents a brief review of the current literature on the economic impact of FASD. In addition it presents some of the major results of a study that provides an economic analysis of the provincial health care, education, and child care costs of children subjected to parental alcohol misuse in Manitoba (Fuchs, Burnside, Marchenski, Mudry, & DeRiviere, 2008). The research reported on in this chapter is the second phase of an empirical study that has already examined the cost of FASD to the child welfare system for children in care. This research builds on a larger body of empirical research on children in care with disabilities (Fuchs, Burnside, Marchenski, & Mudry, 2005; 2007; Fuchs, Burnside, Marchenski, Mudry, & DeRiviere, 2008). Finally, this chapter will discuss the implications of the study results for health and social service policy and programs aimed at providing services to children and families with disabilities.

CURRENT LITERATURE ON THE ECONOMIC IMPACT OF FASD

Over the past two decades, FASD has been increasingly recognized as having far-reaching and costly societal outcomes, including a significant impact on quality of life for affected people. Typically, economic cost

analysis in FASD research has taken three distinct, but related, perspectives based on point of view, including:
- A fiscal *or* government point of view, which includes the costs to the health care or education sectors;
- An individual *or* private point of view, often estimated using a human capital approach in order to calculate productivity effects for affected individuals, which usually refers to the community support structures available to the individual;
- A societal point of view—costs are estimated for various stakeholders in society, such as insurance companies, employers, parents, and relatives of affected children.

During the 1980s and 1990s, some of the earlier economic costing exercises calculated the typical lifetime cost for each child affected by FASD, which was found to be in the range of $596,000 in 1980 (Harwood & Napolitano, 1985) to $1.4-$1.5 million less than a decade later (Klug & Burd, 2003; Lupton, Burd, & Harwood, 2004; Manitoba Child and Youth Secretariat, 1997; Thanh & Jonsson, 2009). Frequently, studies calculate the annual aggregated costs to a province, state, or a nation incurred on behalf of FASD-affected individuals.

More recently, these figures have been revised to $2.0 million in 2002 U.S. dollars and $2.8 million in 2008 Canadian dollars. Fiscal costs comprise approximately 80% of total costs and the balance of 20% is allocated to productivity losses (Lupton et al., 2004; Thanh & Jonsson, 2009). The Harwood and Napolitano (1985) figure of $596,000 in 1980 has recently been adjusted to $2,774,400 in 2008 Canadian dollars (Thanh & Jonsson, 2009). It should be noted that some of the costs cited in this section are undiscounted and, thus, overstated, because they do not account for the monetary value of the time put in by service professional and others in providing services to persons with FASD. Nevertheless, the literature reveals that the fiscal and societal impact of FASD is strikingly large.

In Canada, a limited body of research investigates the economic impact of FASD primarily from a fiscal perspective. However, the most comprehensive Canadian-based study to date, which was conducted by Stade, Ungar, Stevens, Beyenne and Koren (2006), measures both societal and individual costs in 2003 dollars. The cross-country sample includes both FAS- and FAE-diagnosed individuals, thus not limiting the analysis to FAS only, as in other U.S. research. This study examined direct health care costs, prescription medications, special education and social services (respite and foster care), as well as direct costs incurred by the parents of the FAS/FAE-affected children. The impact of externalizing behaviours was also measured. Moreover, the study's costing exercise captured some indirect costs, such as missed workdays for parents, using a human capital approach.

Stade et al. (2006) study findings showed that medical and education costs comprise approximately 63% of total costs. Productivity losses make up 8.1% of the costs, though if the children had been over 21 years of age, these costs would be much higher. Both the severity of the disability and the age of the child were significant and direct predictors of costs. In fact, the costs double for children who have a severe disability compared to those children who are mildly affected. The costs for children aged 6-15 years were highest ($18,988 per annum) compared to the costs incurred by all other groups. Costs were also higher in Central and Western Canada compared to Eastern Canada. It remains unclear to what extent those variables were influenced by the availability of services. Based on a prevalence rate of 3 in 1,000 people, the estimated cost of FASD-affected children up to age 21 is $344,208,000 in 2003 Canadian dollars. The annual average cost for all children combined totaled $14,342.

In other research, Fuchs, Burnside, Marchenski, Mudry, and DeRiviere (2008) estimated fiscal costs in the Manitoba child welfare system for 400 FASD-affected permanent ward children in 2006. These children were in care for 146,000 days in 2006 at a total cost of $9.5 million or $23,760 per annum for each child ($65 per day for each child). Basic maintenance is the first level of funding for all children in care, with or without disabilities. Children in care may also be eligible for special rates as part of the per diem of care, to cover expenditures such as respite, therapy, home visits, as well as some medical and special needs expenses that are not intended to be covered by basic maintenance. A special rate can also include a service fee provided to the caregiver that compensates for the high care demands some children have.

In examining the total children in care population in 2006, on average, children in care required a special rate of $35 per day. However, the analysts found that permanent wards that are FASD-affected had incremental special rate expenditures averaging $43 per day (an average cost of $15,600 per annum for each child). Average expenditures of special needs also increase as the children age. More specifically, special needs costs averaged $10,038 for children aged 0-5 years. However, these costs increased by 80.6% to $18,130 for children aged 16 and older (Fuchs et al., 2008).

In an earlier study, Fuchs et al. (2007) found that children who received a diagnosis of FASD had come into the care of an agency for the first time at an earlier age (2.5 years) compared to children with no disability (3.6 years) and children with other disabilities (4.3 years). Their legal and placement histories confirmed that permanent wards with FASD spend approximately three quarters of their lives in the care of an agency, or about 15% more than any other permanent wards. Consequently, not only are the daily special rate costs higher for this group of children, but also those costs are extended over a longer period of time. Once children in this group come into care, they have a higher probability of becoming permanent wards and in a shorter time period compared to other children, due to their younger age at point of admission to care.

Fuchs et al.'s (2008) estimations of the costs of supporting FASD children in the child welfare system is the first of its kind in Canada. These are not as well-understood as are medical and education costs, as identified earlier by Hutson (2006) in her review of the cost of substance abuse in Canada. Hutson noted a lack of research in two areas that are critical to aggregating accurate costs incurred by the FASD population: the child welfare system and the justice system. Recently, the National Center on Addiction and Substance Abuse at Columbia University (2009) found that the second largest share of federal public spending for children in the U.S. includes the child welfare system for foster care, independent living, and other related programs. These expenditures fall within a larger budget category, referred to as Child and Family Assistance. In fact, child welfare accounts for 3.1% of the total federal budget and 6.2% of state budgets spent on substance abuse and addiction.

Hutson (2006) has asserted that an estimated "50% of children in agency care in Alberta have FAS" and she concluded that FASD-affected children may very well be overrepresented within the child welfare system (Hutson, 2006). In Manitoba, Fuchs et al. (2005) found evidence of diagnosed or suspected FASD in 17% of the children in care in this province. Consequently, gathering accurate costs incurred on behalf of all children affected by prenatal maternal alcohol use in the child welfare system, including non-FASD children affected by parental alcohol misuse, is a critical phase in economic costing research around FASD.

More recently, health analysts in Alberta have estimated two types of aggregated costs in 2008 dollars. The first calculation is the aggregated lifetime costs for FASD-affected children multiplied by the number of affected children born each year. Based on their methodology, the annual long-term costs of FASD range from $130 to $400 million per year in Alberta. In a second calculation, the analysts used an FASD cost calculator developed by colleagues in North Dakota in order to estimate the annual short-term economic cost, which ranged from $48 to $143 million per year in 2008 Canadian dollars. This calculation estimates the annual costs incurred by people who are currently affected by FASD. Though these are rough estimates at best, the study effectively affirms the urgent need for primary prevention strategies in this country (Thanh & Jonsson, 2009).

It should be noted that there are currently no accurate national statistics on the rates of FASD in Canada. However, the incidence has been estimated at 1 to 6 in 1,000 live births (Stade et al., 2006), and women give birth to approximately 3,000-4,000 FASD-affected babies each year in Canada (Hutson, 2006; Thanh & Jonsson, 2009). Moreover, the incidence of FAS is estimated at 1 case in 100 live births, which is thought to be higher than in the U.S. (Stade et al., 2006; Lupton et al., 2004). Two Manitoba studies are noted. Square (1997) estimated the population prevalence in a Manitoba First Nations community to be 55-101 per 1,000 and Williams, Odaibo, and McGee (1999) reported an incidence of 7.2 per 1,000 live births in northeastern Manitoba. In considering these estimates, it is important to remember that the complexity of diagnosis contributes to the delay or even omission of diagnosis (Chudley, Conry, Cook, Loock, Rosales, & LeBlanc, 2005), and prevalence is often determined by diagnostic thresholds (Klug & Burd, 2003).

These cost studies produce a wide variation in estimates. Economic estimates of FASD are highly dependent on a number of study-specific factors (Lupton et al., 2004; Thanh & Jonsson, 2009), including:

- the selected point of view: fiscal, individual, and societal
- time horizon of the analysis (birth to age 18 or older)
- assumed prevalence rates in a region, as well as population growth
- a country's health and social welfare system
- the method by which the cost of service utilization is calculated; for example, in the Canadian health care system, average costs per weighted case are frequently used (Finlayson, Reimer, Dahl, Stargardter, & McGowan, 2009)
- adjusting factors, such as regional inflation rates, net present value calculations, and discount rates which are used to take into consideration the time value of money when conducting economic costing analysis over a period of time
- some analysts have considered the discounted lifetime cost per birth cohort (Lupton, Burd, & Harwood, 2004)

Consequently, on the basis of a limited literature, the Canadian costs range from $344.2 million annually for FASD-affected children ages 1-21 (Stade et al., 2006) or $3-$4 billion per annum if the costs are considered to age 65 (Hutson, 2006), as well as $600 billion over a lifetime for all children currently affected by FASD in Canada. It is sometimes argued that the latter estimate exceeds the national debt (Hutson, 2006; McLean, 2000).

Though there are significant variations in the estimates, these costing exercises are nonetheless useful in that they have informed the knowledge gap around this significant health and social issue. Many costs are thought to be the tip of the iceberg in terms of the true costs. Several studies emphasize a cost avoidance perspective by identifying monetary savings to government for every case of FASD prevented. As a result of the substantial estimations of the cost of care, a common theme in the literature is the need for primary prevention. Primary prevention costs are thought to be lower than the discounted lifetime cost for an alcohol-affected child (Lupton et al., 2004; Klug & Burd, 2003; Stade et al., 2006; Fuchs et al., 2007; 2008). An emphasis on primary prevention would effectively expand the public policy approach to FASD in Canada, as well as creating efficiencies in the allocation of scarce fiscal resources.

Summarizing the literature, we conclude that closing the gap in knowledge around the economic costs of FASD-affected individuals can help to make better public policy, which should focus in part on preventing children from being born with significant disabilities in future. Moreover, from a health policy perspective, there is wide social and political interest in the cost of illness and health care in general. However, the current body of research makes no meaningful link to the notion that substantial health and educational resources may be consumed each year by children living with parents who misuse alcohol. The study which follows this section is a starting point only, but it will provide a more accurate picture of the utilization of resources in one provincial health care and education system (Manitoba). The study is important for addressing future programming in the area of children living in homes where problem drinking is a challenge.

The research focused on in this chapter has been built upon earlier studies of children with disabilities in the care of child and family service agencies in Manitoba, looking particularly at children with FASD. These earlier studies showed that one-third of the children in care of Manitoba's provincial child welfare system had disabilities, many of them related to parental alcohol misuse. Seventeen percent of all the children in care were affected by diagnosed or suspected FASD. Approximately 34% of children in care with disabilities, or 11% of all children in care in Manitoba, had diagnosed FASD. Of the 1,403 children in care with an intellectual disability, 46% had diagnosed FASD (Fuchs et al., 2005).

The objective of this current study reported on in this paper was to compare 2006 provincial health care costs for five groups of children in Manitoba, four of which were children affected by parental alcohol misuse, including three groups of children in care and two groups of FASD-affected children. The fifth group was a sample of children for whom parental alcohol misuse had not been identified, and who were not in child welfare care, used as a comparison population.

The study described in this chapter sought to examine the financial costs of children in care with parental alcohol issues (including FASD) in Manitoba. To gather information on the costs of services delivered outside of the child welfare system, it was necessary to determine what additional services were being provided to children who were either in care or who were involved with a child welfare agency, and at what cost those other services were being delivered.

METHODOLOGY

The researchers collected data from the data repository at the Manitoba Centre of Health Policy (MCHP). The Centre is a research centre of excellence that develops and maintains a comprehensive population-based data repository for the Province of Manitoba. The data found in the repository is derived from administrative records kept by different government departments to deliver health and social services. To meet the objectives of this study, several sample groups were identified using the child welfare database. The cost of services received by the children in the identified groups was calculated with the assistance of the data held by the MCHP and compared with the cost of services received by a comparative sample of the general population.

Child records across databases were linked using a unique consistent identifier which identified individual anonymized respondents across the various health, education, and child welfare service systems. The provincial Child and Family Services database and the population-based data repository at the Manitoba Centre for Health Policy were used to identify data for five population groups of children for the year 2006, which together totaled 6,324 children.

Of the five child populations studied, three general categories were identified: the first general category consisted of three groups of children in the care of provincial child welfare agencies, all of whom were affected by parental alcohol misuse. These three groups are collectively called the Children in Care (CIC) category:

a) Children in care with diagnosed FASD who were permanent wards of the crown; n=603 (CIC-FASD-PW);
b) Children without diagnosed FASD who were permanent wards of the crown and in care due to parental alcohol abuse; n=51 (CIC-PA-PW);
c) Children without diagnosed FASD who were not permanent wards of the crown but in care for some period in 2006 due to parental alcohol abuse; n=587 (CIC-PA).

The second general category consisted of children not in provincial child welfare care in 2006, but affected by parental alcohol misuse and diagnosed with FASD by the Clinic for Alcohol and Drug Exposed Children (CADEC) in Winnipeg:

d) Children with diagnosed FASD; n=119 (FASD-CADEC).

The third category was a sample of the general child population:

e) Children in the general population who were not identified as being affected by parental misuse of alcohol and who did not have an open child welfare file; n=4,964 (general population).

RESULTS

Comparison of Health Care Costs

Children affected by parental alcohol consumption, especially permanent wards with FASD, have higher hospitalization costs than the general population. Of the 6,273 children for whom hospitalization costs were tallied, the CIC-FASD and CIC-PA groups made up 20.9% of the total population. However, their hospitalization costs made up 41.1% of total expenditures.

Average hospitalization cost per capita for the CIC-FASD-PW group was more than three times higher than that of the general population group. The next most expensive group, the CIC-PA children, had an average hospitalization cost per capita more than twice that of the general population group. Girls affected by parental alcohol consumption incurred higher health care costs in mid-to-late adolescence. Females aged 16 and older had a significantly higher number of physician visits compared to males in all age groups, including the general population. This is likely due to female teens accessing physician services for gender-related reasons as they become sexually mature, such as birth control, pregnancy, potential sexually transmitted infections, and the effects of sexual abuse or assault.

The three main conditions causing hospitalization for the four groups of children affected by parental alcohol misuse (including FASD) were diseases of the digestive system, mental disorders, and diseases of the respiratory system. Only 2.9% of the children in the general population were hospitalized for a mental disorder, compared to 14.3% of the CIC-FASD-PW and 15% of the CIC-PA groups. The leading cause of hospitalization for the general population sample was diseases of the digestive system.

Children with FASD are prescribed nervous system drugs at a higher rate than the general population. Children with FASD, whether in care or not, were prescribed nervous system drugs at a higher rate (60%+) than the general population sample (20%). Nervous system drugs were increasingly prescribed to children with FASD as they age. Ritalin and other medications for Attention Deficit Hyperactivity Disorder (ADHD) accounted for a large share of these prescriptions, followed by medications for depression.

In examining the average costs of prescriptions per child and the percentage of children taking prescription medications by group, the CIC-FASD-PW children had the highest average total yearly expenditures on prescription drugs ($641), and also had the largest percentage of children taking prescription medication (74%).

Overall health care costs are much higher for children affected by parental alcohol misuse. Figure 1 illustrates the average costs per child in each group for hospitalizations, physician visits, and prescription drugs. The CIC-FASD-PW and the CIC-PA groups together make up the majority of the average total costs. Cost estimates for both these groups, as well as the FASD-CADEC group, were significantly different from the general population. The average total costs of the CIC-FASD-PW group were 3.5 times higher than the general population. Overall, each FASD-affected permanent ward incurred an additional $1001 in health care costs for 2006 compared to a child in the general population. The average costs

Figure 1. Average 2006 costs per child for hospitalizations, physician visits, and prescription drugs.

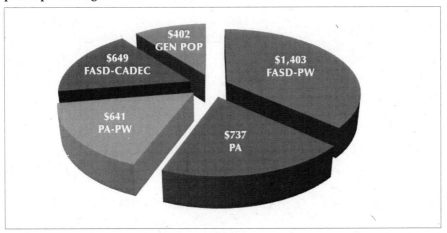

of children in care affected by parental alcohol (CIC-PA) were 1.8 times higher than children in the general population.

Children affected by parental alcohol consumption have more physician visits than the general population. Children in the CIC-FASD-PW and CIC-PA groups had a statistically significant higher number of physician visits than the general population group (Fuchs, Burnside, Di-Riviere et al. [2009], p. 43). This is not surprising, as the physician visits may be related to the abuse and neglect that brought them into child welfare care. Children in the four groups affected by parental alcohol misuse were more likely to visit a physician in 2006 than those in the general population. As noted earlier, higher numbers of CIC-FASD-PW females visited a doctor in 2006 compared to their male counterparts in all age categories.

DISCUSSION

The intent of the Economic Impact Study was to broaden our understanding of the costs associated with FASD and children affected by parental alcohol misuse to include costs of health care, special education, and subsidized child care services. It is widely recognized that children with a diagnosis of FASD present child welfare agencies, as well as the health and education sectors, with an array of complex and variable needs, as a consequence of a range of detrimental health outcomes. These observable facts are corroborated by the empirical findings in this study. FASD-affected children who are permanent wards used more services in all categories that were examined in 2006. The services they used are more costly compared to a random sample of children in the general population. Other U.S. studies have found that children in the care of child protective services have high service needs related to developmental issues, chronic health conditions, and special education (Casanueva, Cross, & Ringeisen, 2008; Ringeisen, Casanueva, Urato, & Cross, 2008).

Compared to the General Population group, the empirical evidence reveals a similar finding of higher costs and service utilization for the PA group of children for whom problematic parental drinking was an identified issue at a child welfare agency. In the categories of physician costs and hospitalizations, the findings revealed that FASD-PW children have the highest utilization and costs, followed by the PA group of children.

However, the FASD-CADEC group is second to the FASD-PW children concerning prescription medications and special education costs. Several of the differences in the estimates between the FASD-PW and PA groups of children are not statistically significant, which implies that many of the estimates did not yield true and reliable differences between these two groups of children.

This is an important finding, since a thesis of this research was that it is short-sighted to only investigate how FASD, the most extreme impact of parental alcohol abuse, affects children. Until the current study, there has been a significant research gap in costing the adverse health and education outcomes for children with no diagnosed FASD who are affected by their parents' misuse of alcohol. This analysis reveals an equally detrimental impact in some cost areas for those children without an FASD diagnosis, but for whom parental alcohol misuse is a risk factor that contributed to their being a child in care. FASD is but one identifiable outcome of prenatal substance abuse. Children who have been exposed to alcohol prenatally, as well as those who have been affected by parental alcohol abuse postnatally, may also be at risk of deleterious outcomes, even if they do not have FASD. Further, given that children with FASD were generally found by Fuchs et al. (2007) to be admitted to care mainly for reasons related to parental conditions or conduct (including substance abuse) and not related to the child's diagnosis of FASD, it is important to consider the impact of both prenatal and/or postnatal parental alcohol abuse on children.

Recent studies by Fuchs et al. examined the effect of FASD on trajectories of care (2007) and the cost of child welfare care (2008). Many of these children with FASD would have come into care with siblings who did not have a diagnosis of FASD yet were in the situation of needing protection from the same parental risk factors as the children with FASD. Additionally, children with a familial history of FASD may also come into care as a result of parental alcohol abuse. As a result of these common familial risks and subsequent admission to care that both children with FASD and those without may experience, it is becoming increasingly important to better understand the experiences of children who do not have FASD but who may have been affected by their parents' use of alcohol.

In the current study, FASD-PW and PA children have similar

estimates for several cost and utilization categories, but there are a few important exceptions. The PA group of children had prescribed medications and costs that mirror the General Population group in contrast to the FASD-PW group. These lower estimates have a tendency to reduce the average total costs for the PA group of children. The other gap in costs is the special education category, which raised aggregated average costs in the FASD-CADEC group. Though there is evidence that the PA group of children have detrimental education outcomes (e.g., higher retention and lower marks compared to the General Population group), any special rate funding is largely allocated to FASD-affected children based on level of functioning. The PA group of children, though potentially requiring additional supports in school, may not be eligible for special services funding in the education system.

The estimates in this study are the tip of the iceberg. They underestimate the outcomes of FASD-affected children and those affected by parental alcohol misuse, since many related social services that are linked to the health and education sectors are excluded due to data limitations.

These outcomes raise the probability that alcohol-affected individuals will have reduced lifetime participation and employment rates in the labour market, as well as lower earnings. The fiscal impact of these educational outcomes is known to be a higher reliance on social services, including housing subsidies and income assistance, for the duration of their lives. Such costs are excluded from the current study, but it is known that children of problem drinkers may have a higher probability of experiencing detrimental outcomes in the labour market, for example, unemployment and lower wages (Balsa, 2008).

SPECIAL EDUCATION AND SUBSIDIZED CHILD CARE COSTS FOR MANITOBA CHILDREN AFFECTED BY PARENTAL ALCOHOL ABUSE

The long-term societal cost of parental alcohol misuse on children in Canada, especially the costs of providing care and education for children with Fetal Alcohol Spectrum Disorder (FASD) who are in the child welfare system, are largely unknown. This section of the chapter summarizes an analysis of the education and subsidized child care costs of children affected by parental alcohol misuse in Manitoba.

The objective of the education and child care costs portions of the study was to compare 2006 costs for education and subsidized child care for five groups of children in Manitoba, four of which were children affected by parental alcohol misuse, including three groups of children in care and two groups of FASD-affected children. The fifth group was a sample of children for whom parental alcohol misuse had not been identified, and who were not in child welfare care, used as a comparison population (Fuchs, Burnside, DeRiviere et al., 2009).

The study showed that the four groups of children affected by parental alcohol misuse, particularly those affected by FASD, were given more special education funding, had higher education costs, and had lower outcomes on a variety of educational success indicators compared to the general population. For example, they had a lower likelihood of completing a full set of credits in the first year of high school, were more likely to be held back a grade, had lower high school average marks, and had lower graduation rates. Children with FASD who were permanent wards had average per capita subsidized child care costs that were twice those of the general population.

Children affected by FASD incurred disproportionately high education costs. The average cost of education funding for the CIC-FASD-PW children was 3.4 times the cost for children in the general population group, and 2.7 times the cost for the FASD-CADEC children (Figure 1). The four groups of children affected by parental alcohol misuse made up 20.4% of the total number of children in the study who were enrolled in school; however, their aggregated costs made up 38.2% of the total education costs of the entire population of children in the study.

Children affected by FASD accessed special education funding at higher levels than the general population. The two groups of FASD-affected children received Levels 2 or 3 of special education funding at much higher rates than those of the CIC-PA, CIC-PA-PW, or the general population groups. Further graduation rates of provincial wards affected by FASD were much lower than the general population.

The percentage of permanent wards with FASD still enrolled in school after age 16 was lower than the percentage for the general population but higher than those affected by FASD who were not permanent wards. The graduation rates and number of credits in grade nine were lower for the

CIC-FASD-PW group compared to the general population.

Children affected by alcohol had lower marks and repeated grades more frequently than the general population. A comparative analysis of average high school marks showed that the four groups affected by parental alcohol misuse had lower marks over a variety of indicators compared to the general population, and were also held back a grade at much higher rates.

Average high school marks for the sample group members who were in high school between the academic years of 2000 to 2006 were significantly lower for the four groups affected by parental alcohol compared to the general population.

A very small number of the two FASD-affected groups were recorded to have written the standard Grade 12 examinations (combined Mathematics and Language Arts). Average marks for the two FASD groups were more than ten percent lower than the general population, although sample counts in the two FASD-affected groups were very low.

CHILD CARE COSTS

Subsidized child care costs for provincial wards with FASD were twice that of the general population. In Manitoba, government-subsidized child care is available for children in the care of child welfare agencies as well as families with special needs, such as those needing medical care or those with low family incomes. When the five population groups were compared, the two CIC groups with the greatest numbers of preschoolers and young children (CIC-FASD-PW and CIC-PA) showed the most frequent use of subsidized child care. The difference between the use of subsidized child care between the CIC-FASD-PW group and the general population was statistically significant.

The average cost of subsidized child care for a child in the CIC-FASD-PW group was $467 yearly, compared to $218 for a child in the general population group. Although the CIC-FASD-PW group made up 10.2% of children accessing subsidized child care, their aggregated costs made up 19.5% of the total costs of subsidized child care for the five populations in the study.

In addition, the study showed that children with FASD who are permanent wards had average per capita subsidized child care costs that were twice those of the general population.

SUMMARY OF THE OVERALL IMPLICATIONS

To summarize, in Phase 1 of the Economic Impact of Children in Care with FASD study, the fiscal costs in the Manitoba child welfare system were estimated for 400 FASD-affected permanent ward children in 2006. These children were in care for 146,000 days in 2006 at a total cost of $9.5 million or $23,760 per annum for each child ($65 per day), which far exceeds the fees covered by basic maintenance. Similar to the findings of the current Phase II study, the average special needs expenditure increased as the children aged (Fuchs et al., 2008).

Given the significant proportion of FASD-affected children in care, as well as the nature of their needs, it is imperative to understand the service demands of this population to agencies, governments, and communities. This study has furthered our understanding of the needs of children whose entry into care is related to parental alcohol misuse, but who do not have a diagnosis of FASD. A major shortcoming of past studies is the lack of emphasis on the intergenerational costs of parental alcohol misuse for children who do not have diagnosed FASD. The findings of this study lead to a conclusion that, not only should the additional information on the PA group of children help to support efforts in preventing FASD, but also parental alcohol use should be addressed at an earlier stage. Too many children with alcohol-abusing parents are ending up in care and suffering serious consequences in many domains of their lives.

CONCLUDING REMARKS

Over the past two decades, FASD is increasingly recognized as having far-reaching and costly societal outcomes. Though FASD is an important area of emphasis for economic costing exercises, it is only one specific consequence of alcohol abuse, which contributes uniquely to the fiscal costs. Until this study, much investigation was lacking on the far-reaching economic impacts when children without diagnosed FASD are adversely affected by problematic parental drinking. A particular strength of this study is the investigation of children in care with parental substance abuse issues, as well as FASD-affected children.

The findings reveal that the FASD-PW and PA groups of children account for the majority of the average total costs of health care, which include physician services, hospitalizations, and prescription medications.

Nervous system drugs, such as anti-psychotics and ADHD drugs, account for a large proportion of prescribed drugs to FASD-affected children, and to a surprisingly high number of PA children. Though there is evidence that the PA children have detrimental education outcomes (e.g., higher retention and lower marks compared to the General Population group), any special rate funding is largely allocated to FASD-affected children based on level of functioning. PA children, though potentially requiring additional supports in school, are not accessing special services at the same rate as the general population in the education system.

To conclude, closing the gap in knowledge around the economic costs of FASD-affected individuals can help to make better public policy, which partly focuses on preventing children from being born with significant FASD-related disabilities in the future. An emphasis on primary prevention would effectively expand the public policy approach to FASD in Canada, as well as creating efficiencies in the allocation of scarce resources. More recently, the costs of alcohol abuse to the federal, state, and local governments were estimated in the hundred of billions in the United States. However, for every fiscal dollar spent to address substance abuse, 95.6 cents is allocated to costs of providing service, for example, in the health care, justice, education, and child welfare sectors. Most of the costs incurred as a consequence of the social problem are potentially preventable, but only 1.9 cents of every dollar was allocated to prevention and early intervention strategies (Califano, 2009).

Moreover, from a health policy perspective, there is wide social and political interest in the cost of illness and health care in general. Until now, the current body of research has not identified that substantial health and educational resources might be consumed each year by children affected by their parents' misuse of alcohol even if they do not have a diagnosis of FASD. Phase I and II of the Economic Impact Study are a starting point only, but this research provides a more accurate picture of the utilization of resources in the Manitoba health care and education sectors, as well as other social services. This research clearly identifies the inordinate and growing economic and social costs of children who been affected by prenatal alcohol use. It is important for prioritizing and addressing future programming in the area of services to FASD-affected children, as well as confronting challenges faced by children affected by problematic parental drinking.

REFERENCES

Balsa, A. I. (2008). Parental problem drinking and adult children's labor market outcomes. *Journal of Human Resources, 43*(2), 454–86.

Califano, D. (2009). CASA* 2009 teen survey reveals: Teens likelier to get drunk, use marijuana, smoke cigarettes if they see parent drunk. New York: Newwire.

Casanueva, C. E., Cross, T. P., & Ringeisen, H. (2008). Developmental needs and individualized family service plans among infants and toddlers in the child welfare system. *Child Maltreatment, 13*(3), 245–258.

Chudley, A. E., Conry, J., Cook, J. L., Loock, C., Rosales, T., & LeBlanc, N. (2005). Fetal alcohol spectrum disorder: Canadian guidelines for diagnosis. *Canadian Medical Association Journal, 172* (5 supplement), 1-21.

Finlayson, G. S., Reimer, J., Dahl, M., Stargardter, M., & McGowan, K-L. (2009). *The direct cost of hospitalizations in Manitoba, 2005/6.* Winnipeg, MB: Manitoba Centre for Health Policy, March 2009.

Fuchs, D., Burnside, L., Marchenski, S., & Mudry, A. (2005). *Children with disabilities receiving services from child welfare agencies in Manitoba.* Ottawa: Centre of Excellence for Child Welfare. Available: www.cecw-cepb.ca/.

Fuchs, D., Burnside, L., Marchenski, S., & Mudry, A. (2007). *Children with FASD involved with the Manitoba child welfare system.* Ottawa: Centre of Excellence for Child Welfare. cecw-cepb.ca/files/file/en/FASD%20Final%20Report.pdf.

Fuchs, D., Burnside, L., Marchenski, S., Mudry, A., & DeRiviere, L. (2008). *Economic impact of children in care with FASD. Phase I: Cost of children in care with FASD in Manitoba.* Ottawa, ON: Centre of Excellence for Child Welfare.

Fuchs, D., Burnside, L., DeRiviere, L., Brownell, M., Marchenski, S., Mudry, A., & Dahl, M. (2009). *The Economic impact of children in care with FASD and parental alcohol issues. Phase II: Costs and service utilization of health care, special education, and child care.* Winnipeg, MB: Faculty of Social Work, University of Manitoba.

Harwood, J. H., & Napolitano, D. M. (1985). Economic implications of the Fetal Alcohol Syndrome. *Alcohol Health & Research World, 10*(1), 38–43.

Hutson, J. (2006). A prenatal perspective on the cost of substance abuse in Canada. *Journal of FAS International, 4*(e9), 1–4.

Klug, M. G., & Burd, L. (2003). Fetal alcohol syndrome: annual and cumulative cost savings. *Neurotoxicology Teratology, 25*(6), 763–765.

Lupton, C., Burd, L., & Harwood, R. (2004). Cost of Fetal Alcohol Spectrum Disorders. *American Journal of Medical Genetics* Part C (Seminar Medical Genetics), *127C*, 42–50.

Manitoba Child and Youth Secretariat. (1997). *Strategy considerations for developing services for children and youth*. Manitoba Children and Youth Secretariat, 1997.

McLean, C. (2000). The fetal alcohol crisis. Report Magazine, September 25, 2000.

Ringeisen, H., Casanueva, C. E., Urato, M., & Cross, T. P. (2008). Special health care needs among children in the child welfare system. *Pediatrics, 122*(1), 232–241.

Square, D. (1997). Fetal alcohol epidemic on Manitoba reserve. *Canadian Medical Association Journal, 157*(1), 59–60.

Stade, B., Ungar, W. J., Stevens, B., Beyenne, J., & Koren, G. (2006). The burden of prenatal exposure to alcohol: Measurement of cost. *Journal of FAS International, 4*(e5), 1–14.

Thanh, N. X., & Jonsson, E. (2009). Costs of Fetal Alcohol Spectrum Disorder in Alberta, Canada. *Canadian Journal of Clinical Pharmacology, 16*(1), e80–e90.

Williams, R. J., Odaibo, F. S., & McGee, J. M. (1999). Incidence of fetal alcohol syndrome in Northeastern Manitoba. *Canadian Journal of Public Health, 90*(3), 192–194.

CHAPTER 11

Awakening the Spirit of Caring by Creating a Community Response for Children with Special Needs: A Presentation of the Innovative Efforts of the Kinosao Sipi Minisowin Agency

Madeline Gamblin and Rachel Barber

INTRODUCTION

The disability rate in the Aboriginal Canadian population is 30%—more than twice that of the non-Aboriginal population (Human Resources and Skills Development Canada, 2009; Ng, 1996). Despite this disparity, disability services targeting Aboriginal populations are limited in number and scope, particularly when looking at services for Aboriginal children (Hanvey, 2002). The federal government funds the community-based Aboriginal Head Start (AHS) program, which aims to enhance healthy early child development and school readiness for Aboriginal children;

SUGGESTED CITATION: Gamblin, M., & Barber, R. (2012). Awakening the spirit of caring by creating a community response for children with special needs: A presentation of the innovative efforts of the Kinosao Sipi Minisowin Agency. In D. Fuchs, S. McKay, & I. Brown (Eds.), *Awakening the Spirit: Moving Forward in Child Welfare: Voices from the Prairies* (pp. 233–248). Regina, SK: Canadian Plains Research Center.

however, this program is intended for children 0-6 years of age, and is not structured to provide specialized long-term supports for children with disabilities (Health Canada, 2010). Individuals with disabilities who are 18 years of age and older living on reserve are able to access home support services through community health providers (Ducharme et al., 2007). However, there has been a major service vacuum for First Nations children (6-18 years) with disabilities residing on reserves. In order to address this unmet service need, the Kinosao Sipi Minisowin Agency Children's Special Services (KSCSS) project was established in the Norway House Cree Nation. It provides services to children with developmental and physical disabilities who live in the Norway House Cree Nation First Nations Community.

This chapter describes the KSCSS program, which was created as a community response to the perceived need for support services for children with special needs and their families within The Norway House Cree Nation Community. The challenges that led to the creation of the program and its beneficial outcomes are discussed. In addition, the chapter discusses the structural and resource issues that the community needed to address in creating a community response for providing services to meet the needs of children and youth with disabilities and their families in their home community. Finally, the chapter identifies some future directions for KSCSS and similar agencies in First Nations communities.

COMMUNITY BACKGROUND

Norway House Cree Nation (NHCN) is one of the largest First Nations in Manitoba. It has a combined on- and off-reserve population of approximately 7,045 people. The community has undertaken a significant number of social and economic development initiatives since 1994, and has developed a number of public resources within the community, including a hospital and personal care home, two schools, apartment buildings, public works facilities, a shopping mall, and a motel (Norway House Cree Nation, 2005). It has continued to expand the education, health, and social services available in the remote rural Northern community. One of the major agencies that have been developed to meet the needs of children and families is the Kinosao Sipi Minisowin Agency (KSMA). KSMA is mandated to provide child and family services to NHCN community members living on and off the reserve.

THE KINOSAO SIPI CHILDREN SPECIAL SERVICES PROGRAM

Mandate of the Program

In 2004, KSMA put in place a program called the Kinosao Sipi Children Special Services Program (KSCSS) to support families in caring for their children in a way that promotes family unity and community strength. This program is based on two fundamental principles:
- Children with disabilities or complex special needs are Norway House Cree Nation members and, as such, deserve to remain in their community; and
- Children with disabilities or complex special needs deserve access to appropriate therapy and therapeutic support services within their community (Ducharme et al., 2007).

Development of the Program

Before this program began, neither therapeutic services for children nor support for First Nations families caring for children with complex special needs were available on reserves in Canada. In Norway House First Nation, families of children with profound and multiple disabilities previously had four options available to them: place their child in institutional care, place their child into the care of Kinosao Sipi Minisowin Agency (KSMA), remain on reserve with no services, or relocate off-reserve to access services.

Typically, children with disabilities were automatically referred to KSMA, a child welfare provider, for services. Under its funding agreement with Indian and Northern Affairs Canada (INAC), KSMA received no funding for special services; however, members felt compelled to support the children and their families. The agency applied for, and received, a grant of $450,000 from the Norway House Cree Nation Master Implementation Agreement Trust Fund to develop and deliver the Kinosao Sipi Children's Special Services program (KSCSS) as a pilot program aimed at providing services for children with special needs on reserve. This KSCSS project was funded by the grant for a period of three years, concluding at the end of 2006.

In subsequent years, the funding of KSCSS was negotiated annually with KSMA, INAC, First Nation Inuit Health (FNIH), and the Province of

Manitoba under the purview of the Department of Family Services and Community Affairs. The KSMA funded the project at a reduced level of service from January 2007 to May 2008, while the province of Manitoba, INAC and FNIH provided funds to September 2008. INAC and FNIH made funding commitments for the 2009-2011 fiscal years, with the final year of maximum funding to conclude on March 31, 2011. Future funding is expected to be reviewed based on the constitutional responsibility of the provincial government to provide child and family services (Manitoba Family Services and Community Affairs, 2011b) and on the federal authorities' responsibility to fund services to First Nations children on reserve (Health Canada, 2007).

Establishing the benefits of the KSCSS program

In 2008, building upon the success of the KSCSS program, Norway House Cree Nation formed a Federal/Provincial Technical Working Group to discuss and evaluate the services provided through the KSCSS pilot project. Two of the main goals of this Working Group were to:

- Collect diagnostic information on the children who received services and determine whether those children would meet the provincial Children's Special Services eligibility criteria; and
- Compare those services against the service menu available through the provincial CSS program delivered by the Department of Family Services and Consumer Affairs (Manitoba Family Services and Community Affairs, 2011a).

The Federal/Provincial Technical Working Group Report was completed in March 2009. In its Observations and Analysis, the Working Group stated:

> ...families of those children [who received services] faced a number of other [socio-economic] challenges... It is not unusual for families living in such circumstances to require a level of service greater than would typically be provided to families living in stable environments where supports are more readily available. (Manitoba Family Services and Community Affairs, 2011b)

The KSMA response to the Working Group was to indicate that, in line with the fundamental principles of the KSCSS, it is the fundamental belief of Norway House Cree Nation that *all Canadian children have the right to access both quality and equality of care and service*, regardless of where they live. NHCN was sceptical of the claim that environmental stability differs between the two groups of children, and although the Working Group suggests that socio-economic challenges may justify a need for an elevated level of service, NHCN maintained that the level of service required by children living on-reserve is neither greater nor lesser than that of off-reserve children with special needs. The agency contended that factors such as family size, parental employment status, presence or absence of other children, and housing situation should not necessarily be at issue when considering access to care and services for a child with special needs (Manitoba Family Services and Community Affairs, 2011a).

It is suggested that the provincial service system in the south and in some northern urban areas of Manitoba can be augmented through the contributions of non-governmental social service groups, volunteer agencies, and other supports that are not accessible in First Nations communities. Alternative funding options have been explored to supplement government funding systems, but as of yet, none offer support on-reserve, including the Society of Manitobans with Disabilities and other child-centred service groups.

Thus, the perspective of the Working Group does not coincide with what is experienced by the NHCN community. The challenges confronted with respect to on-reserve availability and accessibility of resources are not based on a discrepant level of service need; rather, they are related to location of services, the absence of non-governmental support and, most importantly, a fragmented multi-jurisdictional service delivery system that has not yet worked out comprehensive service delivery mechanisms with clear lines of responsibility and accountability (Blackstock, 2010).

What the Program Does

For the first time in a Canadian First Nations community, KSMA's KSCSS provides a single, coordinated, centralized service and referral system that acts in liaison with other programs, including the Health Division and Frontier School Division, to provide the fullest range of services possible within the community for children with disabilities. The CSS in-home and in-community services include: occupational therapy (OT), speech language pathology (SLP), physiotherapy (PT), sign language therapist assistants, non-medical respite, in-home support for medical appointments, in-home care and supervision, in-home and in-community social skills development, computer assistance, parental aid, access to professional services and assessments (audiologist, physical therapist, etc.), recreation planning and assistance, and medical assistance (tube feeding, oxygen). These services are provided using a team approach, involving a program coordinator, a case manager, and core trained therapeutic assistants (service providers) who provide in-home and in-community supports and services to the children and families on an as-needed basis. There are between 24 and 30 service providers at any given time, depending on the assessed needs and therapeutic services required by the children with special needs.

The team works with professionals such as physicians, physiotherapists, occupational therapists, and speech/language therapists to develop a case management plan for each family and child based on individual needs. The professionals diagnose and recommend treatments, while the therapy assistants deliver the one-to-one non-medical in-home services and family supports. The team works with all family members to enable and enhance therapeutic service delivery to the child as well as to provide support for the caregivers.

A full case management approach and structure has been developed and is maintained in a manner that has created a responsive system within NHCN. This involves protocols, procedures, and forms for intake, needs assessment, referrals to specialists, case management planning, staffing and staff training, monitoring client progress, referrals to other programs or agencies, recording and reporting systems.

Due to the limited access to therapists in NHCN, the availability of a network of coordinated therapy resources comparable to provincial services does not exist in the community. KSCSS contracts with external therapists, including PT, OT, and SLP professionals. This continuity of care means that the children are better equipped when they start school, since therapeutic recommendations and provision of care support school readiness, as reported by the staff of Frontier School Division.

Parents of children with a disability and/or complex special needs experience increased levels of parental (caregiver) stress related to the child's disability and chronic care requirements, impacting their ability to cope. The services and supports provided by the KSCSS program contribute greatly to reducing parental stress and increasing parents' ability to cope and provide care for their disabled and/or complex special needs children. Children and families have less stress with the support they receive through KSCSS, which promotes healthier and more functional family units, and, in turn, a healthier and more functional community.

KSCSS links with other existing programs within the community to provide services falling under the mandates and capabilities of the other programs. This is done on a referral basis and includes such things as wheelchair in-community transportation for medical issues, in-home medical services, medical supplies and devices, homemaker (housekeeping) services, adaptive communication devices, Elder services, etc. The services of other programs are coordinated through KSCSS as part of the case management process.

KSCSS provides program services throughout the summer months, when schools are closed, including on-going therapy assistance and summer day camps for the families and children with disabilities and/or special needs. KSCSS has a core of specially trained therapeutic assistants, who deliver in-home services for OT, SLP, PT and other non-medical therapies under the guidance and direction of professionals.

Recent Developments in the KSCSS

Recently, the NHCN director of health and the KSMA KSCSS program coordinator have collaborated to initiate a partnership between community health programs and on-reserve child services in order to increase the menu of services available to the children and families in the KSCSS program. An ad hoc committee—consisting of the KSCSS program coordinator, the director of health, the executive director of KSMA and the band councillor holding the Child and Family Services (KSMA) portfolio—has been formed to advise the coordination of services,. In fact, KSMA is in the process of developing a five-year strategic plan which will ensure that constituents are enabled to have a voice in service delivery.

After the depletion of the initial grant from the Norway House Cree Nation Master Implementation Agreement Trust Fund, KSCSS funding restrictions imposed by INAC and Health Canada forced a reduction in services to the children and families under its care; KSCSS can now offer only the services of therapy assistants (formerly referred to as service providers or respite workers) to provide one-on-one care directly to the children up to a maximum of 25 hours bi-weekly. Currently, therapy assistants provide occupational and speech-language therapies under the direction of professional therapists. Although their focus is on improving the child's strength, coordination, flexibility, and mobility, they also provide opportunities for the child to go on escorted outings to promote in situ socialization and speech-language development.

KSCSS therapy assistants are trained in First Aid/CPR only, and are not certified health care aides. They carry out home therapies according to treatment plans developed by professionals; however, their duties are considerably restricted. In only one case is any homemaker service presently offered, and this consists simply of dusting and mopping floors in the home of a child with respiratory issues. Otherwise, there are no homemaker services or respite hours available or provided to parents living on-reserve.

In response to this insufficiency, services falling under the FNIH funding were opened up to all community members, rather than restricting them to those over 18 years of age. This includes the Home and Community Care (HCC) program, which offers in-home nursing services, homemaker services, home health care aides, and respite services for parents. HCC is in the process of expanding its resources, and program managers meet on a weekly basis to share information, discuss case management, and link program services. Additionally, it is planned to expand the scope of the training for health care aides in order to include a preparatory component on servicing children with special needs. At present, aides are not trained or qualified to do so.

The hospital in Norway House Cree Nation is scheduled to re-open in 2011, with an initial staff of five physicians who can make referrals to appropriate specialists and have them come to Norway House to evaluate and treat the KSCSS children; a physiotherapist now comes regularly to NHCN, and together with the planned integration of a mental health program into current services, children with complex medical needs are less likely to be forced to travel to major urban centres for assessment and treatment. Furthermore, a Wellness/Health Promotion Unit is in the planning stages, which will include a Health Resources manager position and a materials research component, in order to supply informational materials and supports for case managers and other direct service providers.

It is the mandate of both HCC and KSCSS to integrate programs and services. Once HCC staff training has been completed, services can be extended and expanded to include the children currently being provided limited home service under the KSCSS program. This coordination and strengthening of on-reserve organizations can only improve the service delivery to the families and children with special needs within the KSCSS program.

Finally, with respect to collaborative services, the KSCSS program has an on-going partnership with Frontier School Division to provide behavioural assessments and develop treatment plans for behaviour modification, occupational therapy, and speech-language therapy. With the involvement of in-school aides, it is possible to maintain consistency within individualized programming between both home and school environments. These resource collaborations also extend to children not currently able to participate in the school system but who need services delivered within the home. However, regardless of how coordinated the efforts are at the community level, without the federal and provincial departments fulfilling their fiduciary responsibility to fund services to First Nations children on-reserve, service provision remains insufficient to meet the quality of life standards deserved by all children.

Impact of the Program on Norway House

The Norway House Children's Special Services program is innovative in that no such program has been developed or implemented in any other First Nations community in Canada. Children's Special Services in Norway House Cree Nation is the only on-reserve CSS for children with disabilities and/or complex special needs and shows promise in ultimately increasing access to services and developing more equitable service delivery structures compared to off-reserve services. KSMA's KSCSS stands as a model service delivery system for other First Nations communities in Canada.

KSMA Children's Special Services has provided a coordinated linkage/referral system of supports within the Norway House Cree Nation community in liaison with other agencies and programs in the community, such as those under the Health Division and the High Cost Special Education program. This system did not exist and the children received no services prior to the implementation of the Children's Special Services program. To date, a total of 45 children have received services under this program.

Currently, the project is in its seventh year of operation and provides individualized in-home support services through a tri-level model, which is child-centred, family focused, and community-based. While there are many indicators of success, the greatest value of the program to the community is that fewer parents must choose between placing their children in foster care and moving away from their home community in order to access services (Ducharme et al., 2007).

Lack of Influence of the Program in Manitoba and Beyond

Prior to the development of the KSCSS program there was no continuity of care or services for children with disability. Services were fragmented or not available at all. The Working Group stated:

> ...decision-making at the community level mirrors this fragmented approach. In the absence of a continuum of services and mechanisms to ensure consistent service delivery across programs, gaps in services are inevitable.

With the exception of the NHCN Children's Special Services program, no service coordination system exists in Manitoba for children with special needs living on-reserve. Although both federal and provincial governments have openly committed to developing policies and mechanisms for funding such services, to date there has been no agreement reached by the two levels of government beyond that in principle (Blackstock, 2010). Without a structured system in place within the government's health and social services departments, First Nations communities cannot be facilitated in developing their own coordinated systems to meet their children's needs (McKechnie, 2000). In short, a coordinated and comprehensive service continuum can only be realized with the support of coordinated and comprehensive funding mechanisms.

According to the Working Group Report:

> ...the provincial service system, which includes agencies, community organizations and cross-departmental initiatives, delivers service through a coordinated approach where each partner contributes to a fuller system of disability services for children. This coordinated system is not readily available to the children in Norway House Cree Nation. Children with disabilities and their families in NHCN must rely on the spectrum of services available through federal health and social programs. Far more modest than its provincial counterpart and primarily built on a principle of "last resort," funding is often provided for essential components only.

This is a condition of social inequality that must be addressed at governmental levels. As previously discussed, the dearth of support services provided on-reserve by both provincial and non-governmental agencies results in systemic gaps within First Nations community service organizations. Without a comprehensive and coordinated funding system, equal to that provided for non-First Nations citizens, a culturally-relevant and competent continuum of service delivery cannot be provided to serve the diverse and complex needs of the children on reserve (Wright, Hiebert-Murphy, & Gosek, 2005); it becomes an issue of social justice when Canadian families are not enabled to remain intact within their home communities.

In relation to service fragmentation the Working Group reported that:

> ...decision-making and practices at the community level impact access to services. Leadership decisions to prioritize some of its federal funding to address the needs of an increasing elder population living in the community further restricts the availability of certain programs to children with disabilities under the age of 18... similarly, there appears to be limited linkages between the CSS project and other health, social and educational services... resulting in fragmented delivery of service.

CURRENT STATUS OF THE AGENCY AND ITS PROGRAMS

First Nations Inuit Health (FNIH) and Indian and Northern Affairs Canada (INAC) have agreed to share the $450,000 cost of funding the Norway House Cree Nation Kinosao Sipi Minisowin Agency Children's Special Services project to March 2011. Both parties have indicated that this is the final year of funding and that "they are moving towards integration of services" for children with complex medical needs and multiple disabilities. NHCN is seeking clarification as to whether the departments have considered the risks and implications of withdrawing the funding to children and families with special needs.

Both the Province of Manitoba and the Government of Canada have committed themselves to the practical implementation of Jordan's Principle.[1] Jordan's Principle is a child-first principle, named in memory of Jordan River Anderson, that calls on the government of first contact to pay for services for the child and then seek reimbursement later so the child does not get tragically caught in the middle of government red tape (First Nations Caring Society, 2011). Jordan's Principle applies to all government services and must be adopted and fully implemented by the Government of Canada and all provinces and territories.

Referring to provincial funding negotiations, Canadian Health Minister Tony Clement (2008) reassured Manitobans that "services will not in any way be compromised... [officials] will make sure the funds are there and the services will not be interrupted" (telephone interview). In September 2008, the Province of Manitoba reached an agreement with the Canadian government "to implement Jordan's Principle in Manitoba

---

1   Jordan River Anderson of Norway House Cree Nation was ready to go home from hospital when he was two years old, but he went on to spend over two years unnecessarily in hospital as the Province of Manitoba and the Government of Canada could not agree on who should pay for his at-home care. Tragically for Jordan, and his family and the Norway Community, he passed away at the age of four years, never having spent a day in a family home while governments continued to argue. Tragically, First Nations children are still often denied services available to all other children because of payment and jurisdictional disputes within and between the federal and provincial/territorial governments (First Nations Caring Society, 2011).

so that First Nations children with multiple disabilities will continue to receive needed care without delays or disruptions resulting from jurisdictional disputes" (Oswald as cited in Province of Manitoba, 2008, Para 1). A news release from the Province of Manitoba following this agreement cites similar statements from Manitoba's Health Minister, Theresa Oswald, and Healthy Living Minister Kerry Irvin-Ross around the fact that both the federal and provincial governments have expressed the desire to progress quickly to ensure accessibility of services to on-reserve First Nations children with multiple disabilities (Province of Manitoba, 2008). In the same news release, Federal Indian and Northern Affairs Minister Chuck Strahl also affirmed that "this agreement [would] ensure that the necessary care for First Nations children is not disrupted by a lack of clarity of jurisdictional responsibility" (as cited in Province of Manitoba, 2008, para. 7).

Despite these overt promises, as of December 2010, there had been no practical implementation of the principles agreed upon by both governments; continued funding of Children's Special Services in NHCN is still in question. This lack of initiative has created ongoing concern and apprehension on the part of First Nations leaders, as well as the families that support children with complex disabilities. Social inequality and fragmentation continue to permeate current service systems, so NHCN is again seeking clarification as to whether government officials considered the necessarily wider interpretation of Jordan's Principle when discussing funding for children and families with complex needs residing on-reserve.

The intention of the Manitoba/Canada Joint Committee on the Implementation of Jordan's Principle was to determine a process by which to engage First Nations stakeholders in the development of the framework for implementation and operation of Jordan's Principle. Although KSMA, on behalf of NHCN, was instrumental in spearheading the government's adoption of Jordan's Principle, they have not, as of yet, been requested by the Joint Committee to participate as a First Nations stakeholder. NHCN acknowledges that the work of the Manitoba/Canada Joint Committee is an ongoing, time-intensive process; however, the Technical Working Group Report was completed in March 2009, and there has been no significant progress since.

CONCLUSIONS

Norway House has mobilized its own Indigenous social and economic community resources to create a unique service structure to provide a range of necessary services and resources for children and families with disabilities in the community. The importance of this program for families and children in the community cannot be overstated. Prior to the existence of the program, families with children with special needs had to move off-reserve to receive provincial services, or their children were removed from their homes and placed in foster homes off-reserve so that they could access the services and resources that they needed to address their needs. The community, motivated by a commitment to the well-being of its children, took responsibility for developing resources that addressed the needs of the children and families with disabilities on the reserve. The community is now attempting to get federal and provincial governments to assume their fiduciary responsibilities for health and social services to First Nations people to cover the costs of providing these disability services.

The community has faced many barriers on the path toward providing these KSMA programs and services. The authors believe that both the federal and provincial governments must take into consideration the observations of their own joint working group report, which indicated that failing to fund CSS services for the children with complex needs on-reserve would result in significantly higher health care costs, since children and families would have to move off-reserve in order to receive the full range of services available under the provincial system.

FUTURE DIRECTIONS

In keeping with the spirit of Jordan's Principle, Norway House Cree Nation continues to work towards securing the current funding levels for all active cases of children in the CSS program. Furthermore, NHCN is seeking financial support for a sustainable funding system to complete outstanding assessments of many children on the waiting lists and to support the provision of services to those who meet the eligibility criteria. Without an integrated, sustainable funding system, there can be no integrated, sustainable service delivery system. Consequently, the community continues to work with federal and provincial governments and the voluntary sector NGOs to develop a sustainable arrangement to assist in the continued integration of health and social services that will more effectively address the needs of children and youth with disabilities in the Norway House community.

The authors feel it is important to reaffirm the belief that the Norway House community holds that it is imperative that Jordan's Principle be interpreted and applied in the broadest manner possible so that children with complex special needs and their families living on-reserve are able to access resources and services equal to those available to other First Nation children with special needs and their families who reside off-reserve. It is an issue of human rights, equality, and social justice for First Nations children and families with disabilities.

REFERENCES

Blackstock, C. (2010). Indian and Northern Affairs Canada (INAC): Delivering inequity to First Nations children and families receiving child welfare services. Submitted to the Standing Committee on Aboriginal Affairs and Northern Development. Retrieved from www.fncaringsociety.com/sites/default/files/docs/FNCFCS-Submission-SCAND-Dec2010.pdf.

Clement, T. (2008, May 5). Telephone interview by J. Milczarek [Transcription summary]. *Clement offers interim help.* CTV NewsNet, Winnipeg, Manitoba, Canada. Retrieved from winnipeg.ctv.ca/servlet/an/local/CTVNews/20080504/wpg_clement_funding_080504?hub=WinnipegHome.

Ducharme, C., Muskego, D., Muswagon, A., Paupanekis, C., Muswagon, M., Spence, W., & Ramdatt, J. (2007). Kinosao Sipi Minisowin agency: Creating a community response for special needs children. *First Peoples Child and Family Review, 3*(3), 12–20.

First Nations Caring Society (2011). Jordan's Principle Factsheet. Retrieved from www.fncfcs.com/sites/default/files/jordans-principle/docs/JPfactsheet2011-en.pdf.

Hanvey, L. (2002). Children with disabilities and their families in Canada: A discussion paper commissioned by the National Children's Alliance for the first national roundtable on children with disabilities. Retrieved from www.nationalchildrensalliance.com/nca/pubs/2002/hanvey02.pdf.

Health Canada. (2007). About mission, values, activities. About Health Canada. Retrieved from www.hc-sc.gc.ca/ahc-asc/activit/about-apropos/index-eng.php.

Health Canada. (2010). Aboriginal head start on reserve. First Nations, Aboriginal, and Inuit Health. Retrieved from www.hc-sc.gc.ca/fniah-spnia/famil/develop/ahsor-papa_intro-eng.php.

Human Resources and Skills Development Canada. (2009). Chapter 7: Aboriginal people with disabilities. In Service Canada, Advancing the inclusion of people with disabilities: 2007. Retrieved from www.rhdcc-hrsdc.gc.ca/eng/disability_issues/reports/fdr/2007/page09.shtml.

Manitoba Family Services and Community Affairs. (2011a). Children's Special Services. Retrieved from www.gov.mb.ca/fs/pwd/css.html.

Manitoba Family Services and Community Affairs. (2011b). Rural and Northern Services. Retrieved from www.gov.mb.ca/fs/about/org/csd/ruralnorthern.html.

McKechnie, B. (2000). Health Canada FAS/FAE initiative information and feedback sessions: National synthesis report. Retrieved from dsp-psd.pwgsc.gc.ca/Collection/H39-582-2000E.pdf.

Ng, E. (1996). Disability among Canada's Aboriginal peoples in 1991. *Health Reports, 8*(1), 25–32.

Norway House Cree Nation. (January, 2005). A New Beginning. Norway House, MB Unpublished Monograph.

Province of Manitoba. (2008, September 5). Manitoba reaches agreement with federal government to implement Jordan's Principle. News release. Retrieved from news.gov.mb.ca/news/index.html?archive=2008-9-01&item=4376.

Wright, A., Hiebert-Murphy, D., & Gosek, G. (2005). *Final report: Supporting aboriginal children and youth with learning and/or behavioural disabilities in the care of aboriginal child welfare agencies.* Faculty of Social Work, University of Manitoba, Winnipeg, Canada. Retrieved from www.fncfcs.com/sites/default/files/docs/SupportingAboriginalChildren.pdf.

CHAPTER 12

Substance Use during Pregnancy and a Woman-Centred Harm-Reduction Approach: Challenging the Mother and Baby Divide to Support Family Well-Being

Noela Crowe-Salazar

INTRODUCTION

In a recent one-year span of time, one Saskatchewan First Nations Child and Family Service (FNCFS) agency reported that they apprehended nine babies from the hospital after delivery due to problematic maternal substance use during pregnancy. Researchers have noted that First Nations women are often overrepresented in groups of substance-using women (Boyd, 2007; Tait, 2000). Treatment programs that meet the needs of such women during pregnancy and after delivery are not well addressed by existing policies and programs (Applegate, Bradley, Rhodes,

---

SUGGESTED CITATION: Crowe-Salazar, N. (2012). Substance use during pregnancy and a woman-centred harm-reduction approach: Challenging the mother and baby divide to support family well-being. In D. Fuchs, S. McKay, & I. Brown (Eds.), *Awakening the Spirit: Moving Forward in Child Welfare: Voices from the Prairies* (pp. 249–272). Regina, SK: Canadian Plains Research Center.

& Flynn Saulnier, 2001; Boyd, 2007; Hepburn, 2007; Payne, 2007; Tait, 2000). In addition, women who use substances during pregnancy face a number of systemic barriers and, because of this, they tend not to seek health care, treatment, or other services. One of the noted barriers is fear of apprehension of their baby by social services.

Associated with the fear of apprehension, and other barriers to access care, are many poor health outcomes and risks for the mother and child. Payne (2007) reported that mothers who have their babies apprehended at the hospital are discharged to the streets, where the cycle of poverty and homelessness begins again. Substance use continues and women can "re-cycle" via another subsequent pregnancy and child apprehension (see Figure 1). Further exacerbating the issue is that, even when women want to enter treatment, there are few or no existing woman-centred treatment services available for mothers and babies.

Figure 1. Women who use substances during pregnancy—Recycle.

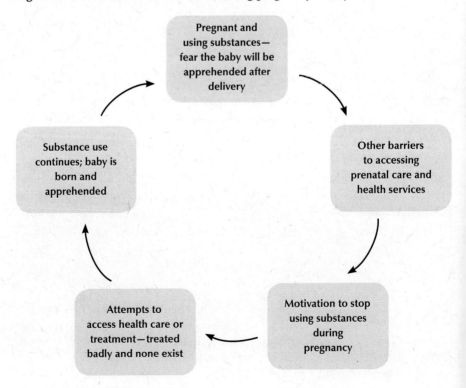

Source: Noela Crowe-Salazar (2003)

In an attempt to address this situation, a Saskatchewan FNCFS agency and one of its affiliated First Nations partnered to review the feasibility of developing a woman-centred harm-reduction program for women and babies. The goal in developing a woman-centred treatment program for women who use substances during pregnancy was to move a step towards keeping mothers and babies together, rather than continuing with practices that foster a mother and baby divide. This chapter provides a literature review on substance use during pregnancy, and summarizes the strengths of four programs that work with pregnant women who use substances. The chapter concludes with an overview of a program description that builds on knowledge that has emerged from the literature and the practice wisdom of other programs. The program description outlines what is needed to support women who experience problematic substance use during pregnancy and their children. Implementing a treatment program like this could offer better health and social outcomes for infants who are apprehended and close the mother-baby divide for women who experience problematic substance use during pregnancy.

LITERATURE REVIEW

A review of academic literature on this topic offers a critical context for understanding the relationships among problematic substance use, women, and pregnancy. The literature review also provides a rationale for the need for woman-centred harm-reduction programs, as well as a glimpse at the essential elements of such a program. The two areas of literature reviewed are substance use and pregnancy, and the treatment needs of women.

Substance Use and Pregnancy

Women who use substances during pregnancy are not well-served by existing treatment programs or related health and social services, and thus they face many barriers to accessing services (Applegate et al., 2001; Bang, Irwin-Seguin, & Bradley, 2007; Carten, 1996; Goldberg, 1995; Tait, 2000). Beginning in the mid-1970s, increased attention and advocacy prompted researchers to look at women as a separate category of substance user (Abbott, 1994; Drabble, 1996; Yaffe, Jenson, & Howard, 1995). Since then, researchers have made a considerable effort toward the analysis and consideration of how best to work with women who use substances. Some of the research in this area has included exploring barriers, prenatal care, perinatal care, gender issues, treatment issues, women's needs, women and co-occurring disorders, parenting, culture groups, feminist perspectives, family or support systems, and children (Alexander, 1996; Bang et al., 2007; Boyd, 2001; Jessup, Humphreys, Brindis, & Lee, 2003; Carten, 1996; Dodge & Potocky-Tripodi, 2001; Drabble, 1996; Finkelstein, 1994; Russell & Gockel, 2005).

Despite the amount of research completed, working with pregnant women who use substances remains a challenge because women who use drugs or alcohol during pregnancy are often stereotyped. For example, the literature references to stigmatization include the following: being viewed as villains who are immoral; sexually promiscuous; weak-willed; negligent to their children; tramps who deserve to be taken advantage of sexually; more disgusting than male addicts; and the enemy to a fetus (Applegate et al., 2001; Finkelstein, 1994; Goldberg, 1995). These stereotypes fuel the argument that drug-using women should not be allowed to have children, which in practical terms is both inappropriate and impossible to implement, and only aids to further punish the disadvantaged (Hepburn, 2007). In addition, drug laws exert a considerable influence on shaping both public policy related to how we deal with pregnant women and substance use, and the social construction of it as seen through attitudes of others (Boyd, 2001).

There has been a long history of misinformation on illicit drugs and drug use. Beginning in the early 1900s, drug legislation in Canada was fuelled by morality, racism, and economic concern (Boyd, 2001). This was evidenced through the writings of Emily Murphy (1920), who won the right for women to be appointed to the Senate and linked opium use to Chinese Canadians and cocaine and marijuana use to southern Blacks (Boyd, 2001; Donovan, 2006). In the February 15, 1920 issue of *MacLean's Magazine*, Murphy wrote an article entitled "The Grave Drug Menace." She stated that her intent was to write about drug addiction and to discuss its relation to insanity, crime, racial deterioration, and social wastage. Although her views are outdated and highly questionable in view of current philosophy and research findings, their impact on the social construction of drug use persisted over time and similar assertions have been presented since then through to this day.

Current references to drug addiction in terms of "insanity" are now more often discussed as mental health disorders, which are classified in the diagnostic and statistical manual of mental disorders (DSM-IV, 1994). The DSM-IV provides clinical criteria for categories of chemical abuse and dependency (Goldberg, 1995; note also that the DSM-5 is being developed online—www.dsm5.org/Pages/Default.aspx—and is scheduled to be completed in 2013). Modern connection to "crime" is evident in the laws and legislation in Canada that continue to deal with drug use from a criminal position (Boyd, 2007). The insanity and crime perspectives have also aided in the construction of drug use and addiction as a medical and legal problem (Boyd, 2001).

Regarding Murphy's reference to "racial deterioration and social wastage," one only has to review the literature that has been compiled on alcohol and drug use to understand that it still has relevance. A great deal of that research focuses on the social downfalls that are often attributed to drug use or to other harms associated with problematic use, and, as Tait (2000) notes, "poverty alone [is] not an indicator for substance misuse by women (p. 39). A considerable amount of the literature on alcohol and drug use focuses on specific racial groups, and this can create further bias or misleading information. For example, although Kaskutas (2000) stated the highest published rates of FASD are among American Indians and African Americans, other researchers have noted the significance of the unpublished rates and the potential bias (Donovan, 2006). Substance use during pregnancy and drug addiction in the United States is less visible among middle and upper income women because they usually give birth in private hospitals that often do not screen for illicit chemicals, and thus much of the research has been with low income women only (Carten, 1996). Added to this is the fact that most of the research on maternal drug use is from the United States, where there has been until recently no universal medical insurance and where poverty is extreme for some of the population (Donovan, 2006). Despite the potential for biases based on race and class, the issue continues to be framed as more significant to American Indians and African Americans. Other research directly opposes this view and finds that, contrary to the stereotypes, substance use and abuse among women occurs at similar rates among poor and non-poor people, and among white people and people of colour (Goldberg, 1995).

In further analysis of the literature on both drug and alcohol use during pregnancy, it is clear there are two distinct bodies of literature that can be found in this area. One addresses women who use substances during pregnancy, and a second focuses specifically on alcohol use during pregnancy and concerns fetal alcohol spectrum disorder (FASD). It is interesting to note that the effect of drug use during pregnancy on the fetus is not found in the literature as predominantly as alcohol use. It is recognized that there are two persons involved, a mother and a child, but the division of the literature and focus on alcohol use—perhaps more functional than intentional—could add to the needs of the mothers and their children not fully being met. In the case of alcohol use during pregnancy, when an FASD diagnosis is applied to children it directly implicates the mother as responsible (Schellenberg, 2007) and it is the only disorder that is named in such a way (Badry, 2009). In addition, putting focus on the fetus/child can lead to an effort to protect the fetus/child, which further implies the mother is an enemy (Applegate et al., 2001). Women who have used substances during pregnancy and were interviewed reveal a predominant theme: the well-being, care, and treatment of the mother and the baby are divided, and the division is evident from pre-conception through to delivery (Hunter, Donovan, Crowe-Salazar, & Pedersen, 2008).

After delivery, a woman's fears are realized when her child is apprehended. Women who use substances are said to make up 80% of those in the child welfare system (Smith, 2006). Child protection workers have identified denial, rationalization, minimizing, and blaming as some of the most frequent challenges they work with (Weaver, 2007). However, given that pregnant women who admit to substance use often have their children apprehended, pregnant women who use substances are not in a position to admit to it. The framework of the child protection social worker–mother relationship creates dissent and inadvertently results in women not accessing prenatal care.

The current systems that deal with substance use and pregnancy are enforced by laws and policies, and these, in turn, influence public attitudes and opinion (Boyd, 2001). It is imperative that health professionals, doctors, nurses, social workers, child protection workers, and addiction counsellors consider the historical foundations on which we have developed these laws, policies, attitudes, and opinions and that we clearly examine the way we actively oppress mothers and children who are already marginalized. As professionals, we need to consider how, through efforts that purport to help, we have developed myriad ways in which mothers who use illicit drugs are regulated via legal, medical, and social professions competing and overlapping in social control (Boyd, 2001).

To engage women who use substances during pregnancy, it is essential that service providers create a continuum of services and a practice framework that is based upon current findings of the needs of women in treatment. Service providers need to know that women are probably more at risk from the social aspects of the use, and the environment they live in, than from the substances themselves. They also need to know that pregnancy offers women a life event that can foster motivation to change (Wright & Walker, 2007).

The Treatment Needs of Women

In 1991, Susan Boyd helped create one of the first woman-centred, harm-reduction programs in Vancouver. The group, called Drug and Alcohol Meeting Support (DAMS), was dedicated to harm reduction, stabilization, and self-empowerment. Family reunification was also a component of the program because most women had at least one child apprehended from social services. The needs for the DAMS program were identified by what a woman prioritized. Stabilization versus abstinence was the goal, and support was diverse. The women in the group were predominantly First Nations women who were mothers. Boyd noted that First Nations women are often over-represented in groups of substance-using women and that they are the most vulnerable to arrest, child apprehension, and poor health outcomes.

Drug and alcohol use is shaped by gender, class, race/ethnicity, sexuality, and culture and, because it is mediated by these factors, the consequences of drug use are not the same for all women (Boyd, 2007). Poverty and social conditions are correlated with outcomes in pregnancy; for example, in one study, mothers who used heroin were matched for social factors and had comparable birth outcomes to similarly vulnerable non-drug-using mothers (Wright & Walker, 2007). However, poverty and related factors do play a role in why some women misuse substances during pregnancy, and services need to address ways women can be meaningfully supported to improve their day-to-day lives (Tait, 2000).

Substance use programs for women must meet women's diverse needs and include programming that reflects the fact that they are women and they are pregnant (Applegate et al., 2001; Bang et al., 2007; Carten, 1996; Drabble, 1996; Tait, 2000). Pregnant women who use substances need to be regarded as pregnant and not as substance users who happen to be pregnant, since this ensures women will receive necessary prenatal and health care as well as treatment services (Hepburn, 2002). Gender-specific treatment has been found to be more effective than mixed-gender approaches (Fitzgerald, Lester, & Zuckerman, 2006). Criticisms against mixed-gender treatment are that pregnant women do not get services related to their pregnancy, nor do they show positive outcomes from traditional, predominantly male-based programming, which have been found to exacerbate women's depression and do not address the violence that is often linked to substance use (Fitzgerald et al., 2006; Russell & Gockel, 2005).

The treatment components for women discussed in the literature are diverse, and offer a range of services for women and often their children and partners. Some researchers have referred to the array of resources as a "complex constellation of interdependent bio-psycho-social factors" (Nina, Uziel-Miller, & Lyons, 2000). More specifically, these components include: services delivered by multidisciplinary teams; services delivered via a multi-agency framework; antenatal/prenatal management; trauma counselling; peer role models; vocational and educational components; reproductive health care; infant-child needs; child protection needs; obstetrician needs; methadone maintenance; role of partners; considerations for domestic violence counselling; FASD; mothering; tobacco cessation; therapy needs; life skills; culture; health; and child care (Bailey, Hill, Hawkins, Catalano, & Abbott, 2008; Carten, 1996; Drabble, 1996; Dempsey Marr & Wenner, 1996; Hepburn, 1993; Wright & Walker, 2007; Martin, Beaumont, & Kupper, 2003; Conners, Grant, Crone, & Whiteside-Mansell, 2006; Nina, Uziel-Miller, & Lyons, 2000; Olson, 2007; Poole, 2007; Roberts, 2007; Russell & Gockel, 2005; Sowards, O'Boyle, & Weissman, 2006). This list is neither exhaustive nor in any relational order, and treatment for women requires flexibility in delivery. Such flexibility provides women with a wide range of options from which those best suited to their lives and families might be selected.

Although there has been a great deal of research and support in the area of women and substance use, a gap remains between what is known and what is applied (Poole, 2007). The diagnosis of FASD has been used for a number of years but, regardless of this, in Saskatchewan there has been no revision or establishment of treatment services that are specific to prevention and reflective of women's needs (Tait, 2008). As mentioned, women are often motivated to change their substance use during pregnancy. Pregnancy is an event in a woman's life that often offers the opportunity and motivation for a mother to change her lifestyle in ways that benefit both herself and her children (Hepburn, 2007). As outlined in the stages of change during pregnancy (see Table 1), many women are at a point of action where they are ready to establish and practise a change in their substance use.

In consideration of the needs and services that could be offered in a woman-centred treatment program, it should be recognized that the treatment needs of women are complex and require many levels of intervention and treatment, including but not limited to socioeconomic, clinical, and systemic (Finkelstein, 1994). Service providers need to be aware of the larger picture and to continually increase their knowledge of special factors affecting substance use by women, particularly during pregnancy (Goldberg, 1995). Further, interventions for mothers and children should be delivered through broad approaches using relationship-based, mother-child models that inspire insights into and progress in the development of mother and child and include the development of the relationship between the two (Leslie, DeMarchi, & Motz, 2007). One application of such approaches is The Centre for Substance Abuse Treatment, which outlines a bio-psycho-social intervention model that includes:

- "Medical interventions and Health Services (including general, gynaecological, and obstetrical health services; infant and child primary and acute care; health education, prevention, and treatment regarding sexuality, HIV, AIDS, and STDs).
- Substance Abuse and Psychological Counselling (including substance-related counselling, as well as counselling based on the

Table 1. Prochaska and DiClemente's Stages of Change Model as experienced by pregnant women and service providers.

STAGE OF CHANGE	CHARACTERISTICS	TECHNIQUES FOR SERVICE PROVIDERS
PRE-CONTEMPLATION	Not currently considering change: "Ignorance is bliss."	• Validate lack of readiness • Clarify: decision is theirs • Encourage re-evaluation of current behaviour • Encourage self-exploration, not action • Explain and personalize the risk Pregnant women present to service providers ready to change. If pregnant women are pre-contemplative they do not seek any services.
CONTEMPLATION	Ambivalent about change: "Sitting on the fence." Not considering change within the next month.	• Validate lack of readiness • Clarify: the decision is theirs • Encourage evaluation of pros and cons of behaviour change • Identify and promote new, positive outcome expectations Due to fears of stigmatism and the apprehension of their baby, pregnant women will most often experience this stage on their own.
PREPARATION	Some experiment with change and are trying to change: "Testing the waters." Planning to act within one month. Non-judgmental care is critical to the needs of the pregnant woman.	• Identify and assist in problem solving re: obstacles • Help patient identify social support • Verify that patient has underlying skills for behaviour change • Encourage small initial steps Pregnant women often show up to a service provider wanting to change their using behaviour. They are open to change techniques, receptive to encouragement and can often make significant initial steps.
ACTION	Practicing new behaviour for 3-6 months. Pregnant women are motivated by their focus on keeping their child.	• Focus on restructuring cues and social support • Bolster self-efficacy for dealing with obstacles • Combat feelings of loss and reiterate long-term benefits Pregnant women are motivated for change; they are often easy to engage and work with.
MAINTENANCE	Continued commitment to sustaining new behaviour post-6 months to 5 years Pregnant women often do not get beyond the 9-month pregnancy and due to apprehension of their child they start to use again.	• Plan for follow-up support • Reinforce internal rewards • Discuss coping with relapse Pregnant women need strong supports as they near delivery of their baby. The collaboration of child protection, maternal health, and other after-delivery supports and services is essential.
RELAPSE	Resumption of old behaviours: "Fall from grace." Pregnant women "recycle" at this point (see Figure 1.)	• Evaluate trigger for relapse • Reassess motivation and barriers • Plan stronger coping strategies Pregnant women do relapse; however, because of the motivation for their baby's health and well-being it is most often after delivery. After-care is critical, but often non-existent.

Adapted from www.cellinteractive.com/ucla/physcian_ed/stages_change.html

relational model in which issues such as low self-esteem, violence, interpersonal relationships, loss and shame are discussed).
- Life Skills Training (including vocational, educational, and parent training).
- Other Social Services (a comprehensive case management approach is recommended including child care, transportation, legal services, and housing)" (Uziel-Miller & Lyons, 2000, p. 356).

Literature Review Conclusion

We do not work well with pregnant women who are using substances problematically during pregnancy. Our lack of effective care and service creates a division between mothers and babies, and promotes the re-cycle of women whose children are apprehended at birth. In our society, we deal with problematic substance use via policy and criminal law. Despite the fact that we know that the current practices and laws do not work well, we do not strive to build a holistic continuum of services and practices that would better serve women, children, and families who are impacted and diminished by problematic substance use.

In a conversation with Dr. Ron Abrahams of Fir Square in Vancouver, the author posed the question: "Where do you see the most deaths related to problematic substance use during pregnancy?" Abrahams responded that, in his experience with Fir Square, most deaths are mothers, by suicide brought on by the loss of a child due to apprehension. Despite known risk and treatment factors, we continue to perpetuate the myths and misinformation, and harm women and children because we believe substance use during pregnancy is most harmful to a baby and that the mother is to blame.

The work of researchers and other scholars strongly suggests that women who use substances problematically during pregnancy need services that are designed for women and are reflective of their diverse needs. A harm-reduction approach is often recommended in the literature, and seems highly appropriate. The foundation of a solid treatment program, then, should be built upon two tenets: woman-centred services, and harm reduction.

To put this plan into action, the social determinants of health need to be addressed as factors highly related to substance use before, during, and following pregnancy. These include level of income, social status, social support networks, education, working conditions, physical environments, biology and genetics, personal health practices, coping skills, health services, gender, and culture. Active and ongoing support by skilled multidisciplinary clinical teams that respond in a woman-centred way (responding to the stated needs and treatment choices of women) are essential. These key elements of a sustainable program model should be very beneficial indeed to women who use substances problematically during pregnancy.

FOUR PROGRAMS AND SERVICES FOR WOMEN WHO USE SUBSTANCES DURING PREGNANCY

There are several programs across Canada that offer services for women who use substances during pregnancy. In this section, four examples are provided that offer a range of successful aspects of services and supports using woman-centred harm-reduction models of care. The section concludes with describing how one local organization developed a community-specific woman-centred program in Regina: Mothersfirst, offered by KidsFirst Regina.

Sheway, Vancouver

Sheway is a Coast Salish word meaning "growth." Sheway is a partnership initiative governed by the Vancouver Coastal Health Authority, the B.C. Ministry for Children and Family Development, the Vancouver Native Health Society, and the YWCA of Vancouver. The program provides "comprehensive health and social services to women who are either pregnant or parenting children less than 18 months old and who are experiencing current or previous issues resulting from substance use" (Vancouver Native Health Society, n.d., par. 1).

Sheway operates in a client-centred, woman-focused environment, and offers highly specialized services to pregnant women who use substances and who have complex needs. Sheway recognizes that the health of women and their children is linked to the conditions of their lives and their ability to influence these conditions. All staff work in partnership with a woman as she makes decisions regarding her health and the health of her child. The program provides health and social service supports to pregnant women and women with infants less than eighteen months old who are dealing with drug and alcohol issues. The focus of the program is to help the women have healthy pregnancies and positive early parenting experiences.

Sheway is located in the Downtown Eastside of Vancouver, often described as the poorest neighbourhood in Canada, in a two-storey building shared with the YWCA. The YWCA shares the main floor with Sheway's community activities and programs. Also on the main floor is a common area with couches; a few small offices and a small eating area surround this. There is a cook at Sheway, and at noon lunch is provided. Mothers can come and eat, then participate in any of the weekly activities that are offered. The second-floor space has examination rooms for the physicians, offices for counsellors, and other services, as well as an open area waiting room. Women who are in the program can have all of their prenatal examinations done at Sheway. A physician is available, and there are nurses.

In addition to the medical aspects of care, there is also an early childhood intervention worker, a drug and alcohol counsellor, social workers, an Aboriginal/First Nations liaison worker, community liaison outreach worker, a nutritionist, cooks, infant development consultants, and other program staff. In addition to this, Sheway works directly with: a pediatrician from Children's and Women's Hospital specializing in developmental assessments and substance-exposed infants and children; an occupational therapist; a physiotherapist; a speech/language pathologist from the Centre for Ability; and music therapists from Vancouver Native Health Society and Fir Square.

Women come into the program by referral from other sources. They complete an application form that contains health information and related information that health systems often require. Sheway works with each woman for a specified amount of time during and after pregnancy. At that point, referrals to other community services and supports are made.

Staff members at Sheway consider their program to be unique. They also consider it to be successful, due in large part to the fact that pregnant mothers using substances would not enter most programs because of stigma and fear of having their children apprehended.

Fir Square Unit – BC Women's Hospital, Vancouver

BC Women's Hospital partnered with Sheway, which was already established in Vancouver's Downtown Eastside, in 1993 with a mandate to offer a detoxification program to women who were pregnant. Ten years later, in 2003, it opened an accompanying harm-reduction unit for the women it served.

Fir Square helps "women and their newborns to stabilize and withdraw from substances" (HealthLinkBC, n.d.). There are five beds available for pregnant women, and six beds for women with newborns. In the latter case, mothers and their infants are housed together, if possible, in a single unit. At times, newborns require intensive treatment, and when this is the case they stay in a nearby nursery.

Fir Square also offers numerous supporting services. For the women themselves, available services include: counselling, life skills coaching (especially looking after a newborn), stress management strategies, parenting groups, spiritual care, and after-care personal support. For accessing community services, women get assistance finding housing, financial assistance, recreation, therapies of various kinds, and other community services. Women are connected with alcohol and drug counselling and related support groups.

These services are offered through a multidisciplinary team of physicians, nurses, social worker, addictions counsellor, nutritionist, and life skills/parenting counsellor. The emphasis is on women themselves taking ownership and direction over improving their own health and the health of their babies, and over sustaining supportive living conditions.

Breaking the Cycle, Toronto

Breaking the Cycle is an early identification and intervention program for women and their children, pregnant women with substance use problems, and mothers who have substance use problems with children under age six (Van Den Broek, 2007). Breaking the Cycle is supported by Mothercraft, which has been a leader in supporting healthy child development since 1931. Breaking the Cycle was designed to enhance the development of substance-exposed children by addressing maternal addiction problems and the mother-child relationship through a comprehensive community model. The program offered the opportunity for existing services to be reorganized and delivered in an improved manner, recognizing that services should be coordinated so that agencies can adapt to families rather than families having to adapt to multiple agencies. Goals identified were to address existing service-system problems and fragmented services for substance-using pregnant women or mothers and their young children. Problems included multiple intake experiences, lack of consistency, multiple service-access locations, and poor conditions of services, particularly between adult and child service sectors.

The program operates through the efforts of seven partner agencies representing a non-traditional collaboration among child welfare, substance-use treatment, health, and child service sectors to address the complex problems of mothering and substance abuse. A single-access model offers integrated addiction counselling, parenting intervention, and health and medical services. External evaluations have taken place since the program began in 1995 and it has been the focus of many research initiatives. Evaluations have reported on the efficacy of both the comprehensive, integrated program model and of a pregnancy-outreach model. The evaluations have also reported on enhanced birth and perinatal outcomes for infants of substance-involved mothers engaged earlier in pregnancy, on enhanced developmental outcomes for the children involved, on enhanced parenting confidence and competence, on enhanced treatment outcomes, and on decreased rates of separation of mother and child.

According to its website (Mothercraft, 2011), "in 2004, Breaking the Cycle was recognized by the United Nations Office on Drugs and Crime as an exemplary program serving pregnant and parenting women with substance-use problems, and their young children" (par. 3).

Mothersfirst, KidsFirst Regina

KidsFirst Regina is "a program that assists families in becoming the best parents they can be, by providing support, enhancing knowledge, and building on family strengths" (Regina Early Learning Centre, 2004). KidsFirst offers a home-visiting component in the form of home visitors who work out of five community agencies in Regina. Participation in the program is voluntary. KidsFirst accepts expectant mothers or those with a child up to the age of one. Families interested in participating in Kids-First will receive a visit by an assessor to determine if they are eligible for the program. A special team made up of a variety of mental health and addictions professionals provides support and training for KidsFirst Regina programs, including the home visitors. KidsFirst is a unique program that provides support to vulnerable expectant and new mothers in Regina (for more information, see Government of Saskatchewan, 2011).

The Mothersfirst component to KidsFirst was established in 2007. The specialized team that offered mental health and addictions services were already providing various programs that would fit with recovery for the women in the program. The idea of integrating those programs into one stream of service grew out of best practice described in current literature. Services were adjusted to meet the full range of needs of the moms in the program, rather than having them access multiple aspects of mental health and addiction care. To plan and carry out this transformation, a working group was struck that consisted of internal KidsFirst program staff and external partners who brought expertise and specialized services. The external partners included public health, the social worker from the Mother Baby Unit at Regina General Hospital, and addiction services.

The initial group was scheduled to be run over eight weeks with women attending three days per week. This schedule allowed the women, as mothers, to have time during the week to care for their families. The group was designed to meet the needs of women who are involved in treatment for problematic substance use and who want to participate in parenting and general lifestyle groups. Priority was given to pregnant women. Available literature has noted that barriers for women entering treatment programs include cost, childcare, transportation, and meals. All of these associated costs are covered by the KidsFirst Regina program. Transporting other children to school was also accounted for and arranged.

PROGRAM MODEL: A WOMAN-CENTRED HARM-REDUCTION TREATMENT PROGRAM

As previously indicated, women's needs are ineffectively met in much of the current programming, particularly for those women who use substances problematically during pregnancy. While there is a body of literature on best practices from which jurisdictions could draw and replicate so as to better meet women's needs, little has been done in most provinces to address this gap in service.

Between November 1, 2007, and October 31, 2008, the author was contracted by a First Nation Child and Family Service Agency in Saskatchewan to develop programming that would address the need for a service for mothers who use substances problematically during pregnancy. The agency had apprehended nine babies from the hospital shortly after delivery due to problematic substance use by the mother during pregnancy. In a file review of the nine cases cited by the agency, all babies went into foster care after discharge from the hospital and they remained in care throughout the first year of their lives and possibly longer. The mothers involved had limited or no extended support systems, nor did they have a venue where they could address their substance use during pregnancy or following delivery. The literature and the programs discussed earlier strongly suggest that access to a treatment program with woman-centred harm-reduction philosophies could have helped these nine women and their infant children remain together.

A woman-centred approach recognizes that women have a choice in their decision-making and that women define their family as whomever they choose rather than by traditional bloodlines. Women's choices are respected, risks are minimized, women are empowered, and recognition of the diversity and complexity of women's lives is given (Payne, 2007). The harm-reduction philosophy that is used in the program is nonjudgemental. It accepts that licit and illicit drug use exists, and it works to minimize its harmful effects rather than ignore or condemn them. Drug use encompasses a continuum from severe abuse to total abstinence, and harm reduction acknowledges that some ways of using drugs are clearly safer than others. A harm-reduction approach does not attempt to minimize or ignore the real and tragic harm and danger associated with licit and illicit drug use.

The program model, designed to be implemented on a First Nation or other community, is illustrated by Figure 2 on the following page. Its philosophical foundation is that local community services and a woman-centred harm-reduction approach should be used in an integrated way. To attain a continuum of services and supports for women, the model relies on teaching people in the existing community what a woman-centred

Figure 2. Program model: Building a home of family wellness.

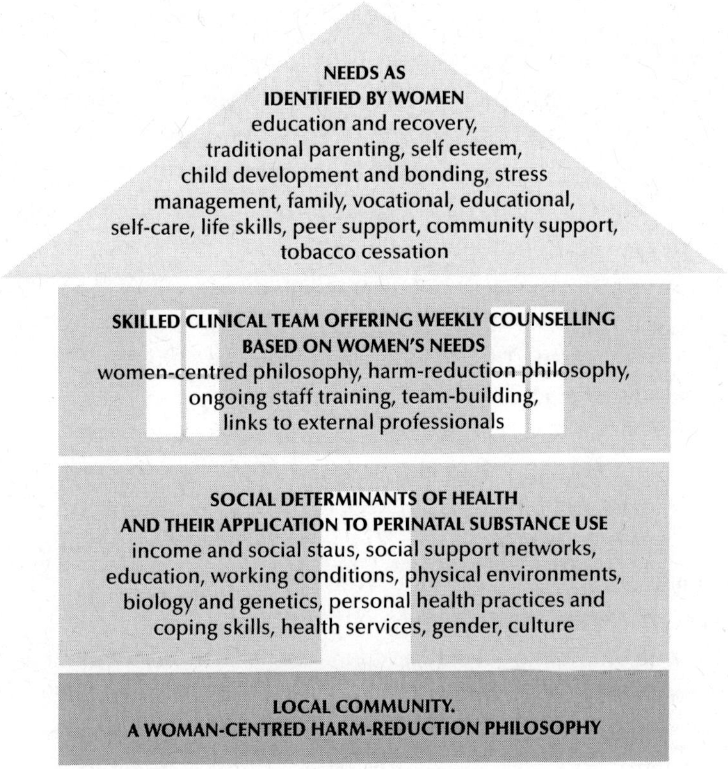

NEEDS AS IDENTIFIED BY WOMEN
education and recovery, traditional parenting, self esteem, child development and bonding, stress management, family, vocational, educational, self-care, life skills, peer support, community support, tobacco cessation

SKILLED CLINICAL TEAM OFFERING WEEKLY COUNSELLING BASED ON WOMEN'S NEEDS
women-centred philosophy, harm-reduction philosophy, ongoing staff training, team-building, links to external professionals

SOCIAL DETERMINANTS OF HEALTH AND THEIR APPLICATION TO PERINATAL SUBSTANCE USE
income and social staus, social support networks, education, working conditions, physical environments, biology and genetics, personal health practices and coping skills, health services, gender, culture

LOCAL COMMUNITY. A WOMAN-CENTRED HARM-REDUCTION PHILOSOPHY

Source: Noela Crowe-Salazar (2003)

harm-reduction approach is. Additionally, service agreements with other services in the community and contracts for service help in integration of services.

The second layer of the model addresses the social determinants of health as applied to perinatal substance use. The social determinants take into consideration the following: income and social status; social support networks; education; working conditions; physical environments; biology and genetics; personal health practices and coping skills; health services; gender; and culture. Each of these is considered in the case of each woman, and in relation to her perinatal substance use. A program is then designed to meet the needs of each woman and her family, based upon her specific needs as she identifies them. Much of this programming continues into the post-care period, from the point of departure from the treatment centre to the ongoing foundational supports and service agreements with the local community.

The third layer of the program's model is the skilled clinical team that offers services, including weekly counselling based on the women's needs identified from the previous list of social determinants. The skilled team offers programming with a woman-centred harm-reduction philosophy as its core. Due to the contrast of this philosophy with other models of treatment for addiction, many clinical teams need ongoing training and opportunities to put into practice what they have learned. In doing so, members of the team become experts in providing the services required by women who experience problematic substance use during pregnancy.

The fourth and final layer, or roof, of the model contains some of the critical elements of the program, such as the shelter and safety that women require, as well as other needs as identified by each woman in treatment. The list is not exhaustive but includes: education and recovery; traditional parenting; self-esteem content; child development and bonding education; stress management (to maintain abstinence); family components; vocational considerations and opportunities for referrals for training; educational GED attainment or other; self-care; life skills programming; peer supports; community support; and tobacco cessation.

CONCLUSION

The four existing programs and the program model, all described above, illustrate various aspects of care for women who experience problematic substance use during pregnancy. These programs allow women to work through their stages of change in individual ways, supported by professionals who understand their unique circumstances. They also illustrate woman-centred services and harm-reduction practices in practical terms. The importance of this cannot be overstated. Sara Payne (2007), writing about Fir Square, put it best:

> We took the risk of believing women with problematic substance use can be good, caring mothers and can care for their babies from birth, despite active substance use

during pregnancy. It is incumbent on all of us who care for pregnant women with problematic substance use to insist on a woman-centred, harm-reduction approach, and to practice it. The lives of many women and infants depend on it. (p. 68–69)

NOTE

This chapter was adapted from a paper written by Noela Crowe-Salazar and available at www.whitebearfirstnation.ca/Substance Use during Pregnancy and a Women Centered Harm Reduction Approach.pdf.

REFERENCES

Abbott, A. A. (1994). A feminist approach to substance abuse treatment and service delivery. *Women's Health and Social Work: Feminist Perspectives*, 19(3/4), 67–83.

Alexander, M. J. (1996). Women with co-occurring addictive and mental disorders: An emerging profile of vulnerability. *American Journal of Orthopsychiatry*, 66(1), 61–70.

Applegate, D., Bradley, C., Rhodes, R., & Flynn Saulnier, C. (2001). Round table discussion on treatment issues of substance abusing women: Consensus, dichotomy, or work in progress? *Journal of Social Work Practice in the Addictions*, 1(4), 117–126.

Badry, D. (2009). Fetal Alcohol Spectrum Disorder Standards: Supporting children in the care of children's services. *First Peoples Child & Family Review*, 4(1), 47–56.

Bailey, J., Hill, K., Hawkins, D., Catalano, R. & Abbott, R. (2008). Men's and women's patterns of substance use around pregnancy. *Birth: Issues in Perinatal Care*, 35(1), 50–59.

Bang, D., Irwin-Seguin, K., & Bradley, N. (2007). A good place to start: What does women-specific substance use treatment look like? *CrossCurrents, Spring*, Centre for Addiction and Mental Health. Retrieved from www.camh.net/Publications/ Cross_Currents/Spring_2007/spring2007crosscurrents.html.

Boyd, S. (2001). Feminist research on mothers and illegal drugs. *Resources for Feminist Research*, 28(3/4), 113.

Boyd, S. (2007). Drug scares and practice: Socio-historical considerations. In S. C. Boyd & L. Marcellus (Eds.), *With child: Substance use during pregnancy: A woman-centred approach* (pp. 20–28). Halifax, NS: Fernwood Publishing.

Carten, A. J. (1996). Mothers in recovery: Rebuilding families in the aftermath of addiction. *Social Work, 41*(2), 214–223.

Conners, N. A., Grant, B. A., Crone, C. C., & Whiteside-Mansell, L. (2006). Substance abuse treatment for mothers: Treatment outcomes and the impact of length of stay. *Journal of Substance Abuse Treatment, 31*(4), 447–456.

Crowe-Salazar, N. (2003). Literature review: Community reinforcement and family training (CRAFT), and addictions programming for the KidsFirst Program in Regina. Unpublished paper for Child and Youth Services, Regina Qu'Appelle Health Region.

Dempsey Marr, D., & Wenner, A. (1996). Gender specific treatment for chemically dependent women: A rationale for inclusion of vocational services. *Alcoholism Treatment Quarterly, 14*(1), 21–30.

Dodge, K., & Potocky-Tripodi, M. (2001). The effectiveness of three inpatient intervention strategies for chemically dependent women. *Research on Social Work Practice, 11*(1), 24–39.

Donovan, K. (2006). Towards an addictions-free province? A closer look at the potential in Saskatchewan's Adderly report and 'Project Hope.' *Circle Talk,* January-April, 22–26.

Drabble, L. (1996). Elements of effective services for women in recovery: Implications for clinicians and program supervisors. *Journal of Chemical Dependency Treatment, 6*(1/2), 1–21.

DSM-IV. (1994). *Diagnostic and Statistical Manual of Mental Disorders. DSM-IV-TR.* Washington, DC American Psychiatric Association.

Finkelstein, N. (1994). Treatment issues for alcohol and drug-dependent pregnant and parenting women. *Health Social Work, 19*(1), 7–15.

Fitzgerald, H. E., Lester, B. M., Zuckerman, B. (2006). *The crisis in youth mental health: Critical issues and effective programs, Vol. 1: The organization and prevention of children's mental health problems.* Westport, CT: Praeger Publishers/Greenwood Publishing Group.

Goldberg, M. E. (1995). Substance-abusing women: False stereotypes and real needs. *Social Work, 40*(6), 789–798.

Government of Saskatchewan. (2011). *Kids First.* Retrieved from www.education.gov.sk.ca/KidsFirst.

HealthLinkBC. (n.d.). *Fir Square Combined Care Unit.* Retrieved from find.healthlinkbc.ca/search.aspx?d=SV000871.

Hepburn, M. (1993). Drug use in pregnancy. *British Journal of Hospital Medicine*, 49(1), 51–55.

Hepburn, M. (2002). Drug use and women's reproductive health. In A. McBride & T. Petersen (Eds.), *Working with substance misusers: A guide to theory and practice* (pp. 285–295). London: Routledge.

Hepburn, M. (2007). Drug use and parenting (Preface). In S. C. Boyd & L. Marcellus (Eds.), *With child: Substance use during pregnancy: A woman-centred approach* (pp. 6–8). Halifax, NS: Fernwood Publishing.

Hunter, G., Donovan, K., Crowe-Salazar, N., & Pedersen, S. (2008, August). We are not asking them to hate us, we want them to help us. *Poverty Profiles*. Regina, SK: Social Policy Research Unit, University of Regina.

Jessup, M. A., Humphreys, J. C., Brindis, C. D, & Lee, K. A. (2003). Extrinsic barriers to substance abuse treatment among pregnant drug dependent women. *Journal of Drug Issues, Spring*, 285–304.

Kaskutas, L. (2000). Understanding drinking during pregnancy among urban American Indians and African Americans: Health messages, risk beliefs, and how we measure consumption. *Alcoholism: Clinical and Experimental Research*, 24(8), 1241–1250.

Leslie, M., DeMarchi, G., & Motz, M. (2007). Breaking the cycle: An essay in three voices. In S. C. Boyd & L. Marcellus (Eds.), *With child: Substance use during pregnancy: A woman-centred approach* (pp. 91–103). Halifax, NS: Fernwood Publishing.

Martin, S., Beaumont, J., & Kupper, L. (2003). Substance use before and during pregnancy: Links to intimate partner violence. *The American Journal of Drug and Alcohol Abuse*, 29(3), 599–617.

Mothercraft. (2011) . Shaping Children's Lives through Learning. Retrieved November 10, 2011 from www.mothercraft.ca/.

Murphy, E. F. (1920, February 15). The grave drug menace. *McLean's Magazine*, XXXIII, Toronto, ON.

Nina, D., Uziel-Miller, N., & Lyons, J. S. (2000). Specialized substance abuse treatment for women and their children: An analysis of program design. *Journal of Substance Abuse Treatment*, 19, 355–367.

Olson, B. (2007). Lessons from the street: One woman's return from the road to nowhere. *CrossCurrents, Spring*, Centre for Addiction and Mental Health. Retrieved from www.camh.net/Publications/Cross_Currents/Spring_2007/spring2007-crosscurrents.html.

Payne, S. (2007). Caring not curing: Caring for pregnant women with problematic substance use in an acute-care setting: A multidisciplinary approach. In S. C. Boyd & L. Marcellus (Eds.), *With child: Substance use during pregnancy: A woman-centred approach* (pp. 56–67). Halifax, NS: Fernwood Publishing.

Poole, N. (2007). Gender does matter: Coalescing on women and substance use. *CrossCurrents, Spring*, Centre for Addiction and Mental Health. Retrieved from www.camh.net/Publications/Cross_Currents/Spring_2007/spring2007crosscurrents.html.

Regina Early Learning Centre. (2004). *Kids First Program*. Retrieved from www.earlylearning.ca/kidsfirst.htm.

Roberts, A. (2007). Common questions about trauma and substance use among women. *CrossCurrents, Spring*, Centre for Addiction and Mental Health. Retrieved from www.camh.net/Publications/Cross_Currents/Spring_2007/spring2007crosscurrents.html.

Russell, M., & Gockel, A. (2005). Recovery processes in a treatment program for women. *Journal of Social Work Practice in the Addictions, 5*(4), 27–46.

Schellenberg, C. (2007). Knowing about women, children, and fetal alcohol syndrome: What knowledge, and whose knowing counts? In S. C. Boyd & L. Marcellus (Eds.), *With child: Substance use during pregnancy: A woman-centred approach* (pp. 106–110). Halifax, NS: Fernwood Publishing.

Smith, N. A. (2006). Empowering the "unfit" mother: Increasing empathy, redefining the label. *Journal of Women and Social Work, 21*(4), 448–457.

Sowards, K., O'Boyle, K., & Weissman, M. (2006). Inspiring hope, envisioning alternatives: The importance of peer role models in a mandated treatment program for women. *Journal of Social Work Practice in the Addictions, 6*(4), 55–70.

Tait, C. L. (2000). *A study of the service needs of pregnant addicted women in Manitoba*. Winnipeg, MB: Prairie Women's Health Centre of Excellence.

Tait, C. L. (2008, March 18). Personal interview regarding substance use during pregnancy and the development of treatment services for women in Saskatchewan. University of Saskatchewan, Saskatoon, SK. Retrieved from www.pregnets.ca/.

Uziel-Miller, N., & Lyons, J. (2000) Specialized substance abuse treatment for women and their children: An analysis of program design. *Journal of Substance Abuse Treatment 19*(4), 355–367.

Vancouver Native Health Society. (n.d.). *Sheway overview*. Retrieved from www.vnhs.net/index.php?option=com_content&view=article&id=49&Itemid=56.

Van Den Broek, A. (2007). Misconceiving mothers: Women-centred care key to FASD prevention. *CrossCurrents, Spring*, Centre for Addiction and Mental Health. Retrieved from www.camh.net/Publications/Cross_Currents/Spring_2007/spring2007crosscurrents.html.

Weaver, S. (2007). Make it more welcome: Best practice child welfare work with substance using mothers – diminishing risks by promoting strengths. In S. C. Boyd & L. Marcellus (Eds.), *With child: Substance use during pregnancy: A woman-centred approach* (pp. 76–89). Halifax, NS: Fernwood Publishing.

Wright, A., & Walker, J. (2007). Management of women who use drugs during pregnancy. *Seminars in Fetal and Neonatal Medicine, 12*, 114–118.

Yaffe, J., Jenson, J. M., & Howard, M. O. (1995). Women and substance abuse: Implications for treatment. *Alcoholism and Treatment Quarterly, 13*(2), 1–15.

Epilogue

In the Foreword of *Awakening the Spirit: Moving Forward in Child Welfare,* Cindy Blackstock likens child welfare today to Hans Christian Andersen's emperor with no clothes. She notes that, like the emperor and all those around him, our current system of child welfare often acts as if it is wearing a beautiful set of clothes, and is too afraid to admit that it really cannot see them, for fear of appearing stupid and incompetent. In Andersen's story, the innocent child who sees the emperor's nakedness breaks the illusion by telling the truth, and Blackstock claims that child welfare, too, needs to listen to the truth of children. This, she concludes, is what is at the core of what we mean by "awakening the spirit."

The chapters in this book all support this view in different ways. The underlying question in the book asks whether we are adhering blindly to values, ways of thinking, policies, and practices that are not as useful as they could and should be in today's world, but are too afraid to question them for fear of appearing stupid or incompetent. Are we acting as if there is merit in these things, even when we cannot see it, because we wrongly believe others can see that merit? We are challenged to awaken our own spirits, to open our own eyes, and to discover the naked truth as it really is. This theme—telling it as we see it, and as it really is—runs throughout this book and is a good and necessary way to start the move forward.

Awakening the *spirit* also reminds us that social work, including child welfare, which is the particular focus of this book, has a philosophical

---

SUGGESTED CITATION: Brown, I., Fuchs, D., & McKay, S. (2012). Epilogue. In D. Fuchs, S. McKay, & I. Brown (Eds.), *Awakening the Spirit: Moving Forward in Child Welfare: Voices from the Prairies* (pp. 273–275). Regina, SK: Canadian Plains Research Center.

and, to a certain extent, a spiritual basis. Humanitarian values, doing what is best for vulnerable children and families and giving them opportunities to both cope and improve, are fundamental to the rationale for providing child welfare services. We are reminded throughout this book that the day-to-day demands of child welfare practice can be onerous, and that this sometimes leads us away from the humanitarian values upon which our professional work is based. To fully awaken our spirit, then, we surely need to awaken and revitalize our own value base. Progress in this area is particularly evident in the initiatives of First Nations communities that are described in many of this book's chapters.

There is also an expanding and revitalized knowledge base in child welfare, as the description of this book's chapters in the Introduction clearly illustrates. Knowledge about factors that contribute to child welfare, new and better service methods, ways to conceptualize child welfare that provide a better fit with both Aboriginal and non-Aboriginal cultural experience, and ways of organizing and disseminating knowledge are all described between these covers. Such knowledge is an essential component of awakening and sensitizing our minds, as well as our spirits, and providing a cognitive stepping stone to begin to move forward.

The book's Introduction also points out that it is critical that the pursuit of new knowledge emerge from the real and expressed needs of the child welfare field, and that new knowledge is based on the findings of research and analysis of best practices. There are many new knowledge needs in Canadian child welfare, but this book helps identify one that is of particular importance: the over-representation of Aboriginal children in child welfare in general, and in out-of-home placements in particular. This issue has received considerable national attention over the past decade—especially from the First Nations Child & Family Caring Society of Canada and the Centre of Excellence for Child Welfare (see Chapter 1) and is an important ongoing focus of the work of the Prairie Child Welfare Consortium. Although much more research is needed to generate new knowledge that is pertinent to both Aboriginal and non-Aboriginal communities, it is encouraging that the efforts of these organizations were supported and supplemented by an inaugural meeting of Aboriginal Scholars at the fifth biennial Prairie Child Welfare Consortium Symposium (see Chapter 2).

Each of the book's chapters, from its own perspective, points toward various paths for moving forward that will be helpful. There are many more paths than the ones included, but these serve as solid examples of how to start off in new directions. They point out that some of the ways of thinking that have shaped policies and service systems are not working as they were intended. New ways of thinking, new policies, and new practices are needed for effective work with vulnerable children and families, and many ideas are provided in this book for change and improvement that may lead us to better places.

Child welfare is a difficult field, focused as it is on troubled families, and the way forward is not always clear. But it is essential that, as we take the next step, we do not start out with the fallacious belief that we are wearing beautiful clothes when we clearly are not. The chapters of this book, like those of the previous two books in this series, are sparkling examples of the various ways we can re-focus on the realities of child welfare today, and awaken the "child welfare spirit" within us. As the action of Andersen's innocent child clearly illustrated, even one voice speaking its truth can strongly impact our future path.

Ivan Brown, Don Fuchs, and Sharon McKay

ABSTRACTS

Legacy of the Centre of Excellence for Child Welfare on Child Welfare in Canada: The Manager's Perspective

Ivan Brown and Nicole Petrowski

The Centre of Excellence for Child Welfare (CECW) operated under funding from Health Canada and the Public Health Agency of Canada from 2000 to 2010. Its four founding partners in Toronto, Montreal, and Ottawa represented French and English, Aboriginal and non-Aboriginal, and academic and practice perspectives of child welfare. Over the years, the CECW partnered with many institutions and organizations in its various research, policy development, and knowledge dissemination activities. One very strong partnership was between the Prairie Child Welfare Consortium and the CECW. Together, these organizations completed several research projects, co-sponsored a number of events, and collaborated on the production of materials. Among the materials produced is the *Voices from the Prairies* series, three books that give voice to child welfare issues that are of particular importance to the three Prairie Provinces. During its ten years of operation, the CECW provided a national voice for child welfare in Canada and created a flurry of activities that stimulated new thinking, research, and useful products that have moved child welfare forward.

A Day's Discourse among Indigenous Scholars and Practitioners about Indigenous Child Welfare Work in Canada

Gwen Gosek and Marlyn Bennett

This chapter reports on a one-day preconference workshop that brought together Indigenous scholars and practitioners for the purpose of identifying and discussing common themes reflected in Indigenous child welfare work and the reality of that work within a Canadian context. While the conversations were comprehensive in terms of the range of topics and related concerns, three main themes evolved from group discussions. The first theme focused on the importance of valuing Indigenous worldviews and cultural ways of being in all areas of child welfare. The second theme identified barriers such as inadequate policies and resources experienced by First

Nations and Métis child and family services in the provision of services. The third theme identified the need for enhanced post-secondary education, which called for: 1) increased Indigenous-based training and education; 2) the inclusion of Elders and ceremonies in the university environment; 3) educators to have an increased level of knowledge related to Indigenous people; 4) academia to link to frontline/grassroots; and 5) an increase in the number of Aboriginal people teaching in universities. The chapter ends with identifying strengths, progress, and recommendations for moving ahead in our shared responsibilities to children, youth, and their families.

The Bent Arrow Study: A Way Forward in Leadership for Child Welfare

Jean Lafrance and Linda Kreitzer

This chapter describes a research project that took place in Alberta from 2007 to 2009 among three different child and family service organizations who work specifically with Aboriginal families. The purpose of the Bent Arrow research project was to provide the opportunity for all three partner agencies to explore, in a supportive environment that allowed for creative thinking, ways to improve child and family practices within Aboriginal communities. Key findings included the importance of relationship in child welfare practice, creativity in practice, and supportive leadership within the organization. This chapter is one of a series of writings that focus on one aspect of the finding: what child welfare workers and their supervisors look for from their leaders. The authors propose that the Bent Arrow experience is a microcosm of what is happening at the macro level concerning leadership in child welfare service systems across the Western world.

Awakening to the Spirit of Family: The Family Group Conference as a Strengths-Based Assessment Process

Donald Keith Robinson

Family group conferencing (FGC) is presented as a model that promotes holistic, strengths-based assessment, cultural safety, inclusion, and decolonization practices with Aboriginal families. This chapter is based on the author's learning experiences as a Family Group Conference Coordinator in an urban setting.

Child welfare work is one of the most challenging careers, with social workers operating in a complex bureaucratic system with demanding caseloads and limited time to do good work with families. FGC offers the possibility and potential for doing child welfare work in a collaborative and empowering way. The intervention creates an opportunity for child welfare agencies to come together differently with families and communities and to work in a way that respects their cultures. Families entering into the FGC process find that they can provide the answers to the problems facing them and regain their self-determination. Communities become involved in widening the circle when and where relevant resources and supports are needed by the family group. Throughout the process, the family as a group asserts their decision-making power in an atmosphere of cultural safety.

It is noted that this model is not a panacea for the challenges of child welfare and that there is much learning that still needs to occur with implementation. The model does encourage a holistic and inclusive way of working that changes not only families but also the others involved in this sacred circle known as FGC.

Cultural Safety and Child Welfare Systems

Eveline Milliken

While named in 1988, "cultural safety" is a term that is only beginning to find its way into Canadian social work literature. This chapter describes the concept of cultural safety as it has come to us from Aotearoa/New Zealand. Cultural safety is contrasted with other terminology with which it is often confused. Five consequences of the so-called synonyms that can have a limiting effect on the helping relationship are identified, and three distinguishing characteristics of cultural safety are outlined.

A key shift of perspective involved in cultural safety is described that will assist educators and practitioners who struggle to move away from systemic inequality toward conceptualizing and operationalizing inclusion, respect, and sensitivity.

Based on research with Aboriginal social work graduates of an inner city Bachelor of Social Work program, ten suggestions are presented through which the child-welfare practitioner may begin to move toward "cultural safety."

A Conceptual Framework for Child Welfare Service Coordination, Collaboration, and Integration

Alexandra Wright

This chapter presents a conceptual framework of service integration in child welfare. A brief discussion of the benefits of service integration is provided, followed by a review of the conceptual contributions of key authors who have examined the issue of service coordination, service collaboration, and service integration. Based on the review, the chapter then presents clear definitions of service coordination, service collaboration, and service integration within the context of the level of service. This conceptual framework may be useful for social services organizations' managers, administrators, and other staff to understand, implement effectively, and manage service coordination, collaboration, and integration challenges.

Fathers in the Frame: Protecting Children by Engaging Fathers when Violence against Mothers Is Present

Carla Navid

This chapter works to uncover how law and policy shape the ways that the Manitoba child welfare system intervenes in cases of violence against mothers. By investigating the dominant discourses of "invisible fathers" and "mothers failing to protect," this paper speaks to how these discourses contribute to the failure of the current system to hold the perpetrator accountable for his violence. It sets out to confirm the argument that men need to be included as both risks and assets in the frame of our child welfare lens when assessing risk for children in order to realize a feminist perspective in our work with families. Discourse analysis methods from a number of sources were drawn on to reveal and analyze how the discourse of 'mothers failing to protect' has emerged, and how it informs child welfare practice and policy in ways that harm mothers and children.

Hitting the Target: Transitioning Youth with High-Risk Behaviours

Kathryn A. Levine and Rick Rennpferd

This chapter addresses policy and practice issues with a particular group of "at-risk" youth: adolescents who have been diagnosed with intellectual disabilities (ID) who demonstrate sexually offending and other challenging behaviours. Adolescents with intellectual disabilities and these types of high-risk behaviours present a complex challenge to the service system. One of the key factors that hinders successful transition planning is the absence of disability-specific knowledge within child welfare systems regarding children and adolescents with ID. This, in conjunction with contradictory mandates of service systems with potential involvement, prevents professionals from responding to these youth in a thoughtful and planned manner. Using a case example as the basis for analysis, this review describes the major issues in transition planning within the Manitoba context, and discusses implications of these issues for service provision and risk reduction for this population.

Fetal Alcohol Spectrum Disorder Communities of Practice in Alberta: Innovations in Child Welfare Practice

Dorothy Badry, William Pelech, and Sandra Stoddard

There are many challenges in meeting the needs of children and youth in care with Fetal Alcohol Spectrum Disorder (FASD) and in their transition to adulthood. In 2002, with this challenge in mind, staff of Alberta Children and Youth Services (ACYS) in Region 1 (Lethbridge and area) initiated the development of casework policy and practice standards for children in care with, or suspected to have, FASD. It was at the instigation of staff in this region that new ways of child welfare practice emerged for children and youth with very high needs.

In 2003, Region 1 staff contacted the Faculty of Social Work, University of Calgary to seek assistance in developing a research project to determine if, indeed, the new policies and practices developed would be effective. In the initial project the term "practice standards" was utilized. In the current research project, which began in 2009 and is highlighted in this chapter, the term practice standards has evolved and is now known as "promising practices." The pilot project had positive results and became the impetus for a much larger project known as the Fetal Alcohol Spectrum Disorder Communities of Practice (FASDCoP) carried out in Alberta between 2009 and 2011, involving five regions (1, 7, 9, and 10 as study regions and 6 as a comparison region) of ACYS. Ethics approval was obtained for this project from the Conjoint Faculties Research Ethics Board at the University of Calgary. The FASDCoP involved researchers from the Faculty of Social Work in partnership as a team with two senior managers from ACYS, and this partnership developed into a very effective research model.

The term "promising practices" also identifies a philosophical shift in child welfare caseload management that risks need to be taken to benefit children and youth with FASD who face multiple struggles in their lives and in care, and live with a lifelong disability. The broad goals of the FASDCoP included a commitment to children and youth with FASD in care having permanent placements; transitional plans on record by their sixteenth birthdays; assessment for suspected cases of FASD; provision of 48 hours respite minimally per month per child/youth; collaborative support plans developed with caseworkers, foster care support workers, and foster parents; minimal training of 12 hours required prior to placement and respite care; and case workers required to meet at least once a month with foster parents. In this chapter, early and promising results of this research are profiled, as well as the importance of considering a new model of practice for children and youth in care with FASD. Appendix 1 has a glossary of terms, acronyms and links that will benefit the reader.

Awakening the Caring Spirit for Children and Youth with FASD: Social and Economic Costs to the Child Welfare System in Manitoba

Don Fuchs, Linda Burnside, Shelagh Marchenski, and Andria Mudry

This chapter presents a brief review of the current literature on the economic impact of Fetal Alcohol Spectrum Disorder (FASD). In addition, it presents some of the major results of a 2009 study that provides an economic analysis of the provincial health care, education, and child care costs of children subjected to parental alcohol misuse in Manitoba. The research reported on in this chapter is the second phase of an empirical study that has already examined the cost of FASD to the child welfare system for children in care. This research builds on a larger body of empirical research on children in care with disabilities. Finally this chapter will discuss the implications of the study results for health and social service policy and programs aimed at providing services to children and families with disabilities.

Awakening the Spirit of Caring by Creating a Community Response for Children with Special Needs: A Presentation of the Innovative Efforts of the Kinosao Sipi Minisowin Agency

Madeline Gamblin and Rachel Barber

The Children's Special Services Program was created by the Kinosao Sipi Minisowin Agency to meet the requirements of special needs children and their families in the Norway House Cree Nation community of Manitoba. While the program itself is an excellent resource, its creation highlights the challenges faced by Aboriginal children with special needs and their families in regards to accessing services. Specifically, the creation of the program draws attention to the service vacuum that Aboriginal children with special needs must face. The chapter discusses the structural and resource issues that the community needed to address in creating a response for providing services to children and youth and their families. The authors point out that the value of the program to the community cannot be underestimated; because of this program fewer parents have to make the choice of either placing their children in foster care or moving from their community in order to access services. Finally, the authors highlight the importance of Jordan's Principle in providing direction for the sustainability and ongoing development of the Children's Special Services Program.

Substance Use during Pregnancy and a Woman-Centred Harm-Reduction Approach: Challenging the Mother and Baby Divide to Support Family Well-Being

Noela Crowe-Salazar

Although there are some effective programs in Canada to support pregnant women who use substances and mothers who use substances and their babies, these are few, and many are not well-developed. As a result, there exists a mother and baby divide, where many babies are apprehended from substance-using mothers by child welfare authorities at birth. Existing literature focuses on substance use during pregnancy and the treatment needs of women, and strongly suggests that systemic barriers are in place—especially blaming of women themselves—that discourage pregnant women who use substances to seek support. It also strongly suggests that support programs should be woman-centred and focus on harm reduction. Four examples of effective programs in various parts of Canada are provided, and a comprehensive program plan is suggested from knowledge garnered from these programs and from the scholarly literature.

CONTRIBUTORS

DOROTHY BADRY is a professor in the Faculty of Social Work, University of Calgary, and lead co-principal investigator on the FASD Community of Practice Research. Research interests focus on Fetal Alcohol Spectrum Disorder, child welfare, disability, birth mothers and children living with FASD. Professional memberships include the Canada Northwest FASD Research Network Action Team on Women's Health, Prairie Child Welfare Consortium, and the Canadian Disability Studies Association. Dr. Badry has received project funding from the Alberta Centre for Child, Family and Community Research, Public Health Agency of Canada and the First Nations & Inuit Health Branch.

RACHEL BARBER has worked with individuals with disabilities for over 15 years in a variety of capacities. She has been involved in research at the Hospital for Sick Children and Holland Bloorview Kids Rehabilitation Hospital in Toronto and has presented at a number of conferences on topics such as health self-advocacy and social well-being. She has an undergraduate degree in Health Sciences and a master's degree in Disability Studies from Brock University, and also has lifelong friendships with individuals with autism.

MARLYN BENNETT is a member of Sandy Bay Ojibway Nation in Manitoba, and has worked in the field of child welfare as a researcher for over 14 years. Marlyn is the director of research for the Winnipeg-based office of the First Nations Child and Family Caring Society of Canada and the coordinating editor of the *First Peoples Child & Family Review*. She is currently an Interdisciplinary Ph.D. student, focusing on the transition of First Nations youth from First Nations child welfare care in Manitoba. Current professional interests include missing children and sexual exploitation of children. Marlyn serves on the boards of the Canadian Centre for Child Protection, Animikii Ozoson Child and Family Services, and Sandy Bay Child and Family Services; she is the president of Elizabeth Fry Society of Manitoba.

CINDY BLACKSTOCK is the executive director of the First Nations Child and Family Caring Society of Canada and an associate professor at the University of Alberta. A member of the Gitksan Nation, she has worked in the field of child and family services for over 20 years. An author of over 50 publications, her key interests include exploring and addressing the causes of disadvantage for Aboriginal children and families by promoting equitable and culturally based interventions. She currently holds fellowships with the Atkinson Foundation, the Ashoka Foundation and the J. W. McConnell Family Foundation.

IVAN BROWN is a senior research associate in the Factor-Inwentash Faculty of Social Work, University of Toronto, and a professor (adjunct) in the Centre for Applied Disability Studies at Brock University. He acted as the manager for the Centre of Excellence for Child Welfare from 2000–2010. Dr. Brown is an internationally recognized expert in disability and quality of life. He has published widely in the academic literature and has written or edited eleven scholarly books, including the internationally-used text *A Comprehensive Guide to Intellectual & Developmental Disabilities*. He has initiated several major quality of life studies, and has demonstrated active leadership in international organizations in the field of intellectual disabilities.

LINDA BURNSIDE is a social worker whose career has focused on the needs of children, youth, and families involved with the child welfare system. A specific area of interest is children with disabilities involved in child welfare, including children affected by FASD. After more than 25 years of employment with the child welfare system and with disability programs in Manitoba, including eight with the provincial Ministry, Dr. Burnside now works in private practice with Avocation: Counselling, Consulting, Research and Training.

NOELA CROWE-SALAZAR is a member of Cowessess First Nation in southern Saskatchewan. Noela is the proud mother of Skyler and Alexa. She holds a B.A. in Geography and a B.S.W. from the University of Regina. She is currently a master's candidate in the Faculty of Social Work at the University of Regina. Noela has worked in community organizations, child welfare, and mental health. She is currently on secondment from the Ministry of Social Services in Saskatchewan, and working with Touchwood Child and Family Services Inc. and Yorkton Tribal Council Child and Family Services Inc. to develop an urban program for First Nations families involved with child welfare off-reserve.

DON FUCHS is a full professor in the Faculty of Social Work at University of Manitoba. He has conducted extensive research on the role of social network and social support in strengthening parenting ability in families and preventing child maltreatment. His current program of research focuses on establishing the prevalence of children with disability in care and examining the determinants which result in children with disabilities (particularly FASD) coming into care and their experiences while in care. He has done extensive international social development work in Russia and Ukraine for the past twelve years as part of CIDA-funded projects. He has served as dean of the Faculty of Social Work at the University of Manitoba for eleven years, and was a founding participant in the development of the Prairie Child Welfare Consortium. He has been instrumental in the development of a B.S.W. option in Child and Family Services at the University of Manitoba.

MADELINE GAMBLIN is an Aboriginal woman, born and raised in Norway House Cree Nation in northern Manitoba, Canada. Her first ten years of life were spent learning how to survive in fishing camps and hunting grounds in the resource area of Norway House. Her family would migrate from camp to camp, being careful not to overuse the available resources (firewood, ducks, geese, fish, rabbits, etc.) of one camp before moving on to the next. Many more life lessons were learned and many sacrifices made in the following 30+ years, which led to acquiring certificates in the helping professions as well as a Social Work degree. Of course, none of this would have been possible without the shared patience of her beautiful family and others too numerous to mention. Madeline continue to advocate for our most precious resource, Our Children.

GWEN GOSEK is a Cree-Dene woman from Lac La Ronge First Nation in northern Saskatchewan, Canada. Gwen has been working with the Faculty of Social Work at the University of Manitoba since 1998 and is currently a Ph.D. student at the University of Victoria. Before coming to the university, Gwen worked in the Indigenous community in several capacities, which included both front-line support work and agency management positions.

LINDA KREITZER began her social work career in the U.S. and in Britain. After working for 12 years with British social services she taught social work in Ghana for two years. In 1998, she received her M.S.W. with an international concentration from the University of Calgary. Her thesis was a phenomenological study concerning Liberian women in a refugee camp in Ghana. After working for a year in Armenia with the American Red Cross, she pursued her Ph.D. at the University of Calgary, looking at culturally-relevant social work curriculum in Ghana. Since 2005, she has worked for the University of Calgary, Central and Northern Region, and is associate professor. She continues to be involved in issues concerning social work in Africa.

JEAN LAFRANCE has been involved in child welfare work for over 45 years, beginning with front-line social work in northern Alberta in 1964 and serving in various leadership roles in northern, central, and southern Alberta, as well as in Edmonton and Calgary. He has also worked in staff development, policy and program development, and strategic planning as an assistant deputy minister, capping his 33 years in government as Alberta's provincial children's advocate. He earned an M.S.W. at Carleton University in 1970 and a Ph.D. in Social Work from the University of Southern California in 1993. He joined the Faculty of Social Work with the University of Calgary in 1997, where he is now an associate professor with a keen interest in child welfare work with Aboriginal communities.

KATHRYN A. LEVINE is currently an associate professor with the Faculty of Social Work at the University of Manitoba. Her practice and research interests focus on family violence issues, child and adolescent mental health, and the promotion of resilience in at-risk youth. She has extensive experience as a clinical social worker and has provided a wide range of therapeutic and clinical services to individuals, families, and groups within the child welfare, child and adolescent mental health, and public school systems. Her current research projects include an examination of the cumulative impact of violence exposure on adolescent girls, and exploring factors that promote family involvement in the career development processes for children.

SHELAGH MARCHENSKI. After many years of social work practice in northern Manitoba providing direct service to children and families through both mandated and non-mandated organizations, Shelagh has turned her focus in the direction of research and policy. She has been an active participant in research describing children with disabilities, especially FASD, involved with the child welfare system. She is presently working under Manitoba's Children's Advocate as program manager of the Special Investigation Review Unit responsible for child death reviews.

SHARON MCKAY is professor emerita, Faculty of Social Work, University of Regina. Her teaching career began at Lakehead University School of Social Work, following ten years of full- and part-time practice in the fields of child and family services and mental health. She served as dean of the Faculty of Social Work, University of Regina, from 1990–2000, and is a founding member and steering committee chair of the Prairie Child Welfare Consortium (1999–2011). She served as president of the Canadian Association of Social Work Education (2002–2004). She is an active member of current provincial and national child welfare initiatives.

EVELINE MILLIKEN is an associate professor in the Faculty of Social Work at the University of Manitoba. Eveline lived and worked in Aboriginal communities in Manitoba's Interlake region and in northern Manitoba with the J. A. Hildes Northern Medical Unit, Faculty of Medicine, University of Manitoba. She returned to northern Ontario as executive director of a district mental health program. She subsequently worked in Alberta in a family therapy centre and in the child welfare and justice systems. There she assisted in founding Red Deer's first women's shelter, and was coordinator of a multi-disciplinary Child Abuse Intervention Team. Eveline has been recognized with Outstanding Teacher and Community Service Awards. She currently chairs the Faculty of Social Work's B.S.W. Committee, and sits on the board of the Manitoba Institute of Registered Social Workers (MIRSW), as well as on several community committees.

ANDRIA MUDRY is a nutritionist and social worker who has worked with children, families, and seniors in a variety of social and health programs. Her current area of interest is research and evaluation for children with disabilities and their families. She is presently working for the Government of Manitoba, Children's Disability Programs.

CARLA NAVID completed her M.S.W. degree from the University of Manitoba in 2009, where she developed her feminist research project on father absence and mother responsibility in the child welfare system when violence against women is present. She has worked as both a front-line child welfare worker and supervisor. Currently, she maintains a private practice in Brandon, Manitoba.

WILLIAM PELECH is a professor in the Faculty of Social Work and lead co-principal investigator on the FASD Community of Practice Research. His practice focus has primarily been in the area of rural and Aboriginal communities, as well as the development and leadership of the Virtual Learning Circle B.S.W. curriculum and program. Professional memberships include the Canada Northwest FASD Research

Network Action Team. Dr. Pelech has research interests in FASD, group practice, and Aboriginal concerns. He has received research grants from Canadian Institutes of Health Research, Social Sciences and Social Sciences and Humanities Research Council and the Alberta Centre for Child, Family and Community Research.

NICOLE PETROWSKI is a child protection consultant in the Statistics and Monitoring section at UNICEF headquarters in New York, NY. She was the projects coordinator and a research associate for the Centre of Excellence for Child Welfare (CECW) from 2008–2010 and a site researcher on the Canadian Incidence Study of Reported Child Abuse and Neglect (CIS-2008) from 2009–2010. Nicole has published in academic literature and wrote and edited several of the CECW's publications. Nicole completed her undergraduate studies at the University of Manitoba before undertaking her master's degree at the University of Toronto.

RICK RENNPFERD has been executive director and therapist for Opportunities for Independence, Inc., since 1988. Rick has extensive training and experience developing programs and working directly with developmentally disabled adults and adolescents who have a history of sexually inappropriate behaviours or who are in conflict with the justice system.

DONALD KEITH ROBINSON, a Cree man from the Bunibonibee (Oxford House) First Nation in northern Manitoba, is a graduate of the University of Manitoba. Don has been involved in the helping field for over 25 years, in the areas of child welfare, mental health, and community development. Since 1996, he has been a social work educator, teaching regularly for the University of Manitoba; as a consultant and trainer he has worked for many organizations and First Nations communities. He retired in July 2011 and is focused on developing his business (www.inninewconsulting.com).

SANDRA STODDARD works within the education system and has specific interest in children living with FASD. She was the project lead and a research team member on the FASD Community of Practice Research in Alberta (2009–2011) and continues to work in educational settings with students living with the challenges of FASD. Dr. Stoddard is also interested in policy and practice for children in educational settings.

ALEXANDRA WRIGHT is an associate professor with the Faculty of Social Work at the University of Manitoba. Her research and teaching interests include social services organizations (and related issues such as effectiveness, leadership, culture and climate), family-centred practice (in the context of child welfare services and services for children with special needs), and policy analysis, implementation, and evaluation.

Subject Index

NOTE: The lowercase letter "n" following a page number indicates that the citation is in a footnote. For example, 244n1 is footnote 1 on page 244.

A
Aboriginal Head Start (AHS) program, 233–34
Aboriginal people. *see* First Nations
Abrahams, Ron, 259
adolescent offenders with intellectual disabilities: barriers in transition to adulthood, 167–71; challenging behaviours of, 158–60; how social workers deal with, 162–67; implications for practice of, 172–73; risk factors for, 160–61; transition to adulthood, 159, 161–62, 165–67, 172–73
Alberta, Government of, 182–83
Alberta Centre for Child, Family and Community Research (ACCFCR), 181–82, 191–208
Alberta FASD Cross Ministry Committee (FASD-CMC), 182–83
Anderson, Jordan River, 244, 244n1
apprehension of babies, 250–51, 254, 259
Atlantic Canada Child Welfare Forum, 17

B
balance of power, 100, 103–4, 109
Beckford, Jasmine, 41
Beckford report, 41

Bent Arrow research project: and Aboriginal values, 44–45, 62–63, 65–66; and co-location, 56–62, 67; described, 37–39; factors effecting collaboration, 47–55; ideas for improving leadership, 46–47, 64–66; methodology, 45–46
Berube, Mary, 181, 182
Blackstock, Cindy, 6, 16
Boyd, Susan, 256
Breaking the Cycle, 262–63
Brown, Ivan, 6
bureaucratization of social work, 43–44, 53–55

C
Campbell Collaboration, 13
Canada, Government of, 29, 33–34, 235, 244–45
A Canada Fit for Children, 3
Canada Northwest FASD Research Network, 182
Canadian Child Welfare Research Portal, 15, 18, 19
Canadian Human Rights Tribunal, 33–34
Canadian Incidence Study of Reported Child Abuse and Neglect (CIS), 8, 13, 145

289

Canadian Research in Brief (CRIB), 15
Caring Society, 6
The Centre for Substance Abuse Treatment, 257, 259
Centre of Excellence for Child Welfare (CECW): accomplishments, xix, 12–17; legacy, 18–21; mandate, 7; origins of, 1, 3, 4–6; priorities, 7–12
Centres of Excellence for Children's Well-Being Program, 3–4, 19, 21
Chamberland, Claire, 5
child abuse: and changes in welfare practice, 39–43; and CIS, 13, 145; and Family Group Conference, 84, 86–87; and intellectual disability, 169
Child and Family Services Authority (CFSA), 180–81
Child Welfare League of Canada, 5
child welfare system. *see* social work/social workers
Chotalia, Shirish P., 33
Clarren, Sterling, 181
Clement, Tony, 244
co-location, 56–62, 67, 127
collaboration partnerships, 168, 241. *see also* teamwork
colonization, 2, 44–45. *see also* decolonization
Colwell, Maria, 40
Community of Practice (CoP), 180–82, 183–91, 195
creativity, 50, 51, 123
cross-cultural approach, 28, 97–101, 104–5, 112–13
cultural competence, 96–101, 104–5
cultural safety: contrast with other cross-cultural terms, 96–101, 112–13; definition, 76, 94–95; integration of, 105–12; qualities of, 101–4; resistance to, 93–94; in social work literature, 95–96
culture, 25, 26–28, 81

D
Debolt, Donna, 181, 182
decolonization, 84–86, 110
developmental disability, 158
differentiated response models, 154
discrimination, 33–34, 162–63. *see also* racism
documentation, absence of, 170–71
domestic violence: blaming mothers for, 135–36, 137; failure to protect concept, 147–49; in Family Group Conference, 80, 83; fathers' inciting of, 135, 136–37; and high-risk situations, 139, 154; legislation on, 144–47, 151, 154; in Manitoba social work policy, 144–47; suggestions for better social work on, 149–53
Drug and Alcohol Meeting Support (DAMS), 255
Dudding, Peter, 5

E
elders, 32, 51, 80–81, 85
emotional abuse, 145–46
evaluation strategies, 11–12

F
failure to protect concept, 143–44, 146, 147–49
Family Group Conference (FGC) model: case example, 86–87; and decolonization, 84–86; described, 71–72; how it works, 75–81, 82–84, 88; origins of, 74–75
FASD. *see* Fetal Alcohol Spectrum Disorder (FASD)
fathers: causing domestic violence, 135, 136–37; and failure to protect concept, 143, 144; in Family Group Conference, 83; missing from child welfare cases, 135, 136, 137, 138–42; suggestions for working with, 147, 149–53

Subject Index 291

Fetal Alcohol Spectrum Disorder (FASD): current research project on, 191–208, 229–30; described, 179–80; development of Communities of Practice for, 180–82, 183–91; economic impact of, 214–20, 226–29; Manitoba Centre's economic study of, 221–26, 229–30; needs of children with, 184–85, 213–14; prevention of, 219, 230; rates of, 218; research into, 181–82, 253, 254; using diagnosis of, 257
Fir Square, 259, 262
First Nations: and Aboriginal Head Start program, 233–34; Bent Arrow view of values, 44–45, 62–63, 65–66; CECW action on, 8–9, 16, 19; and children with disabilities, 233–34; complaint against federal government, 29, 33–34; and cross-cultural awareness, 100; and cultural safety, 105–6; demographics of, xviii, xxiii; in FASD projects, 186, 190–91; and intellectual disabilities, 161, 166; as percentage of child welfare system, 23–25; and poor service integration, 123; situation of substance-using pregnant women, 249–51, 256. *see also* Norway House Cree Nation (NHCN)
First Nations Child & Family Caring Society of Canada (FNCFCS), 5–6
First Nations Inuit Health (FNIH), 235–36, 240, 244
First Nations Research Site, 13
First Peoples Child & Family Review, 15, 19, 31
foster care, 184–85, 188, 189, 198–99

G
Glode, Joan, 85

H
harm-reduction philosophy, 255, 259, 265
Henry, Tyra, 42
high-risk children, 62
high-risk situations, 52–53, 139, 154, 165

I
Indian and Northern Affairs Canada (INAC), 235, 244
intellectual disabilities (ID): barriers in transition from adolescence to adulthood, 167–68; case study of transition to adulthood, 169–71; definition, 158; how social workers deal with, 162–67; and sexual offenses, 158–63; transition from adolescent to adult, 159, 161–62, 165–67, 172–73
interdisciplinary research, 182–83
Irvin-Ross, Kerry, 245

J
Jordan's Principle, 244–45, 247

K
Kepple, William, 40
KidsFirst Regina, 263–64
Kinosao Sipi Children Special Services Program (KSCSS): development and funding of, 234–36, 242–45; evaluation of its services, 236–37; future of, 246–47; importance of, 237–39, 241–42; mandate, 235; recent developments in, 239–41
knowledge dissemination, 10–11, 12, 14–15
Knowledge Transfer and Exchange (KTE), 12

L
Lands, M., 99–100
leadership issues: in Bent Arrow study, 38–39, 44–45, 46–47, 49, 54–55, 63, 64–66; and service integration, 128–29, 130
legislation, 144–47, 151, 154, 163–64
Lorrington, Beverley, 41

M
Ma Mawi Wi Chi Itata Centre, 30, 74–75, 86
management: Bent Arrow findings on, 48, 54–55; and service integration, 118, 126–27, 128–29, 130
Manitoba, Government of, 244–45
Manitoba Centre of Health Policy (MCHP), 221–29
men. *see* fathers
mentors, 47–48
mother-blaming, 135–36, 137, 142–43, 147, 149–50
Mothercraft, 262
MotherFirst, 264
Murphy, Emily, 252, 253

N
National Association of Social Workers (NASW), 97
National Expert Advisory Committee (NEAC), 4
National Outcomes Matrix (NOM), 8, 13
Neil, Andrew, 42
network of professionals, 10–11, 15–17
New Zealand, 74, 94–95
Norway House Cree Nation (NHCN): creation and development of KSCSS, 235–37; current status of programs at, 244–45; described, 234; future of, 246–47; impact of KSCSS on, 241–43; what KSCSS provides for, 237–41

O
Orvis, Wendy, 85–86
Oswald, Theresa, 245

P
parental alcohol misuse, 221–26, 226–28, 229–30
parental stress, 185, 238–39
Participatory Action Research (PAR), 45–46
Patten, John, 42
physical space, 57–58
placement, 164–65, 188, 189, 204–7
policy: on adolescent intellectual disabilities, 172–73; CECW advice on, 14; on domestic violence, 144–47, 151; and service integration, 128–30
post-secondary education, 29–30
Prairie Child Welfare Consortium (PCWC), xvii–xviii, xxiii–xxiv, 17, 25–33
pregnancy and substance use: literature and research on, 251–55, 259–60; needs of, 256–59; program model for, 264–67; programs and services for, 260–64; situation of First Nations', 249–51, 256
prenatal alcohol exposure (PAE), 179–80
Prochaska and DiClemente's Stages of Change Model, 258
Public Health Agency of Canada (PHAC), 3–4
Public Sector Service Delivery Council (PSSDC), 128

R
racism, 30, 109, 252–53
Reconciliation conference (2005), 16
reconnecting children, 30
Regehr, Cheryl, 6
rehabilitation, 41–43
Research Watch (RW), 15
residential schools, 24
respite, 188, 198–99, 201–2, 203
risk behaviours, 203–4

S
Saini, Michael, 6
security, 39–43

service collaboration, 119, 121–28
service coordination, 120, 121
service delivery, 120, 123–25, 128
service integration: benefits of, 122–23; challenges to, 125–28; conceptual framework for, 123–25; difficulties with, 118; implementing, 128–30; review of terms in, 118–21
sexual offenses and intellectual disabilities, 159–68
Sheway, 260–61
Shlonsky, Aron, 6
Sixties Scoop, 24, 25
social work/social workers: and bureaucracy, 43–44, 53–55; case study of intellectual disabilities transition from adolescence to adulthood, 169–71; challenges of, 72–74; and co-location, 56–62, 67; and cultural diversity, 28, 29–30; and cultural safety, 95–96; development of Communities of Practice for FASD, 180–82, 183–91; and domestic violence policy, 144–47; factors effecting collaboration, 47–55; and failure of cultural competence, 96–101, 104–5; and FASD casework, 199, 201, 202; feeling culturally unsafe, 110–12; findings from Bent Arrow on, 46–47; and focus on security, 39–43; implications for practice with intellectual disabilities, 167–68, 172–73; proposals for education in, 66; and responsibility to protect concept, 143–44, 147–49; staff turnover in, 61–62, 166–67; suggestions for dealing with domestic violence, 149–53; usual response to ID offenders, 162–67; working with fathers, 138–42, 147, 149–53; workplace environment of, 59–60
special education, 226–28
Steinhauer, Paul, 4–5
stereotyping, 28, 98, 252

stories, 32, 84
Strahl, Chuck, 245
substance use and pregnancy: literature and research on, 251–55, 259–60; needs of, 256–59; program model for, 264–67; programs and services for, 260–64; situation of First Nations', 249–51, 256
surveillance, 41–43, 55

T
teaching circles, 86
teamwork, 50–51, 61, 122–23, 152–53. *see also* collaboration
Touchstones of Hope, 9, 16
traditionalism, 92
tragic incidents, 52–53, 111
Trocmé, Nico, 5, 6, 14

V
victimization, 169

W
workplace environment, 59–60, 126, 129
world views, 26–28, 39, 49–50, 65–66, 98

Y
Yates, Andrea, 144

Author Index

NOTE: The lowercase letter "n" following a page number indicates that the citation is in a footnote. For example, 244n1 is footnote 1 on page 244.

A

Abbott, A. A., 251
Abbott, D., 166
Abbott, R., 256
Aboriginal Nurses Association of Canada, 96
Adams, C. (Harbin et al., 2004), 127
Adams, P., 126
Aiken, M., 118
Alaggia, R., 151, 154
Alexander, M. J., 252
Al-Krenawi, A., 97
Allan, R., 159, 160
Anderson, A. (Lindsay et al., 2004), 159
Anderson, G., 108, 112, 113
Anderson, M., 126
Andrew, G., 180
Applegate, D., 249, 251, 252, 254, 256
Aronson, M., 184
Asamoah, Y., 97
Astley, S. J., 180
Atkinson, L., 158
Austin, M., 118, 119, 123, 126, 128, 130
Autti-Rämö, I., 185

B

Badry, D., 180, 181, 188, 194, 254
Bailey, J., 256
Balcazar, E., 162
Balsa, A. I., 226
Bancroft, L., 137, 140, 141

Bang, D., 251, 252, 256
Barr, H. M., 193
Bastien, B., 45
Batty, D., 40, 41, 42
Beaumont, J., 256
Beck, S. (Carmichael Olson et al., 2009), 185
Beckford Report, 41
Beech, A., 163, 165
Bennett, M., 23, 27
Benton-Banai, E., 31
Bertsch, M., 25
Beyenne, J., 215–16
Bickman, L., 206
Bidgood, B.A., 25
Binyamin, S., 44
Birchall, E., 118
Black, T. (Trocmé, Fallon, et al., 2005), 145
Blackstock, C., xviii, 23, 24, 27, 29, 32, 44, 65, 237, 242
Boer, D., 165
Bookstein, F. L., 193
Bourassa, C., 167, 168
Boyd, S., 249, 250, 252, 253, 254, 255
Boyd-Franklin, N., 82
Bradley, C. (Applegate et al., 2001), 249, 251, 252, 254, 256
Bradley, N. (Bang et al., 2007), 251, 252, 256
Brannan, A. M., 206

Briggs, H. E., 119, 120
Brindis, C. D., 252
Briskman, L., 44
Brown, A., 165
Brown, I., xxiv, 27, 159, 161
Brown, J., 165
Brown, J. D., 185
Brown, K., 97
Brown, L., 74, 83; (Strega et al., 2008), 135, 139–40
Brownell, M. (Fuchs et al., 2009), 180, 224, 227
Bruder, M. B. (Harbin et al., 2004), 127
Bry, B. H., 82
Buckley, E., 86
Burd, L., 215, 218, 219
Burford, G., 72, 77, 80
Burnside, L. (Fuchs et al., 2005), 214, 217-18, 220; (Fuchs et al., 2007), 164, 172, 217, 219, 225; (Fuchs et al., 2008), 214, 216, 217, 219, 229; (Fuchs, Burnside, DeRiviere et al., 2009) 180, 224, 227; (Fuchs, Burnside, Marchenski et al., 2009), 180
Burrus, S., 122

C
Califano, D., 230
Callahan, M., 142; (Brown et al., 2009), 83; (Strega et al., 2008), 135, 139–40
Calley, N. G., 168
Campbell Collaboration, The, 13–14
Canadian Institute of Child Health, 158
CanFASD Northwest, 182
CASW (Canadian Association of Social Workers), 123, 127
CASWE (Canadian Association of Social Work Education), 164
Carleton-LaNey, I., 97
Carmichael Olson, H., 185
Carriere, J., 25, 30
Carten, A. J., 251, 252, 253, 256
Casanueva, C. E., 224
Casey, R. E., 189
Castello, H., 94
Catalano, R., 256

Chandler, M., 44
Charles, G., 159
Chiefs of Ontario Office, 96
Chinitz, S., 180, 184
Chotalia, S. P., 33
Chudley, A. E., 180, 213, 218
Clarren, S. K., 180
Clement, T., 244
Coates, J., 28
Colapinto, J., 72
Collings, S., 152
Comer, D. P., 82
Compton, B., 97
Conners, N. A., 256
Connolly, M., 80
Conroy, K., 152
Conry, J. (Chudley et al., 2005), 180, 213, 218
Cook, J. (Chudley et al., 2005), 180, 213, 218
Cossette, L., 158
Craig, L., 159
Crone, C. C., 256
Cross, T. P., 224
Crow, G., 77, 78, 80
Crowe-Salazar, N., 254
Csiernik, R., 167
Curnoe, S., 159
CWLA (Child Welfare League of America), 126

D
Daciuk, J. (Trocmé, Fallon, et al., 2005), 145
Dahl, M. (Finlayson et al., 2009), 219; (Fuchs et al., 2009), 180, 224, 227
Daniel, B., 138, 153
Darmoody, M., 160
Davies, L., 152, 153
DeMarchi, G., 257
Dempsey Marr, D., 256
DePalma, R., 195
DeRiviere, L., 214, 216
Desmeules, G., 72, 75, 77, 79
Developmental Disabilities Association, 158

Dewar, J., 167
Dewar, R., 118
Dexter, P., 86
Dinnebeil, L., 122
DiTomaso, N., 118
Dodge, K., 252
Dominelli, L., 100; (Brown et al., 2009), 83; (Strega et al., 2008), 135, 139–40
Donovan, K., 252, 253, 254
Doyle, D., 160
Drabble, L., 128, 251, 252, 256
Dressler, W., 46
Dromgole, L., 167
Drye, S., 195
Ducharme, C., 234, 235, 242
Duclos, E., 158

E
Edwards, R., 163
Emerson, E., 158
Emerson, J., 160, 165

F
Fallon, B., 24, 145
Fals Borda, O., 45
Farmakopoulou, N., 118
FASD CoP Team, 197
Featherstone, B., 153
Feduniw, A., 24n2
Felstiner, C. (Trocmé, Fallon, et al., 2005), 145
Ferguson, C., 119
Ferguson, H., 150–51
Finkelstein, N., 252, 257
Finlayson, G. S., 219
First Nations Caring Society, 244, 244n1
Fitzgerald, H. E., 256
Fleet, C. (Strega et al., 2008), 135, 139–40
Flynn Saulnier, C. (Applegate et al., 2001), 249–50, 251, 252, 254, 256
Foy, J. M., 59
Friesen, B. J., 119, 120, 122
Fuchs, D., xxiv, 164, 172, 180, 214, 216, 217, 219, 220, 224, 225, 227, 229
Fulcher, L., 94, 95, 96, 101, 102
Furber, M. (Zon et al., 2004), 109, 111–12

G
Gabbard, G. (Harbin et al., 2004), 127
Galaway, B., 97
Garrod, A., 95
Gelo, J., 185
Giwa, S., 27
Glaser, W., 160
Glisson, C., 126
Glode, J., 85
Goard, C., 142, 144
Gobeil, S., 126
Gockel, A., 252, 256
Goffin, S., 119
Goldberg, M. E., 251, 252, 253, 257
Golub, S., 119
Gordon, L., 142
Gosek, G., 123, 243
Gough, P., 83
Government of Canada, 3
Government of Saskatchewan, 264
Govindshenoy, M., 164
Graham, J., 97
Grant, B. A., 256
Graveline, F. J., 44
Gray, M., 28
Green, B., 122
Green, P., 126
Greene, R., 104
Greenwood, S., 109
Griffiths, D., 162
Gunderson, K., 77

H
Haaven, J., 165
Habbick, B. F., 189
Hage, J., 118
Hale, L., 122
Hall, E., 98n3
Hallett, C., 118
Hamilton, A. C., 32, 127
Hanna, S. (Law et al., 2003), 127
Hanvey, L., 233
Harbin, G., 127
Harries, M. (Lonne et al., 2008), 52, 67
Harwood, J. H., 215
Harwood, R., 215, 219

Hassett, S., 118, 123, 126, 130
Hawkins, D., 256
Hayes, C. (Zon et al., 2004), 109, 111–12
Health Canada, 234, 236
HealthLinkBC, 262
Healthy Child Manitoba, 166
Heffernan, K., 144
Heflinger, C. A., 206
Heinonen, T., 39, 40, 97
Henry, F., 30
Hepburn, M., 250, 252, 256, 257
Herbert, M., 73
Hernandez, M., 119
Heslop, P., 166
Hess, P., 152
Hetherington, T., 28
Heyd, T., 31
Hickey, N., 160
Hiebert-Murphy, D., 123, 243
Hill, K., 256
Hill-Tout, J., 164
Hodges, S., 119
Hogan, F., 150–51
Hogg, J., 160, 164
Hollins, S., 161
Hollis, M., 43
Holt, S., 153
hooks, bell, 44–45
Horwath, J., 38, 44, 56, 120–21, 127
Hostler, S., 127
Houck, T., 127, 130
Howard, M. O., 251
Howe, D., 39, 40, 41, 42, 43, 46
Hudson, B., 118
Hudson, J., 72, 74
Hudson, P., 27, 30
Hughes, H., 95
Human Resources and Skills Development Canada, 233
Humphreys, J. C., 252
Hunter, G., 254
Hurley, P. (Law et al., 2003), 127
Hutchison, E. D., 142
Hutchison, R., 159

Hutson, J., 217, 218, 219
Hyde, C. A., 44, 46

I
Irwin-Seguin, K. (Bang et al., 2007), 251, 252, 256

J
Jaffe, Peter, 140–41
James, L., 126
Jamous, H., 40
Jaskyte, K., 46, 123
Jeffery, D., 27, 28
Jeffs, L., 95
Jenney, A. (Alaggia et al., 2007), 151, 154
Jenson, J. M., 251
Jespersen, E., 195
Jessup, M. A., 252
Johnson, P., 73
Jones, K. L., 179
Jonsson, E., 215, 218
Josewski, V., 95–96
Joyce, M., 95

K
Kadushin, A., 97
Kadushin, G., 97
Kagan, S., 119
Kahn, K. B., 59
Kalland, M., 185
Kanter, J., 184, 189
Kaskutas, L., 253
Kaufman, E., 97
Keeling, J., 165
Kegan, R., 77, 78
Kendall, E., 95–96
Kertoy, M. (Law et al., 2003), 127
Keys, C., 162
Kimelman, E. C., 73
King, G., 119–20, 122, 123; (Law et al., 2003), 127
King, S. (Law et al., 2003), 127
Klug, M. G., 215, 218, 219
Knoke, D., xviii, 24

Konrad, E. L., 119, 121
Koponen, A., 185
Koren, G., 215–16
Krajewski-Jaime, E., 97
Krane, J., 143–44, 153
Kreitzer, L., 38n1, 46
Kupper, L., 256

L
LaDue, R., 99
Lafrance, J., 38n1, 45, 46
LaLiberte, T., 164
Lalonde, C., 44
Lambrick, F., 160
Langevin, R., 159
Larsson, M., 122, 128,
Laskow Lahey, L., 77, 78
Lau, A., 184
Lavallée, L., 24n1, 28
Law, J., 159, 160
Law, M., 127
LeBlanc, N., 180, 213, 218
Lederman, J., 72
Lee, K. A., 252
Lee, M., 123
Leslie, M., 257
Lester, B. M., 256
Lightfoot, E., 164
Lindeman, M. (Zon et al., 2004), 109, 111–12
Lindsay, W., 159, 160, 168
Litrownik, A. J., 184
Locust, C., 25
Lonne, B., 52, 67
Loock, C., 180, 213, 218
Lowe, K., 164, 171
Loxley, J., 29
Lupton, C., 215, 218, 219
Lyons, J. S., 256, 259

M
Macgowan, M., 97
MacLaurin, B., 24; (Trocmé, Fallon, et al., 2005), 145

Madsen, W. C., 81, 83, 84, 86
Magen, R., 152
Manitoba Child and Youth Secretariat, 215
Manitoba Family Services and Community Affairs, 236, 237
Marchenski, S. (Fuchs et al., 2005), 214, 217-18, 220; (Fuchs et al., 2007), 164, 172, 217, 219, 225; (Fuchs et al., 2008), 214, 216, 217, 219, 229; (Fuchs, Burnside, DeRiviere et al., 2009), 180, 224, 227; (Fuchs, Burnside, Marchenski et al., 2009), 180
Marsh, P., 77, 78, 80
Martin, S., 256
Martinson, M., 126, 127
Mathews, F., 160
Matusov, E., 195
Maxwell, G., 74
Mazzarella, C. (Harbin et al., 2004), 127
Mazzuca, J. (Alaggia et al., 2007), 151, 154
McCrory, E., 160
McDonald, K., 162
McDonald, M., 159
McDonough, E. F., 59
McEwan-Morris, A., 168
McGee, J. M., 218
McGowan, K-L., 219
McIntosh, P., 109
McKay, S., xxiv, 24, 83
McKechnie, B., 242
McKenzie, B., 27, 30
McLean, C., 219
Merkel-Holguin, L., 77
Meyer, K., 119–20, 122, 123
Milliken, E., 96, 105, 106, 108
Mills, L., 152
Mills, S., 142
Milner, J., 142, 150, 153
Minuchin, P., 72
Minuchin, S., 72
Mirabla, K., 82

Mirsky, L., 74, 81, 85
Mogro-Wilson, C., 129
Morris, A., 74
Morrison, F., 168
Morrison, T., 38, 44, 56, 120–21, 127
Mothercraft, 263
Motz, M., 257
Mudry, A. (Fuchs et al., 2005), 214, 217-18, 220; (Fuchs et al., 2007), 164, 172, 217, 219, 225; (Fuchs et al., 2008), 214, 216, 217, 219, 229; (Fuchs, Burnside, DeRiviere et al., 2009), 180, 224, 227; (Fuchs, Burnside, Marchenski et al., 2009), 180
Munro, E., 142–43
Murphy, E. F., 252, 253
Muskego, D. (Ducharme et al., 2007), 234, 235, 242
Muswagon, A. (Ducharme et al., 2007), 234, 235, 242
Muswagon, M. (Ducharme et al., 2007), 234, 235, 242

N
Nanson, J. L., 189
Napolitano, D. M., 215
National Association of Social Workers, 97
Navid, C., 136
Nelson, K., 126
Nesman, T. (Hodges et al., 2003), 119, 122
Netting, F. E., 44
Newton, J., 167
Newton, R. R., 184
Neilson, C., 168
Ng, E., 233
Nielsen, H., 109
Nina, D., 256
Nixon, K., 154
Nixon, P., 77
Norman, D., 180, 181, 188, 194
Norway House Cree Nation, 234
Nøttestad, J., 161

O
O'Boyle, K., 256
O'Connor, M. C., 44
Odaibo, F. S., 218
Olson, B., 256
O'Malley, K., 179–80
O'Neill, A., 167
Oti, R., 185

P
Panciera, A., 152
Papin, T., 127, 130
Park, J., 119, 120, 127
Parton, C., 39, 42
Parton, N., 39, 40, 42, 52
Paupanekis, C. (Ducharme et al., 2007), 234, 235, 242
Paymar, M., 139
Payne, S., 250, 265, 267–68
Pedersen, S., 254
Pelech, W., 180, 181, 188, 194
Peled, E., 139
Peloille, B., 40
Pence, E., 139
Pennell, J., 72, 76, 80, 83, 97, 108, 112, 113
Pithouse, A., 164, 171
Poertner, J., 120, 122
Polaschek, N. R., 94, 95, 96, 100, 101, 103, 109, 110
Poole, N., 128, 256, 257
Potocky-Tripodi, M., 252,
Prakash, T., 29
Press, S., 193
Pritchard, E., 119
Province of Manitoba, 245
PSSDC (Public Sector Service Delivery Council), 128

Q
Quinn, K., 159, 160

R
Rabin, C., 82
Ramdatt, J. (Ducharme et al., 2007), 234, 235, 242

Ramsden, I., 94, 95, 96, 101, 103
Rasmussen, K., 161
Redmond, M. (Alaggia et al., 2007), 151, 154
Regina Early Learning Centre, 263
Reich, K., 150
Reid, M., 25
Reilly, T., 118, 119
Reimer, J., 219
Richardson, C., 84
Ringeisen, H., 224
Risley-Curtiss, C., 144
Rivero, H. K., 195
Rhodes, R. (Applegate et al., 2001), 249, 251, 252, 254, 256
Roberts, A., 256
Rockhill, A., 122
Rodger, S., 185
Romney, S. C., 184
Rosales, T. (Chudley et al., 2005), 180, 213n1, 218
Rose, J., 165
Rosenbaum, H., 82
Rosenbaum, P. (Law et al., 2003), 127
Ross, D. (Zon et al., 2004), 109, 111–12
Routhier, G. M., 72, 74
Rule, S., 122
Russell, M., 252, 256

S
Sampson, P. D., 193
Saunders, D., 139
Scarth, S., 30
Schact, A. J., 82
Schaef, A., 93
Schellenberg, C., 254
Schibler, B., 167, 168
Schulman, A. L., 189
Scott, D., 119, 121
Scourfield, J., 141, 143, 150–51, 153
Sens, M., 82
Sequeira, H., 161
Sethi, A., 27
Shangreaux, C., xviii-xix, 24
Shenk, C., 165
Sherrard, I., 95

Shore, S. E., 59
Shulman, L., 180, 184
Silver, J., 30
Silverman, J., 137, 140, 141
Simon, B., 152
Simpson, M., 160, 164
Sinclair, C. M., 32, 127
Sinclair, R., 25, 100
Sivak, P., 77
Smart, N., 160
Smith, A. (Anne H.), 159, 160, 168
Smith, A. (Astrid), 159
Smith, B. (Brenda), 129
Smith, B. (Bridget), 27
Smith, C., 167
Smith, D. W., 179
Smith, L. T., 31
Smith, N. A., 254
Smye, V., 95–96
Snyder, R. E., 189
Sobsey, D., 164
Søndenaa, E., 161
Sowards, K., 256
Spearman, L., 39, 40, 97
Spence, N., 38, 59
Spence, W. (Ducharme et al., 2007), 234, 235, 242
Spencer, N., 164
Spero, L., 161
Spoonley, P., 103
Square, D., 218
Stade, B., 215–16, 218, 219,
Staff, I. (Harbin et al., 2004), 127
Standal, O. F., 195
Stargardter, M., 219
Statistics Canada, 158
Steele, L., 160
Steinhauer, P., 4-5
Stermac, L., 160
Stevens, B., 215–16, 218, 219
Stoddard, S., 196, 197
Strega, S., 83, 135, 138, 139–40, 148–49, 153, 154
Streissguth, A. P., 179–80, 184, 189, 193
Strier, R., 44
Stroul, B., 119, 121

Sue, D., 97
Swift, K., 153
Sylvester, K., 150

T
Tafoya, N., 82
Tait, C. L., 249, 250, 251, 253, 256, 257
Tator, C., 30
Taylor, J., 138, 153
Thanh, N. X., 215, 218
Thoburn, J., 52, 67
Thomas Prokop, S., 24, 83
Thompson, S. A., 195
Thomson, J. (Lonne et al., 2008), 52, 67
Toubeh, J., 123
Tough, S., 165
Trocmé, N., xviii, 23, 24, 145
Trute, B., 123
Tudway, J., 160
Tupara, H., 95
Turnbull, A., 119, 120, 127
Tutty, L., 142, 144
Twigg, R., 185

U
Ulleland, C. N., 179
Ulrich, D., 59
Ungar, W. J. (Stade et al., 2006), 215–16, 218, 219
United Nations General Assembly, 3
Urato, M., 224
Uziel-Miller, N., 256, 259

V
Vancouver Native Health Society, 260
Van Den Broek, A., 262
Van Reyk, P., 38, 59
Vassar, D., 82
Vaughn, P., 159
Veneziano, C., 160
Veneziano, L., 160
Vig, S., 180, 184
Vizard, E., 160

W
Wabano, M., 27
Wagner, R., 38, 59
Waites, C., 97
Waldegrave, C., 59
Waldfogel, J., 154
Walker, J., 255, 256
Walmsley, C., 30; (Brown et al., 2009), 83; (Strega et al., 2008), 135, 139–40
Walsh, F., 79, 83
Watkins, M., 104
Weaver, S., 254
Weedon, C., 136
Weil, M., 97
Weissman, M., 256
Wenner, A., 256
West, B., 162
Whitbread, K. (Harbin et al., 2004), 127
Whiteside-Mansell, L., 256
Wien, F., 29, 85
Williams, A. (Zon et al., 2004), 109, 111–12
Williams, J., 59
Williams, R. J., 218
Wright, A., 123, 127, 243, 255, 256
Wright, T., 109

Y
Yaffe, J., 251
Young, I., 104, 112
Yu, D., 158

Z
Zeitz, G., 118
Ziefert, M., 97
Zon, A., 109, 111–12
Zorfass, J., 195
Zuckerman, B., 256